Necessity for Light

by
Lester Wingate
Mouthpiece

Necessity for Light
Copyright © 2019 Lester Wingate
Masterworks BookMakers Publishing Company

All rights reserved. No part of this book may be reproduced or transmitted in any form or by any means without written permission from the author.

ISBN: 9780983332558

LCCN: 2019918247

Lester Wingate
Email: elijahblue_15@outlook.com
www.sardiusstone.com

Authors Note

Writing is a sequestered journey navigating through the channels of our imagination. It is an expression of freedom captured in the power of our words. Writing is born from the depths of provocation; yearning of our hearts in search for value we assign to the meaning of life. It is a suggestion of movement; an examination of our introspections and patterns of thoughts capturing our world of imagination defining our reality. Like a torrid river thrusting with power of creativity, the imprint of our experiences, dreams, and visions are garnered motivating a response from our gifting. Our articulations will unfold as our perceptions of truth creating a clear path to pursue life's purpose with a reverence preserving the treasures of our innermost feelings.

*And we have the prophetic word confirmed, which you do well to heed as a **light** that shines in a **dark** place until the day dawns and the morning star rises in your hearts; knowing this first, that no prophecy of Scripture is of any private interpretation, for prophecy never came by the will of man, but holy men of God spoke as they were moved by the Holy Spirit.* [1]

Table of Contents

Forward   vii
Acknowledgement   ix
Prophets Corner   xi
Preface   xiii
Introduction   xix

The Longest Day

Chapter 1	From Darkness to Light	1
Chapter 2	Mystery of Faith	9
Chapter 3	Father of Lights	37
Chapter 4	The Man From Eden	51
Chapter 5	Can Trees Talk	89
Chapter 6	Rivers	117
Chapter 7	Isle of Patmos	135
Chapter 8	Sixth Sense of Prayer	163
Chapter 9	Open Heaven	177

Now and Then

Chapter 10	Side-Meat Beans and Biscuits	197
Chapter 11	Bacco	221
Chapter 12	Where Healers Fail	253
Chapter 13	Lawfulness vs. Lawlessness	289
Chapter 14	Return of Babel	321
Chapter 15	The Constitution *"A Variable Conception"*	347

Just as an eagle glides effortless with its wings stretched across the shadows below, the wings of faith covered the face of Heaven for an enrapturing encounter revealing mysteries hidden in secrecy of "God's Creative Spirit"

FOREWARD

*"For **flesh and blood** has not revealed this to you, but My Father who is in heaven."* [1]

As I pondered writing this book, it was not my intention to levy criticism against anyone or to be condescending. I sought desperately to make plain the simple; to remove the shroud of heaviness embedded in words bringing to the surface revelations with clarity and simplicity of thought. It was a struggle bringing together the patterns of faith almost to the point I considered not releasing this book. I wrestled with great difficulty attempting to capture prophetic images formed in my imagination and paint them into pictures for interpretation viewed in our mind's eye. Indeed, this is my most daunting endeavor.

The metaphoric interpolations of *"Necessity for Light"* are literal abstractions of *"God's Creative Genius"*! In the far reaching distance of time and eternity, pulsating waves of invisible currents with energy greater in intensity than erupting forces emitting from a volcano's inferno, lies a hidden stream of celestial power that gave witness to the day of God's creation.

*I fed you with **milk** and not with **solid food**; for until now you were not able to receive it.* [2]

Acquisition of spiritual revelations is a birthing struggle nourished in its beginnings from a diet of milk and honey. Maturity of solid food is not purposed for development of babes. To produce the finest of wheat requires a retreat from the intangibles of materiality to capture the prophetic images of faith through a sequestered life of prayer.

"Teach my eyes to see through the dark and train my spirit to move in the light."

Acknowledgement

I dedicate this book to the warriors of faith; faithful pioneers persecuted while sacrificing their lives to apprehend such an enduring promise. Faith is a sacrifice; a price not so easily embraced when we truly consider the cost of its requirements. Measurement of the success of our sacrifices is determined by the degree by which we give. The spiritual principle of faith demands relinquishing of *"Everything"* to attain the perfect good of the Kingdom.

> *Then Peter spoke up, "We have left **everything** to follow you!" "Truly I tell you," Jesus replied, "no one who has left home or brothers or sisters or mother or father or children or fields **for me and the gospel** will fail to receive a hundred times as much in this present age: homes, brothers, sisters, mothers, children and fields along **with persecutions** and in the age to come eternal life. But many who are first will be last, and the last first.* [1]

We give with the reciprocal principle of expectation; *"Give and it shall be given"*,[2] but the greatest value of giving is without reciprocation. Giving is an action born of love seeded in the compassion of faith. The *"Law of Love"* is spiritual, agreeable; freed from the burden of materiality. Love is a guarantee of greater productivity yielding its greatest reward in the harvest of faith.

Prophets Corner

Every name is uniquely empowered with seeds of vision for this journey called life. As in the case of all human beings; I did not unexpectedly appear without cause or purpose but as destiny would prevail, I became a living reflection of a word encapsulated in the womb of God's Creative Thought. Though obscured in a flux of aspiring ideas concerning my future, I emerged with a conviction of faith centered in a belief that continues to sustain me.

Time is of precious value only realized in fullness when we truly consider its end. It is only given to us *"once"* to define the meaning of our human experience. Throughout the journey of life, the result of time intersects with our gifts and talents to fulfill a destiny prophesied before our time. It was *"Our Creator"* who knew us in our formation before we knew ourselves and launched us on a path to resolve life's meaning by the motivating power of faith. Every man is endowed with a measure of faith. It is by that same faith we believe, searching to apprehend accomplishment of God's faithfulness and comfort of peace He brings to our struggles.

"I will no longer drive out before them any of the nations Joshua left when he died. I will use them to test Israel and see whether they will keep the way of the Lord *and walk in it as their ancestors did."*

Judges 2:21-22 NIV

Preface
Can You Hear Me Now?

IN one of my night seasons a few years back, I had a remarkable vision. It is pressed upon me to speak it again. The Spirit of God revealed to me the image of a church being restored from its ruins to its original form. It was rather significant that the work began from the Altar to the pulpit; from the pulpit to the pews; from the pews to the doorway; from the doorway to the steps leading into the sanctuary; inside out from top to bottom. After completing restoration of the inner chambers, then the work continued repairing the outer structure. After all the work was done, the image of a cross was placed on top of a steeple which was mounted high above the *"Church"*. What followed spoke volumes into my spirit.

The steeple started vibrating; reverberating like the quaking of Earth just like the thunder at Mt. Calvary when Jesus surrendered His obedience to the Cross releasing the dead from their graves. I began to hear the sound of a symphony like a coronation of angels trumpeting from above! I looked up and there was a Cross illuminating in an array of lights pulsating at a compelling frequency. The Cross was broadcasting for the world to see God's prophetic intent. In bold vibrant colors serenading in light, I saw the word *"CLARION"*! It was so compelling I needed to resolve its meaning.

It soon became clear what the Lord was revealing to His Church. The vision was indicative of a revolt; a spiritual revolution with a mandate to get God's House in order. The trumpeting call for spiritual restoration was prioritized from the inner house to the outer appeal; from inwardness of our living tabernacle to the outer extensions of our gifts. When the Church was restored back to its original order, I made a profound discovery; *"There was no more pulpit; Only an Altar"*. No more of man standing in the way of God! It was as if the Church was revisited with a *"Corrective Whip"* likened to when Jesus cleansed the Temple indicating the true purpose of His Father's House;

"A House of Prayer"

When will that day come when we realize provisions of God's grace are in our submission and boldness to present ourselves before the *"Throne of Grace"*? It seems rather remarkable how we have neglected the Altar. For so long now, we have been inundated with distractions away from the center of God's attraction; far beyond His acceptability. Centered in the heart of faith, the Altar of our submission is often contested when we bow in surrender to a power much greater than ourselves. With a renewed commitment to prayer, impediments in the path of faith will be minimized.

But yet we still are continuing down the highway of prosperity *"Churching"* from one worship place to the other. *Our house is on fire! Can't you smell the fumes?*

Perhaps, it would be in our best interest to invest in *"Smoke Alarms"* to detect fumes at the source of our inactions. We are in desperate need of the detecting power of the *"Holy Spirit's discernment"* who constantly surveils intruding influences that seems to have us consumed with the sedations of this world. God can awaken our spiritual eyes while availability of His grace still exists if we are motivated to pray.

> *And the priest shall burn them on the altar as food, an offering made by fire for a sweet aroma; "All the fat is the LORD's".*
> **Lev. 3:16 NKJV**

God has given us provisions for our sustainment. But have we forgotten; there is a part we owe to Him in exchange for His faithfulness? We, the Body of Christ are suffering from a serious condition of *"atrophy"*. We talk the good talk of faith all day long; breaking bread pernicious in our presumptions but lack performance of our gifting to make a difference.

"Church, we have lost our Spiritual Fat"! Without the marbling of faith, the attracting aroma of our sacrifices will lack the fragrance of our prayers to entreat the *"Ear of God"*. With our lives prostrated on the Altar of Fire, submissively we offer our sacrifices in exchange for His provisions. The enticing aroma surfacing from our yielded hearts attracts the Ear of the Lord to our surrender. But with no more fat to render, we have nothing left to buffer the fire as our lives are laid bare on the Altar of submission.

Spiritual Drought

The drought of God's Words, *"His Prophetic Word"*, has silenced the voice of many of the chosen who have pursued a path away from the burning Altar of Fire. The parched land of their inner ear lies dormant in the *"desert sands of infertility"*. What was once a sprawling vineyard of the ointment of olives and fragrant spices has almost disappeared with no one to tend.

Spiritual drought has caused some of God's chosen to pursue a path of vanity; blinding their sight, muting their voices. Without a fertile cavity to receive God's revelations, planting of His Word falls upon deafened ears eluding wisdom necessary for their judgments. Their outer man has become dormant ruling the sense and body with corruption and inner turmoil. Doctrines of man and his secular beliefs have colluded with the spiritual principles of faith and we are struggling.

On one of my mission trips to Africa, I *"watched"* a segment of a BBC documentary concerning the state of the Church in Europe which by all accounts was in a spiritual freefall. It was indeed quite shocking to hear how secularism had replaced the spiritual role of the Church. Foundationally, the Church had eroded to the point of disrepair. What's left is merely a shell of the Church Christ envisioned. When the Anointing of God is removed from our presence, we will unquestionably enter into His judgment. The broadcast went on to say what happened in Europe was a precursor to events that would come to America. Yes we are next in line but with a greater consequence because of the seeds of division and greed that have taken root in our culture. Signs of change are rapidly emerging and it is rather frightening to watch how blinded we have become to the spiraling decline taking place in our culture.

Spiritual pollution is fumigating our airways to the likes of agnosticism and apostasy which only serves to confound *"God's Grace"* necessary for our survival. Our actions are indicative of a ship in raging seas that has lost its rudder. The idea of *"common sense"* is not such a common thing at all. The seductive offerings of man's interpretations are no substitute for the natural order of our senses unique to the lives of all human beings. Commonality of our senses and the God given sense to discriminate between what is the good and acceptable thing to do is a battle we must fight. By all accounts we are *"backwards thinking"* inundated with the persuasions of materialism which are conflicting with God's original objectives.

Generationally, we are losing the battle of faith in a rapid descent as our moral base sways amid clouds of uncertainties. You can readily see evidence of erosion as the winds of change are beating upon traditions of old brandishing weapons of convenience substituting for truth. Truth is not ambiguous! But somehow we've been anesthetized by deceptive powers ravaging our understanding of God's intended purpose for our lives! Time is an enemy of change; it waits for no one! While observably we remain saddled in our indecisions; time does not guarantee an extension to complete the hopes of today for tomorrow's rewards of faith.

There is a generation that **curses its father, And does not bless its mother.** *There is a generation that is pure in its own eyes, Yet is not washed from its filthiness.* **There is a generation oh, how lofty are their eyes! And their eyelids are lifted up.** *There is a generation whose teeth are like swords, and whose fangs are like knives, To devour the poor from off the Earth, And the needy from among men.*
Proverbs 30:13-14 NKJV

So are the ways of **everyone that is greedy of gain;** *which taketh the life of the owners thereof. Wisdom crieth without; she uttereth her voice in the streets: she crieth in the chief place of concourse, in the openings of the gates; in the city she uttereth her words saying, How long you simple ones, will ye love simplicity? And the scorners delight in their scorning and fools hate knowledge? Turn you at my reproof; behold, I will pour out my spirit unto you, I will make known my words unto you.*

Because I have called and ye refused; *I stretched out my hand and no man regarded; But ye have sat at nought all my counsel, and would have none of my reproof:* **I also will laugh at your calamity; I will mock when your fear cometh;** *When your fear cometh as desolation, and your destruction cometh as a whirlwind; when distress and anguish cometh upon you.* **Then shall they call upon me but I will not answer;** *They shall seek me early, but they shall not find me.* **Proverbs 1:19-28 KJV**

Introduction

N*ecessity for Light* is written as a guide into the spiritual principles of faith. It is an inward journey to diminish if not to conquer barriers of hindering influences existing in violation of God's blueprint for humanity. *"Necessity for Light"* makes a compelling attempt to unify the mind, body, soul and spirit into *"inseparable oneness"* with the Spirit of Christ. He is an interweaving Spirit with the ability to unify our hearts in a new awakening of faith.

As a lamp of guidance illuminating the path before us, the Spirit of Christ shines from within revealing a paradigm targeted in our preparations to fulfill the mandate of faith. The requirement of a unified heart immersed in His Spirit is the only triumphant power that can produce His success. Just as chaos persisted in creation before settling in peace, reformation of our inner man continues in pursuit of the journey of faith; searching for fullness of God's redemptive life.

The Hidden Particle

> *In the beginning God created the heavens and the earth. The earth was without form, and void; and darkness was on the face of the deep. And the Spirit of God was hovering over the face of the waters.*
>
> *Then God said,* **"Let there be light"**; *and there was light. And God saw the light, that it was good; and God divided the light from the darkness. God called the light Day, and the darkness He called Night. So the evening and the morning were the first day.*
>
> *Then God said, "Let there be a firmament in the midst of the waters, and let it divide the waters from the waters." Thus God made the firmament, and divided the waters which were under the firmament from the waters which were above the firmament; and it was so. And God called the firmament Heaven. So the evening and the morning were the second day.*
>
> *Then God said, "Let the waters under the heavens be gathered together into one place, and let the dry land appear"; and it was so. And God called the dry land Earth, and the gathering together of the waters He called Seas. And God saw that it was good.* [1]

The *"Word of Light"* was a concealed thought in the mind of our Creator. It incubated as a hidden particle of faith bearing the seeds of creation. At the command of His Spoken Word, invisibility morphed into visibility revealing the beginnings of creation as an image born of His imagination. Void of diminishing return, the *"Word of Light"* set in motion a revolution shattering all darkness exposed to His power. As the Spirit of God brooded upon the waters of creation, there was no conceiving end of His exploration. With the heavens erupting displaying remnants of exploding stars, a celestial celebration burst forth in brilliancy of power, illuminating as a garment of visibility of the spoken Word of Faith. With quickening power that brought such terror to darkness, seeds of life emerged bursting forth as a benefactor of *"Light"*.

Before emergence of light, Earth was without form, void and darkness covered the face of the deep. And the Spirit of God hovered over the face of the waters just as a mother of hens stands guard over a brood of eggs. All life is born in darkness, concealed in secret beginnings invisible to our sight. When light appears, the restraining cavity of darkness disappears behind a veil of invisibility. Contrast of darkness gives visibility to our sight to discern the beauty of creation only revealed by *"God's Creative Light"*. The Light of eternity continues the journey of the spoken *"Word of Faith"*.

The eternal visibility of God is embedded in radiant waves of illumination emanating from His Presence. His productive life fuels our understanding from the source from where all power stems. Spiritual power morphs perpetually never ending in constant evolution of God's ability to deliver Light into our humanity as *"His Originality"*. He continuously pursues our gifts to manifest visibility of *"His Presence"* into existence.

Discovery is a source of empowerment unfolding as a *"transformative agent"* to reveal some of the greatest wonders yet to be discovered. There is nothing new under the sun; that which began in the beginning is an eternal seed reflective of our Father's creativity and expansion of His authority given to man.

> *"In the beginning, God created the heavens and the earth".*[3] *"Be fruitful and increase in number; fill the earth and subdue it. Rule over the fish in the sea and the birds in the sky and over every living creature that moves on the ground."* [4]

In the *"thought"* of God, the spoken Word of Light is an envisioning of the inseparability of divinity and humanity where Heaven and Earth coalesced under one expression of His authority. The spoken word, the Word of Faith was intended to bring the Presence of God as a habitation here on Earth. God is the Light of all seen realities: *"The Father of All Lights"*.[5] Visibility of His Presence and Authority exist in all of creation. In every moment of our wakening day, we should have a conscious presence of His Existence in our lives.

The Cross of Christ bore witness as an image of *"That Light"* pointing *"vertically"* upward into Heaven, the dominion of God's rulership with side post pointing *"horizontally"* east to west covering all the Earth as a redeeming action of His love. The revelation of Christ continues to bring us closer to the transfixing Cross to experience the unity Jesus had with His Father from the beginning of creation before being commissioned as the object of our redemption. His life was given as a sacrificial gift of love. God's plan unfolded nearly two thousand years ago as the *"Greatest Gift"* that ever proceeded from Heaven. Love is a sacrifice; a costly price that was fashioned to a *"Cross"* of martyrdom testifying of God's divinity in search of our humanity:

> *God so loved the world that He gave His only begotten Son that whoever **believes** in Him should not perish but have everlasting life.* [1]

Image of Unity

Our thoughts possess glimpsing power to create visualizations of the spoken word. Images framed in our imagination are non-contiguous. Fragmentation disrupts our ability to propagate God's Image into the center of our conscience. Unity of our mind, body, soul and spirit must coalesce into a reflective image born of *"His Thought"* with authority to rule in His Spirit over everything through love and love's creative power.

Our thoughts aren't fluid; compartmentally drifting *"to and fro"* from variability of our soul causing undo separation of God's intent of love to unify our hearts to His desire. Love unifies as a compilation of our beliefs, faith and passion consecrated in our innermost being. It is pure; the true Light of power to perform beyond where our understanding has settled. Love is spiritual pulsating in the heart of faith; living and breathing as confirmation of God's Existence in our lives. Exhibition of love perceived through the eyes of faith is evidential of *"things we believe by performance of things we do"*.

While in *"Communion with the Spirit of God"*, our lives exist as an extension of eternity ready to deliver His solutions from an image born of *"His Thought"*. We are Heaven's agents, light bearers assigned to bring exposure of His Presence into a world void of light. All of Heaven and Earth are groaning for emergence of the true sons of God to take their rightful place and rule with the same authority Adam decided against. We are compelled to bring *"Light of His Revelation"* into our sphere of influence. It is the same light of truth that emanated from the *"Tree of Life"*;

> *He who has an ear, let him hear what the Spirit says to the churches. To the one who overcomes I will grant to eat of the Tree of Life, which is in the paradise of God.* [1]

The Requirement of Faith

The exhibition of faith is an unlimited expression of things we *"Believe"*. Faith without results centered in belief is an indication of fragmentations in our inner man failing to connect to the reservoir of strength lying within us. Without proper connectivity, it is impossible to please God; delivering evidence that says; *"He Said"*. Impediment to Heaven's authority gaining dominion over our lives resultantly is the lack of faith to believe.

Faith displays our belief as an exhibition of things spoken from time beginning. It is a receptor of the spoken Word of God's Spirit for inspirations of divine life to flourish in our hearts. As an operating principle, acceptance of faith is necessary for release of God's provisions to facilitate completion of what we are called to do. For without it our achievements will fall short of fully completing the call of our destiny.

God's Spirit is an enterprising power of invisibility; invisible to our senses but recognizable by evidence in all of His creation. His spiritual substance adorned an image as a garment of visibility as evidence of His creativity. It was the Word of Faith; *"In the beginning was the Word and the Word was with God and the Word was God."* [1] We have the same *"draping power"* of creativity actualized by the spoken Word of Faith. It is a decorated power that brings visibility to the things we believe.

The content of faith is a reservoir of immeasurable creative power. It is unlimited, but yet we continue to struggle in an attempt to connect to an abundance of prophetic promises. Unsymphonic distortions vibrating in our inner man exist as disruptive forces of great peril that continues to impede our walk of faith.

> ***Now*** *faith is the substance of things hoped for, the **evidence** of things not seen.* [2]
>
> *For assuredly I say to you whoever says to this mountain be removed and be cast into the sea and does not doubt in his heart but believes that those things he says will be done, he will have whatever he says.* [3]

What more evidence do we need other than the things that we say! We're all either climbing upward toward the pinnacle of achievement or coming down after having completed the call of faith. *"Everything God instructs us to do is an assurance of His authority but believe"!* Believe in the Word of Faith and believe in yourself with the hope for *"evidence of things not seen"!*

Faith always speaks in the present tense; it is what we are actively doing to bring about results. Hope however is a projection into the future we attach to the production of our faith. God's Faith framed the worlds! It will take our faith uniting with His Spirit to release power of His Word to bring visibility of His Existence into everything He has commanded us to do.

Divine Purpose

"Necessity for Light" is an inner cry of hope that will excite investment of God's gifts connecting with our faith. Flow with me and dig a little deeper while we continue the journey through tributaries that provides a passageway into our inward treasures. There is a secret fire burning dispersing revealing light upon our conscience penetrating at the core of faith. There are discoveries waiting for our encounter, an encounter of truth to unveil a transparent path into the motivations fueling our decisions.

Time is a filter, a discriminate judge of our choices as we pursue life's destiny to justify means to an end. It is given to us as a gift born from the revelation of God's creativity. In the time given to perfect what He has called us to do, our existence must be realized as a spiritual investment to manifest *"His Purpose"* into visibility from the opportunities faith provides.

1

From Darkness to Light

But where can wisdom be found? And where is the place of understanding? Man does not know its value, nor is it found in the land of the living. [1]

Darkness is extreme without measurement of its depth. It is condensed; non-dilating with an undercurrent of evolving light beneath its surface that incubated the time and seasons of our lives. Unraveling the outer layer of darkness requires a power greater in intensity to reveal the essence of things hidden from our sight. Just as *"smelting"* of a refiner's fire extracts treasures exposed to the surface mined from an unknown interior life; the process of *"Revelation is also preexisting mined from the depths of darkness by an illumination exposing what already existed."* Shrouded in mystery of an un-awakened life, we all have darkness within us that's been incubating since our conception; pulsating with the urgency of a beating heart yearning for revelation of God's Light of *"Discovery"* to enlighten our destiny of faith. Treasures hidden in the path of faith will unfold yielding fruit with seeds harvested from our labor.

If we had the ability to make the voyage across the barriers of time and eternity, now and then, we would discover unseen dimensions of our beginnings; a place of thought unique in the creative mind of our Creator. There is no separation between thought and the word of life it was sent to produce.

> *So shall My word be that goes forth from My mouth; It shall not return to Me void but it shall accomplish what I please, And it shall prosper in the thing for which **I sent it**.* [1]

Darkness is monolithic, rigid in uniformity just as the hardness of a stone of sapphire harvested from cavities buried within the Earth. Darkness also exists as a disguise; a protector of secrets of all preexisting life as in the day of creation. It is restrictive of freedom camouflaged in a non-reflective shroud of invisibility. Darkness is equal in value but not in strength to the advancing of light sent to pulverize its surface. The curtain of darkness shelters treasures and mysteries only revealed by a *"Light"* greater than its power.

Darkness is not a shroud of emptiness conforming to itself. However, it shares the same properties of light coexisting in a unique balance of creation. *"We can see darkness but lack the ability of our senses to see in darkness!"* Void of an identifiable spectrum of light to penetrate beneath its cover, the unknown treasures of darkness remains hidden until exposure to light. Light is illuminating; *"the conceiving power of our perception relative of our ability to recognize its genius"*.

"The Light of God is the universal reflection of His Existence." He has appropriated seasons to walk in His Light with a designation of time for implementation of His desired intentions. After completion of life's destiny of time; from dust we came and dust we shall return with no further need for the fulfillment of Light.

As light enters our mind's eye, our conscious is enlightened by its brilliance in a display likened to the sun; glowing in the day before surrendering in the night. As the sun retreats, darkness reemerges from its shelter in preparation for new discoveries concealed behind a cloud of creativity. The night seasons of our lives are intended to do the same; searching deeper in the secret dimensions of faith for new presentations in our awakening day.

As a seed buried beneath the surface, it contains an encasing of life and is nourished by light within its shell until the day of its revealing. Life is contained within though surrounded by darkness. Darkness only serves as a protector, an incubator until the true life of its enclosure emerges as a fulfillment of light.

Secluded in darkness, instigated by declining rays in the shade of evening, ignites a feeding frenzy of invisible creativity nourishing throughout the night. In silhouette, flowers of the evening fields receive strength from the waters below with their roots penetrating the streams of faith but yet at the reappearance of the sun; their pedals migrate upward drawn to a greater power of awakening. Our universe is a self-balancing dynamo; always retreating under the cover of darkness then re-emerging with fresh vigor at the reappearance of light adorned with treasures born in the night. Light and darkness bear the secrets of eternity; coexisting in a dominion of their own with exception of a migrating eclipse when the performance of darkness temporarily transcends any competitive light.

Darkness is a preparatory place; a brooding ground for development of life with an anticipation of light to reveal the content of things hidden away from our sight. Darkness is neither a misfortune nor deficiency of our perception. It has a purpose; without it there would be no need for discovery. It is intended as a concealment of preparation yielding its greater value in cooperation with the communion of light.

God's advancing Light penetrated darkness creating a distinct separation of enlightenment enhanced with power to manifest visibility to our senses. We believe to see from darkness to light; invisibility to visibility; from hope to evidence our faith produces. We have power within us to speak to our dark surroundings by the Word of Faith; *"believing to see"*. We walk by faith and not by sight!

Glory Within the Light

Our beginnings were sequestered in hidden places before being awakened by illumination of penetrating light. Emerging from a thought of God's Originality, life began to flourish just as a seed buried beneath yearns for revival before budding into a blade transfixed to the sun's perfect light. True Light is an attraction of faith securing a performance of our imagination to believe. Just as God envisioned our lives, our visualizations substantiate the possibility of faith. *"The potential of faith has imaging power that's capable of capturing the conscience of our beliefs unfolding as our perceptions of truth."* It patterns the image of faith with invigorated hope of things yet to come evidential of what we truly believe. When the suppression of faith is lifted and our eyes focused on the destiny ahead, we will discover preserved since our beginnings; *"the treasures of life"* we so desperately defend bearing the imprint of our hearts belief; our dreams and visions suspended upon the pedestal of faith.

Glory and the Light

True light is blinding. Our natural eyes lack ability to sustain its power. As Apostle Paul discovered on the Road to Damascus; to encounter Light emanating from the *"Countenance of Christ"* is as a two-edged sword; it is blinding to your past but illuminates a path forward towards fulfilling your purpose. Our ambitions and talents will succumb to the greatness of His power.

> *As he journeyed he came near Damascus, and suddenly a **light shone around him from Heaven.** [1] And he said, "Who are You, Lord?" Then the Lord said I am Jesus, whom you are persecuting, It is hard for you to kick against the goads. [2] So he trembling and astonished said, "Lord, what do You want me to do?" Then the Lord said to him, "Arise and go into the city and you will be told what you must do". [3]*

> *And when I could not see for **the glory of that light**, being led by the hand of them that were with me, I came into Damascus.* [1]

Where there is Light there is a Glory to be found. Apostle Paul detailed in his encounter that he could not see because of the Glory of the Light and had to be led by the hand of those who were with him. It seems rather amazing a light could shine so bright in glorified intensity that no one else but Saul was blinded. In our spiritual encounters, there is a uniqueness embedded in God's revelation concerning our destiny. When God speaks concerning His plan for our lives, His Words are not generically amplified but specifically targets what He has envisioned. If we walk in the Light of God, we will discover His Glory. *"His Glory is His Anointing"* that delivers power to the Light! As He reveals Himself through the Light of His Word, He will lighten our path but we need His Glory!

> *And they that were with me saw indeed the light, and were afraid; but they heard not the voice of him that spake to me.*
> **Acts 22:9 KJV**

Those that were traveling with Saul did not hear God's private instructions to him but did in fact see *"The Light"* shining around him. Even though they heard a voice, they had no recognition of *"The Voice"* speaking into his destiny. They could only stand as a witness of his encounter. *"The Revelations of God are impressions of His Reality."* They are not ascertained peripherally and never at a distance apart from Him. As a central feature of faith; *"His private instructions are customized with a demand of obedience for the performance of every Word He releases into our lives."*

Saul, first blinded by The Light later recouped and his eyes did open. But he was still blind; immersed in God's Glory with so great a power that it would take him three days to fully recover.

> *And the men which journeyed with him stood speechless, hearing a voice, but seeing no man. And Saul arose from the earth; and when his eyes were opened, he saw no man: but they led him by the hand, and brought him into Damascus. And he was three days without sight, and neither did eat nor drink.* [1]

Likened to the moon that has no light of its own but dependent on the light of the sun for exposure; the same is the presence of darkness relational to the exposure of light to unveil its covering. Transparency of light when reflected upon a darkened canvas has conversion power. When Saul encountered the *"Light of Heaven"* shining upon his darkened conscience; it created a revolution in him that changed his religious ambitions from Saul, the Chief Obstructer of Faith to Apostle Paul; one now convicted of God's sovereignty. Paul would spend the rest of his days as a witness of the *"Revelation of Christ"*.

"Necessity for Light" instigates humility of faith to cry out as Paul; *"Lord, what do You want me to do?* [2] Have you seen the Light? Were you enraptured in the

experience of God's Glory as a transforming testimony bearing witness of the power of His Light? Revelation of Christ will blind you from looking into your past by the transfixing Glory of His Presence. In exchange of willingness for recovery of our sight to see, we must accept guidance of *"God's Anointing; the Holy Spirit; the Glory and Power of His Divine Presence"*. Under His ruler-ship, the power and passion of love centered in our hearts releases faith as an exercising agent of His Spirit living within us to control activity of our gifts. If we are able to connect to the center of His Indwelling Presence, a continual outpouring of His Spirit would flow as a dynamo releasing *"The Oil of Heaven"* as a precious resource needed for our journey.

Mystery of Faith 2

"The performance of faith executed by the Holy Spirit's guiding influence is of greater value than any accomplishments motivated by our intellect and talents."

Faith truly is an enigma existing as a shroud of invisible power. When rightfully used, it becomes a transcending instrument of creativity. It fuels our imagination as an accelerant to replicate an image of thought conceived in the mind of our Creator. Every vision has the imagining of faith as a resource of great wealth capable of turning our dreams into a tangible reality. Without the imagination of faith, we lack the ability to exceed the beaten path where others have trod before us. The speculations of life seeded into faith can't be achieved without the trusted path of the Holy Spirit's guidance. He will lead us in discovery of the perfect will of God purposed for our lives.

By God's design, our lives are intended to be the collective conscience of His Existence here on Earth with given authority and the tool of faith to replicate His Image. Written upon the scrolls of faith, there are vaulted testaments of spiritual experiences that have preceded our existence. When we interrogate faith, it creates a provocation to dig a little deeper for clarity of truth. Discovery of God's true plan He intended for humanity becomes much clearer as our understanding becomes aligned with the proven protocols of faith.

The Day of Adam

Throughout our daily interactions as we contend with circumstances laid in our path, our thoughts are in a struggle separating the powers of *"Good and Evil";* warring of our spirit versus our flesh. Uniqueness of war is a contest of ownership always resulting with a winner and a loser. At times, a settled compromise of coexistence may occur when our battles are unsettled and the war of *"betwixt opinions"* challenges our faith in pursuit of resolution.

The natural man, laden with scenic interpretations, opposes the *"Spirit of Christ's dominion-ship"* as God's authority to operate in our lives. In the unrelenting battle of absolutes, *"Flesh vs. Spirit";* unity of the heart and soul of man lies in the balance of his decisions for choice of governance. To accept God's governance, constituted as the anchor of our beliefs; our mantle of faith must rest beneath the Anointing to exercise His authority. An inner life of unity communing with God's Spirit is a nucleus of invincible power eradicating any threat of darkness shadowing our beliefs.

While communing with the Spirit of God, I was compelled to consider the fragmentations of my beliefs which were biased by years of fluctuating testimonies of my successes and failures. I discovered variances that surfaced from an inequality of results emerged from my battles. We all are spiritually contested where our conscience is buffeted by resistive forces of the lesser order of our natural inclinations. However, the Holy Spirit is God's protector capable of conquering any deception of darkness lurking in our path.

While scrutinizing the testimonies of Adam's early beginnings in the Garden, I discovered the peace and unity he experienced consumed with the love of God before his fall. I made an examination of his response to love before his fatal decision to abandon an eternal hope while still occupied in perfection of God's design. It was a source of guidance as I ventured to deepen my faith with a nostalgic view of my spiritual beginnings.

Necessity for Light

While sifting through memories of yesterday, when faith was still hidden in the dark trenches of discovery, I was confronted with a need for *"Necessity for Light"* to unveil my destiny in life. After years of waiting for a response through interrogations of my faith, I arrived to embrace the fate of obedience to a call much bigger than me. My ears were opened to God's instructions and my eyes fixed on an uncharted destiny laid in the path before me. I took comfort in the Light of God's Revelations that was so needed in my life. I discovered revelation lifts the curtain of darkness sheltering our understanding and ushers in clarity of light dispelling the dark cloud over our imaginations and dreams.

I re-examined revelations God gave to Moses on top of Mount Sinai opening a curtain for a glimpse into eternity past. When God removed the veil revealing the beginning of humanity, there was no evidence of life before Him which can be articulated. His beginnings, the *"Genesis of Creation"*, were within the boundaries of a creative thought with enough imagination to fuel our existence. God has an imagination but unlike ours, He connects *"His Creativity"* to a divine purpose.

Moses bore record of humanity's beginnings looking prophetically backwards into the day of creation. It was a revelation of how we got here; where we're going and how to get there. Moses recorded his testimony, the *"Pentateuch, Torah; a record of God's Theocracy"*. He looked as far back as time would allow as a witness to revelations of God's testimony to mankind of His Creation. I wonder did Moses entertain the thought that his prophetic encounter on Mount Sinai would still be broadcast from the tops of every mountain known to man.

> *Then I saw a new heaven and a new earth, for* **the first heaven and the first earth had passed away**, *and the sea was no more. And I saw the holy city, New Jerusalem, coming down out of heaven from God, prepared as a bride adorned for her husband. And I heard a loud voice from the throne saying,* **"Behold, the dwelling place of God is with man.** *He will dwell with them, and they will be his people and God Himself will be with them as their God.* [1]

Just as Moses traveled the tributaries of revelation past, Prophet John in the Book of Revelation saw far into our distant future. From one revelation to the next; *"**It is but One Truth; One Dwelling Place**"* in the heart of humanity. Eternity past and present is but one thought; one event in the mind of our Creator. It is the truth of yesterday, today and forever in the conscience mind of His unchangeable Spirit.

God's *"thoughts"* are quite intimidating. Your head would explode if you tried to harness His power! It will consume you with babblings if you tried to articulate His reality. Your lips would stammer uncontrollably as the inside of you would burn with unquenchable fire. Truth is, God's words are radioactive likened to the core of Earth and the nuclear fusion of the sun. They both derived their power from Him through the Spoken Word of Faith; *"The Light of His Existence"*. Do you realize, the words of faith we speak are radioactive as well to bring blessings and curses upon others as well as ourselves? That's why we are to be mindful of the things we speak; *"Our words bear seeds of life"*. And they do have consequences.

To communicate with us, God gave us *"revelation"* by His Words proportional to what our senses could handle. Some understood; some knowingly dismissed; *"But they deliberately forgot that long ago by **God's Word** the heavens came into being and the Earth was formed out of water and by water."* [1] Very profound! The spinning of water mixed with dust shaped from darkened matter is within the realm of His Creativity.

Scripture teaches; *"If we desire wisdom, God has an availability of answers delivered as a promise of faith to our prayers"*. But there is a caution; don't ask amiss meaning don't ask in vanity of your curiosity. Too much of His wisdom can have an overloading affect. The testimony of Solomon bears witness to this truth.

> *Behold, **I have done according to thy words**: lo, I have given thee a wise and an understanding heart so that there was none like thee before thee, neither after thee shall any arise like unto thee.* [1]

In an exceptional moment of meditation, I emerged with a very provocative question: *"How many billions of years did it take for me to get here? How far did I have to travel?"* Now that's the kind of stuff where your head will definitely explode! Only the wisdom of eternity has the answer. But the provocative nature of my thoughts were actualized in the deep trenches of meditation to accept a truth; *"God's thoughts are eternal"*! Essence of all that I am came from His original thought. He spoke me into being by an expression of His Creativity by the spoken Word of Faith *"let there be light"*.[2] Truth being; *"I came with the light"*. It just took me a while to get here. There is nothing new under the sun. We all came from the same Light of His Existence. I am a conceived thought in the mind of my Creator and so are you. We are not here by accident or the product of some cosmic failure but by extension of His Breath He breathed into the nostril of man as the *"Spirit of Life"*.

In the Beginning

It all began from a spoken word when God defined the boundaries of time and seasons and produced us as the object of His desire. All life belongs to God! All men are the product of His imagination and we all draw our life from Him. The purpose of our beginnings was intended to be a reflection of His Image defined by impressions of His love. It was a gift unto Himself; the making of humanity bearing the seeds of creation with instructions to reproduce in the likeness of Him.

Adam was first introduced into a virgin garden born of God's imagination. Unification of his inner man connected with God's outer perfection as a source of power and authority with creativity only bound by his choices. He was sanctioned with *"freedom of choice"* to rule in a stream of purity embedded in his conscience. Adam received a set of simple instructions which his obedience could not fathom the depth of the failing consequences of his refusal to comply. We should be pointing the finger at ourselves; we are no different.

> *And the LORD God commanded the man, "You are free to eat from any tree in the garden; but you must not eat from the tree of the knowledge of good and evil, for when you eat from it **you will certainly die**."*
> **Genesis 2:16-17 NIV**

What is the sentence of death to one who has never experienced it before? Certainly, Adam would find out! Ultimately his resolution to invalidate the eternal good of God is no different than a decision we would make. *"Flesh born of flesh is powerless without God's Spirit as the eminent authority."* As a consequence, failure of our willingness to adhere to the principles of obedience will render self-judgment of our choices. Periodically, when pursuing our goals, we fail in steadfastness to address the demons of temptation constantly lurking in our path. Adam proved to be no exception. By disobeying God's instructions, He made a decision violating God's creative experience instigating judgment upon us all.

The garment of the Image of God's Likeness that was bestowed upon Adam lost its connectivity to the stream of eternal life that flowed from the fountain of God's Everlasting Love. Disobedience is a separator, a consequential result of the betrayal of love. Seeded in temptation, it clouds our understanding diminishing the true Light of God's Revelation as a mimic of truth. Adam had only one law to consider; it was simply the *"Law of Obedience"*. It would be the same law Jesus would fulfill giving credence to the domination of spirit over corruptible flesh.

Tend and Guard: Do's and Don'ts

> *And the Lord God took the man and put him in the Garden of Eden to* **tend and guard** *and keep it. And the Lord God commanded the man, saying, you may freely eat of every tree of the Garden but of the tree of the knowledge of good and evil and blessing and calamity, you shall not eat it, for in the day that you eat of it you shall surely die.*
> **Genesis 2:15-17 AMPC**

Adam's original commission was consummated in his instructions; *"tend and guard"*. There's a difference between tending and guarding. Hopefully I am able to differentiate between the two. *"Tending is the complete comprisal of faith; full consummation and sum total of obedience to God's center of attraction."* Tending also suggests movement; cultivating the Tree of Life for continual expansion which needed Adam's undivided attention. Tending the Tree of Life; God's Eternal Fire, demanded an unwavering commitment of faith for a life of permanence to the extent his obedience allowed.

You've heard the statement and even have said in defense of your time; *"I'm tending to my business"*; which implies our ability to gravitate, migrate towards something perceived to be of greater importance than mundane encounters surrounding our lives. Tending is *"object dependent"* meaning the total focus and distribution of our thoughts, feelings, actions and our motivations. Inclusively, tending defines our purpose; fully encased with instructions targeting our faith in pursuit of God's chosen path. In our obedience; we surrender with our faith immersed into the center of His attraction terminating pursuit of our own agendas. Tending is a sacrifice; a burden of faith no different than burden of the cross we bear.

Tending establishes a relationship of a dependent object bearing accountability to its sustaining source. As an object which is dependent related, the influence at the center of its sphere of attraction as the Earth which locks the moon in its orbit by its gravitational power both share a mutual relationship. It's the same as the gravity of faith; attracting our lives to the call of obedience. We tend to things that are most precious to our survival; our families, homes, money, relationships and even our faith; things of our greatest concerns. Tending also invokes a level of trust. Just as God has promised, we take no thought in doing His bidding knowing He will supply whatever is needed in pursuit of faith. Hope, anchored in belief is a secured trust of God's ability to do exceedingly above and beyond what we ask or think. By accepting this truth we will avert compromise and contempt levied against our faith.

Guarding however is statically positioned to defend as a protector from intrusions. Just as a soldier stands watch in defense of a protected treasure; we guard against penetrating forces trying to compromise our faith. When our perceptions are actualized to a given set of instructions, we vigorously defend what we are assigned to do. Most often, it's the action of what we are defending against in keeping God's entrustments.

The guarded stance of faith is a burden to bear amidst never-ending confrontations in our pursuit of faith. Scripture teaches that we must guard our heart; *"Everything we do flows from its center"*. It's imperative we defend against variances orchestrated to dampen our hope of faith. If we allow them to take root, they develop into warring factions challenging our resiliency to remain standing. Immersed in the weariness of our battles, the settled peace of Christ continues as a chaperon of comfort settling any dispute of the heart.

> *Be anxious for nothing, but in everything by prayer and supplication, with thanksgiving, let your requests be made known to God; and the peace of God, which surpasses all understanding will guard your **hearts and minds** through Christ Jesus.* [1]

The heart of faith is precious in the eyes of God. It is the key to treasures waiting for discovery through our pursuit of faith. God's greatness dwelling within will protect us, settle us and keep us from falling. Not only will he keep our hearts but He will keep our mind in perfect peace. As our hearts are being cultivated to His desire and our meditations remain centered on the hope of faith; radicalization of our motivations propels us towards the path of an unwavering defense of truth.

In the mind of faith, battles are waged fighting for supremacy of our *"conscience and wavering thoughts"*. The weapons of our warfare are contriving not born of human carnality but are uniquely spiritual. Like a shelter, the Holy Spirit will defend against arguments of faith but our thoughts must be punished for any variance of truth. If allowed to linger we could suffer a dislocation of faith at a time we so desperately need it opening the door to fanaticisms and exaggerations.

> *But the weapons of our warfare are not carnal but mighty in God for pulling down strongholds, casting down arguments and every high thing that exalts itself against the knowledge of God, bringing every thought into captivity to the obedience of Christ, and being ready to punish all disobedience when your obedience is fulfilled* [2]

In Adam's instructions, what was he commissioned to do? Was it to protect the trees that were good for food? NO! Was he to put on his battle helmet and stand guard on the perimeter away from the center of his delegated responsibility? Really! Then what was his commission? He was tending the *"Tree"* that would sustain him (*Tree of Life*) and guarding against the *"Tree"* purposed to destroy him (*Tree of Good and Evil*).

> *And out of the ground the* **God Made every tree grow** *that is pleasant to the sight and good for food. The tree of life was also in the midst of the garden, and the tree of the knowledge of good and evil.* [1]

Was it too much to ask of Adam to tend and guard? Could he not think and chew gum at the same time? Are we still to assume his role was simply that of a farmer; tilling? Was he instructed to just grow crops or was it a much greater commission of maintaining and increasing what God had already initiated?

Adam's instructions were non-burdensome and quite simple; *"Tend and Guard"*. God didn't need a farmer; He was the farmer *"In-Chief"*. He put Adam in **"His Garden manufactured from the soil of His Own creation"**. The Earth was in perfect balance. It was after Adam had sinned and excommunicated to the field he was to till the Earth with labor and sweat.

While in a moment of meditation, I was envisioning Adam's physical appearance of his days in the Garden. I know that sounds really crazy but I was challenging my imagination seeking an understanding of the why of things. Have you had peculiar thoughts you couldn't share because of how the *"self-righteous"* would judge your perceptions? Images formed in our imagination will develop into pictures of life initiating power from the pictures they paint. And indelibly they will leave an impression seared into our imagination and if not *"rightfully"* filtered, will take root as an action of our faith. *"As a man thinketh, so is he."*

However, I had my filters on and the thought still reverberated; *"Eyebrows"!* What is their purpose? Have you ever taken thought why they are suspended above your eyes? Despite for appearance, particularly women exemplifying their uniqueness by designing contour lines of distinction, eyebrows keep sweat from falling into our eyes.

"Did Adam have eyebrows?" Subjectively, there is inference that he may not have. He didn't need them! God's Garden existed in an ambient environment void of sweat; no rain and definably no tears. Only when Adam entered the world of sweat and labor to till the ficlds did man evolve with hair as a means to temper the flow of sweat forming in his brow! Salinity of sweat falling into your eyes can be quite irritating. It will temporarily obscure your vision. Salinity of sweat from the pain of labor and excrement of salty tears when our hopes are dampened still exist as a measurement of Adam's disobedience. Have you noticed; the amount of stress put on your body will produce an array of consequences. You could lose your hair and it will

never come back. Stress also can cause your anxiety level to shoot through the roof making it impossible for you to sleep. Aches, pains, wear and tear taking its toll on our fragile bodies; they all cause an imbalance of hormonal distribution due to exertion of stress. But more significantly, stress compromises your immune system with a host of vulnerabilities. So when you look into the mirror take special note of your *"Eyebrows"*. My daughter has. She shaved them off!

> *Thorns also and thistles shall it bring forth to thee; and thou shalt eat the herb of* ***the field****; By the sweat of thy brow shalt thou eat bread, till thou return unto the ground; for out of it wast thou taken: for dust thou art, and unto dust shalt thou return.* **Genesis 3:18-19 KJV**

Adam was evicted from the Garden to do labor in the fields of Earth. What a remarkable departure! How long was his tenure in the Garden before his eviction? We will never know! But one thing we do know; he was living by *"God's eternal clock"* before the clock of death initiated a new sequence of time. After his expulsion, God assigned a new guardian; a host of *"Cherubims"* at the east of the Garden and a flaming sword protecting God's Eternal Tree of Life. Cherubims are spiritual so is the blinding light of a flaming sword. Spirit matter is a distinct separation of visibility from all physical properties share in our reality.

> *So he drove out the man; and He placed at the east of the Garden of Eden Cherubims, and a flaming sword which turned every way* ***to keep the way of the Tree of Life.*** [1]

When Adam failed to keep the instructions of faith, there was no further need for him to guard against the theme of death emanating from the Tree of Good and Evil. He already had consumed it! It was now part of his constitution. He brought it into the world we are now living in; *"metastasized"* while leaving behind the tree our world so desperately needs; *"The Tree of Life"*.

Adam obstructed God's plan for His Presence to continue as the centerpiece of His Creation in the midst of the Garden. If he had continued fanning the flames of *"God's Eternal Fire of the God Given Life"*, eternity would exist in all of us. God's Life is eternal life! As *"ministers of reconciliation; guardians mandated to distribute His Fire"*, we are commissioned to fan the flames of His Redemptive Life to all living in darkness.

> *There was a man sent from God, whose name was John. The same came for a witness, to bear witness of the Light that all men through Him might believe. He was not that Light but was sent to bear witness of that Light. That was the true Light, which lighteth every man that cometh into the world.* [1]

John the Baptist succeeded as a witness waiting in the wings of faith for Revelation of Christ to emerge to shine the Light of God upon all humanity. Ever since the epic days of Adam's betrayal, the Revelation of Christ had been incubating behind a protective shield of Cherubims until the Cross of Calvary was mounted as the object signifying God's eternal life. The Cross of Christ is symbolic of *"The Tree of Life"* hewn from Earth's humanity in search of God's divinity.

In the Garden, The Tree of Life was purposed to sustain Adam throughout eternity but the Tree of Good and Evil if consumed, would bear the seeds of a *"pandemic"* the world had never seen. The power of temptation is a force to be reckoned with. You can get too close to what God has commanded you to stay away from and you could get singed. Just ask Moses! He had an encounter;

> *And the Angel of the Lord appeared to him in a **"flame of fire"** from the midst of a bush. So he looked, and behold, the bush was burning with fire, but the bush was not consumed. Then Moses said, **"I will now turn aside and see this great sight, why the bush does not burn."** So when the Lord saw that he turned aside to look, God called to him from the midst of the bush and said, "Moses, Moses!" And he said, "Here I am." Then He said, **"Do not draw near this place."** Take your sandals off your feet, for the place where you stand is Holy Ground.* [1]

When Moses turned aside in his query pondering why the bush didn't burn, he encountered a flame of fire beyond recognition of his senses. The shadow of God's Presence, the fiery angel in the burning bush is the same fire occupying our hearts as the Holy Spirit *"Living Within"*. The *"Upper Room"* experience when the disciples were yielded in prayer at the Altar of Faith, *"Eternity Came to Dwell Within the Heart of Man"*. The Holy Spirit expanded God's Existence in the Earth by a exponential factor spreading from heart to heart as a unifier; *"Into Oneness of Eternity Living Within"*.

Revelation of Life

As a fully conceived thought of Earth's beginnings, Revelation of Life drifted in the patient streams of time for the mystery of creation to reveal its purpose. It is the revelation of divine rulership of a King and His Kingdom with a *"humanity"* created to occupy in His authority. The plan of God continued to evolve even beyond Adam's failure for the Revelation of Christ to be revealed to all of His creation.

> *And He said to me, "It is done!" I am Alpha and Omega, the beginning and the end. I will give of the fountain of the water of Life freely to him who thirst. He who overcomes shall inherit all things and I will be his God and he shall be My son.* **Revelations 21:6-7 NKJV**

After Adam's fall, God initiated a plan of redemption to restore humanity back into the center of His vision evidenced by the Cross of Christ that lifted high on a pinnacle as a beacon of hope to draw all men back into His Kingdom. When redemption came, it came with a choice to all men to accept the sacrificial blood that was purchased on the Cross as the expense for sin. As an identifying garment for our salvation, the fabric of our conscience is stained by the Blood of Christ as an action of His redeeming grace. As Believers, we are a living signature of sufferings of the Cross evidenced in our walk of faith. The obedient will of Jesus fulfilled the destiny of faith; now it is our turn to take identity of the Cross. It's a matter of choice. *"Pick It Up!"*

God's government by rule of law which existed for thousands of years because of Adam's betrayal guided us into a new standard that we are now made children of God through *"faith in Jesus Christ"*. To redeem the sacrificial offerings of the Cross, it necessitated a New Birth but with a different protocol of selectivity;

> *But as many as **received Him to them** gave He power to become the sons of God even to them that **believed on His Name**.* [1]

From one man's choice that declined permanence in the estuary streams of continual flowing waters to a generation in thirst of the *"True and Living Water"*, we are now made sons through Jesus by faith established for our redemption. It is not a work of our flesh but an acceptance of the *"Word of Faith"*.

A New Awakening

The arousal of our spiritual conscience migrates towards the path that secured our beginnings in the *"Garden of God's Creation"*. It's like the salmon in the ocean returning to the source of their first migration seeking to fulfill completion of their purpose.

God's original design of humanity was interwoven with seams stitched by His unifying power to create an *"image of singleness"* conceived in His thought. After marring of the mantle of faith by the blemish of sin, His design of perfection no longer prevailed exclusively centered in trust. The result of sin introduced a new demand for a greater power of compliance than the ability of dust and soul. It was of greater value than what restrictions of the law could produce initiating a new creativity of faith; the *"burden of belief"*.

> *For God so loved the world that He gave His only begotten Son, that whosoever **believeth** in Him should not perish but have everlasting life.* **John 3:16 KJV**

Adam's tenure in the Garden was defined as being the first Adam, a living being, a place holder in time until the *"Revelation of Christ"*, the second Adam, a life giving spirit was manifested. The creation of Earth is a habitation for the *"Revelation of Christ who personifies God's Existence as Father of all Eternity"*. Christ is the identifying image of God! In the day of creation, Christ was with God as an entity of Trinity. As a vacuum of flesh with value no more than a dead man's dust being reclaimed by the Earth; our hollow chambers of dust and soul were created to give identity to the image in the Likeness of Christ as a visible image born of His Spirit just as the likeness of Christ was born of God.

> *And so it is written, "The first man Adam became a living being"; the last Adam became a life-giving spirit. However, the spiritual is not first, but the natural and afterward the spiritual. The first man was of the earth made of dust; the second man is the Lord from heaven. As was the man of dust, so also are those who are made of dust; and as is the heavenly man, so also are those who are heavenly. And as we have borne the image of the man of dust, we shall also bear the image of the heavenly man.* [1]

> *This is the book of the genealogy of Adam. In the day that God created man, He made him in the **likeness of God**. He created them male and female, and blessed them and called them Adam in the day they were created.* **Genesis 5:1-2 NKJV**

Adam first appeared on the scene with no prior life of preparation; he was matured born in perfection of the *"Likeness of God"*. Perfection needs no preparation. *"It Just Is"*. The declarative *"Is"* has infinite power that requires no other sponsorship. *"It is what it is."* Adam never had the opportunity for trials and errors of faith as we have; his instructions were absolute, without any exceptions.

Adam's world existed in the comfort of peace born from the fellowship of God's Presence. In his world of introduction, he had opportunity to experience what you and I will not see until our souls are reclaimed to know the *"true"* purity reflected in the light of God's character. In a sense, I am quite envious of Adam. He experienced the Presence of God in His purest form with the Tree of Life (*The Tree of Eternity*) emanating from His Presence. To have known God in the intimacy of our understanding and then suffer a self-inflicted wound of betrayal is life shattering when you consider irrevocably, you have lost everything. It's no different than having the Presence of the Holy Spirit lifted from our lives. How unbearable that would be! As Believers, God's stewards of faith, our existence in His Kingdom is non-perishable securing eternal life for habitation in a new Earth as a reward for our obedience.

The Cross of Christ was a transactional event for reinstatement of eternal life to all who would believe. It's a measurement of the depth of love Christ endured for the salvation of humanity. *"Eternal life is the woven strength of eternity"*. It is an endless boundary of time encased in an ovum of ever evolving inner life. Though the foundation of God's Kingdom is without end, His circumference is illuminating as a power defining the countenance of *"His Appearance"*. Although Moses was not allowed to see the full revelation of God on top of Mount Sinai, he was privy to a rear view perspective of Him (*revelation of time beginnings*). However, the day will come when we all will see Him face to face. He has already made preparation for an eternal occupation enjoined with His Presence.

The Image of Love

"God's love is eternal and cannot be recalled." How remarkable; a never-ending gift fueled by the power of the greatness of His love. True love is a fixation on the value of trust; synonymous as not to separate one from the other. The uniqueness of trust exemplifies the character of love exercised by our ability to submit. Trust espouses a willingness to obey indicative of our hearts humbled in submission.

Centered as a feature of love along with forgiveness, longsuffering and kindness of compassion which are the building blocks for the expression of a greater love is patience. Patience measures the degree of love we attribute to ourselves as well as others. Often in our haste we can inflict discouragement upon others by our unsettled response to patience. Patience is waiting. The anxiety of waiting can be punishing; punishing everybody and everything crossing our path if we are not careful. Anxiety is a causation of insensitivities in considerations of others when we are suspended in the balance of our indecisions while waiting. Waiting is not always easy and can be quite trying to our faith.

So often in the middle of our battles, a test will arise putting on full display our determination to wait; waiting for us not to get ahead of ourselves to make a blunder of our faith. Before we can determine where the road ahead is leading us, it is required of us to wait in *"contentment of faith and rest in the peace of God and He will preserve our visions and dreams"*.

Patience measures time which is given as grace to discover and gain strength for the unknown battles concealed in our path. We don't always know what the future will hold but through patience it allows us time for preparation to move beyond our inadequacies to rightfully reclaim legitimacy to our faith. Our lives are not lived in a day; it is a journey. We are living in a time ordered with a sense of hurriedness, forgoing the need for patience. It is edifying to see results from the investment of faith knowing the end did come but we never should be in such a hurry to see its end. Value gained from the stilling affect of patience is in our preparation; redeeming our time. *"Set your affection on things above, not on things on the Earth. For ye are **dead** and your life is hid with Christ in God."* [1]

Love Never Fails

Despite Adam's heartbreaking betrayal reversing the intended good designated for his life, the love of God still continues mending the wounds scarred by Adam's indulgence of faith. God's love is *"irrevocable, forgiving and ever evolving"* as an attraction that can never be apart from Him. After Adam disrupted the plan laid before him, the Image of Faith purposed as guidance into the center of God's appeal has evolved throughout the ages. The path of faith was vindicated outside the gates of Calvary on Golgotha's Hill for the *"Revelation of Christ"* to complete His call.

God is continually drawing men back into His Kingdom through the *"attraction of His Magnetism"*. Love is magnetic; in essence, *"God is Love"*! [1] It is His Existence. The recklessness of Adam's disobedience violated the boundaries of God's trust which was given as a commitment of love. The veil of Glory resting upon his mantle of authority was blemished by corruption of sin that has lasted throughout the ages. From end to end, Scripture teaches us that love will never fail but will testify of our inability to apprehend its principles. *"Love is perfect in its conception."* It is impossible to dissect for distribution into any other format.

The Image of Love was ever so wounded in Adam's disobedience. It ushered in so much disparity and pain developing to be the source of our tears and sufferings that continue to beset our faith. But the mercy and kindness of God's faithfulness is forever present to re-center our faith to His imperishable promise. It is a promise exceeding our grief and fears with a hope borne by acceptance of His grace that's surely needed in our daily encounters.

In the Garden; Adam had an interwoven experience fellowshipping in the Presence of God; not by mandate of faith but by the intuitive power of love actualized where trust and faith synergized into *"communion"!* What an awesome relationship? In our prayer life, we have an exceptional opportunity to achieve that level of togetherness habitable by our willingness to accept God's olive branch of peace as a miraculous life of His giving. Living in true fellowship with His Spirit, peace and love emanating from His Presence will impact our lives with an abundance of power. *"The closer we are to God; the more demonstrative are His Exhibitions."*

In our encounters dealing with others, we all have a tendency of exalting our self-righteousness pointing a finger at other people's failings without knowledge of their circumstances. We are so predictive surmising of our future in what lies in the path before us, but don't truly count the cost required for *"knowing"* which can only be achieved through fellowship and humility of prayer. It's a place we often neglect cultivated for our surrender where our passions are sensitized to the spiritual impressions of faith. Prayer is a capitulation of our will in search of our Father's heart. He knows the true path and will expose any impediments that can bring a hindrance to our faith. God has more of an investment in the destiny of our lives than we realize; for it was He who created us with His purpose in mind.

Ask a rich man on his dying bed, who hoarded all his wealth and never gave to the poor and needy; there is a question I would ask; *"Can your wealth secure you a path into the afterlife? Can one dollar of your fortune buy one breath of soul God has withdrawn from you?"* The answer is quite frankly, No! So why does a man spend his time trying to gain the whole world only to lose his soul? The doorway is narrow and much easier for a camel to go through the eye of a needle than the burden of man and his wealth to enter in. I know we all desire to get as much out of this life as we can without any regrets of un-fulfillment. But it's a choice!

I have often put myself in Adam's shoes to consider my own response to faith;

> *What need or desire do I have that could usurp the authority of God's Presence that could lay claim aborting fulfillment of my destiny? What attachment have I acquired that is more valuable than life itself I would risk the squander of so great a promise? What overwhelming influence or deception could cloud my understanding, evicting me from perfection centered in His love?*

"For all have sinned and come short of the Glory of God." [1] Take a close look in the mirror; it is by God's grace we are being preserved or even considered in the redemptive power of His love. *"We all have sinned"* is an indictment in direct response of our actions which is inclusive; meaning we all have our own failings. So save your judgment of others; *"Judge Yourself"*!

Hidden Within

Life without purpose and instructions to achieve its highest good is a life still laden as a seed buried in darkness struggling to emerge as a benefactor of light. *"Life is a projection of urgency for completion of faith."* Resolutions to impeding issues that often obstruct our progressions are determined by our response to the inner battles lying beneath a surface we often tend to disguise. Usually, by the time they emerge, evidence of their existence is indicative of untold circumstances surrounding our lives. *"My mother once told me; don't let the world see your tears."* That's to say; one would never know of our private battles unless we gave them a purview into our lives. A vexing inferno could be brewing in our spirit; raging beneath our projections as a developing testimony we are reluctant to share. If we are not grounded in our beliefs and proven by the execution of faith, like the flickering flame of a candle, we will lack the power of God's interpretation intended to illuminate our testimonies.

Hidden Life

A hidden life is necessary to maintain fervor of the Holy Spirit's burning flame of fire centered in our hearts. God requires visibility of our faith as a beacon of hope to reach those searching in the dark. We are light bearers with a torch of fire igniting liberating flames for all who have succumbed to the emptiness of night. *"Is a lamp brought to be put under a basket or under a bed? Is it not to be set on a lampstand?"* [1]

The Light of Christ shedding abroad in our hearts attaches to our introspections creating an opportunity for discovery of what God has purposed for our lives. It compels us toward an inward journey searching every possibility hidden in the channels of faith. The broad scope of faith created by His Occupying Presence gives us greater hope for success to complete our journey.

Life's Redundancy

There is a constant in our human experience we cannot escape; *"History has made us all captives as a prisoner of time"*. Usually, in making decisions we tend to follow the same path where our past has led us. Life is an unpredictable series of events; from one day to the next never to be determined from experiences of yesterday what a new day will bring. The offerings of today could be results of carried events of yesterday but each day has its own opportunities.

Often we miss the wisdom of God's Revelations for our lives because of distractions keeping us away from resolute of silence. Typically, our testimonies are veiled in silence buried beneath years of layering. At times, circumstances surrounding our lives are so compelling summoning a greater expression of our faith gained from our secret battles. With wisdom, we have a better chance pulling together fragmented pieces of our hopes and dreams that were scattered in disarray.

Our spiritual composite is the same as a song of prose with no defining structure but is evidenced by its own creative measures. It is very difficult to grasp the substance of spirit which is no different than our failing attempts to redeem the fleeting moments of a broken dream. You stand a better chance trying to harness activity of the wind. The functionality of God's Spirit is a conveyance of power that brings recognition of His Presence as the controlling influence governing our lives. Evidence of His embodiment is reflected in our gifts executed in the synergy of faith.

"The solace of our spirit and the soothing fires of ambience pulsating from our soul will bring a glow to our countenance as the reflective Image born of God's Presence."

3
Father of Lights

Every good gift and every perfect gift is from above, and comes down from the Father of lights, with whom there is no variation or shadow of turning. Of His own will He brought us forth by the word of truth, that we might be a kind of firstfruits of His creatures. [1]

God is the giver of every good and perfect gift descending from above. All power comes from Him; the *"Father of Lights"*, who reveals all mysteries made known to man. We are Heaven's gift of the good and perfect expression of His Resplendent Glory. Revelation of humanity is a kind of *"firstfruits"* when God created man in the Image of His Likeness. In all that proceeded from Heaven, Earth was God's destination for *"Revelation of His Divinity"*. Divinity without humanity is the existence of the likeness of Heaven reverting unto itself before the creation of man. The dominion of Heaven is spiritual; everlasting unlike the perishing materiality of the temporal domain of Earth. God's divinity was originally intended to be a seamless stream of eternal life for all of humanity.

"Of His own will He brought us forth by the Word of Truth, that we might be a kind of firstfruits of His creatures." [2]

The Word of Truth manifested by faith is the given *"Light"* of the victorious power of our Creator. Enriched with gifting of wisdom and understanding to make one wise, we are creatures born of *"His Destiny"* in pursuit of the lighted path where there is no variation of truth nor turning away into the shadow of darkness. Hidden at a distance, obscured from revealing power of light, our gifting and the treasures of life remain undetected until the penetrating light of discovery brings to the surface recognition of our gifts as a service purposed for humanity.

Morning Dew

At the morning glow of day while sitting in my chair meditating upon silent reflections of yesterday; I began to ponder as the stars of heaven started disappearing at emergence of the sun's blinding light. In the light of day, our vision of the darkened sky loses its power to see the captured body of stars in the distant heavens. When the darkened canvass of night encounters the morning light, it changes its color from black to blue. In my ponderings, I realized the light of the sun is only a prism of colors empowering our eyes with sight to see from morning to night.

The universe is so vast enveloped in a canvas of darkness with illuminating stars descendant from the light of creation. Without the shining light of the sun and the generation of stars fragmenting the heavens, we would see creation before the beginning; a world void of light.

Blackness is the restrainer of darkness but lost its clutching hold at the command of the spoken word of faith; *"Let there be! And so it is and will be until God reclaims the heavens".* From darkness we came and darkness we shall return drawn to a greater power of light waiting at water's edge of a new beginning. Light is a sponsor of the Spoken Word of God's Creativity; the same Light of power giving visibility to faith.

Time

Time is a recycling of eternity; an ever evolving cycle completing its call as the host of God's Creation. The strings of time and eternity will continue to restrain Earth upon its pedestal until the cycle of its fulfillment comes to an end. Creation of our time beginnings was established upon six sequential building blocks; God's six days of creation from formation of the heavens and Earth to the finishing of man as an occupying steward of *"His Creative Adventure".*

Revelation of time is embedded in light. If we had the ability to dissect light and sustain its power, we would come to know the purity of God. Light as we know it is an instrument of the spoken Word of Faith. It was the *"Word of Beginning"* that created a window of opportunity into the measurement of our existence. The emergence of light was the *"Light of God"* breaking through the cover of darkness that had shielded the substance of His Creation. The empirical Light of God is the creative energy of His Existence and is only bound by limits initiated by His spoken Word.

Throughout scripture, the question remains of time, its purpose and connectivity to our humanity. Our days are filled with numbers of adding one to another. From days to years; from minutes to hours; from price for sight to the fathom depths of faith, we expense time as an occupying presence consuming our existence. From the hourglass to the sundial, clocks to watches, analog to digital, we have incremented time into a burden of our human activity. In the thought of God, the past, present and future is one event; *"That which is has been is now, and that which is to be has already been and God requires that which is past"*.[1] There is nothing comparable to time; it is an analogy unto itself embedded with a consciousness of its own completion.

Man has harvested time turning it into a business by selling off its measurements. We are compensated not only for services rendered but through negotiations of hourly, monthly and yearly expectations of the management of time. It induces an obligated burden of anxiety, a disturbance of peace immersed in waves of confusion beating upon the shorelines of our destiny. In our hurriedness of time, it can produce fluctuating circumstances impeding upon our spiritual priorities.

Seasons

> *Then God said, Let there be lights in the firmament of the heaven to divide the day from the night; and let them be for signs, and for seasons, and for days, and years.*
> **Genesis 1:14 NKJV**

Even though time is a constant, it is not timeless. It is only a measurement separated from the endless life of eternity. The seasons of our lives are unpredictable transitional events of time. It may take days or even years from one season to the next for the fulfillment of its purpose. Nature itself is suspended in a balance of reoccurring seasons as a symphony of time migrating from one season to the next. The Laws of Nature are consistent from labor of summer to the harvest of fall; from rehabilitation of winter to blossoming of spring. It is a redundant cycle that continues as a reminder of God's replenishing grace.

The seasonal path of nature is reflective throughout the animal kingdom. Through our observations, if we take a moment and withdraw from the complexities (*compound simplicities*) of managing our lives, nature will teach us through changing of seasons that our lives follow the same pattern. In our discovery, we can ascertain wisdom purposed for our instructions. We will discover why salmon follow the same migrating route from the day of their beginning and die after spawning; why bears store up fat for hibernation of winter and give birth to their cubs in a cave; why birds don't fly at night and live in silence at the setting of the sun; why buffalo migrating across the Serengeti follow the same dangerous path crossing rivers infested with danger; and why deer rut at the changing of fall in reckless pursuit to connect with their nature. There is so much nature can teach us; down to the smallest "*ant*" but inquisitiveness of nature must be activated.

There is a difference between our selective process and that of animals in consideration of the seasonal events of our lives. Animals move in seasons without time's increments but our lives are micro managed to the ticking of the clock. When God put the lights in the firmament of heaven and separated the day from the night, He gave us a clock from the rising sun in the east to the twilight of dusk. It is His clock given as measurement for everything required of us to do; from sun up when we were born to sun down at evening pause of our journey.

"Time is given to purpose". It is a truth we all must consider for without it, there would be no justifying cause for our existence. Seasons without respect of time is as an oasis of our imagination to believe the content of our lives have no defining purpose.

Seasons are calendar events of the expectations of faith. To everything there is a season, a time for every purpose under Heaven. Even Heaven has a time that is waiting for the fulfillment of *"time"* and so do our lives. There are two things with certainty we cannot change: *"A time to be born and a time to die."* [1] In between, the Bible says; *"work out your own salvation with fear and trembling"* [2] guided by our choices as the clock of our lives continues to tick.

From bitterness of winter to restoration of spring; from heat of summer to the sabbatical of fall, seasonal events of our lives are always fluctuating in dynamic movement from one season to the next. Seasons never remain the same always delivering freshness to the expectations of life. However, attached to our mortality they do have a defining end. Swaying in my conscience in reflection of time and eternity, I am somewhere in between sequestered in a time to live. Betwixt of its beginning and where it will all end, I'm journeying the path in the security of time waiting for the finishing of my faith on a course that has not completed its end.

> *"As a child I spoke as a child; it was the only response I knew to the guidance of love. But through the transitioning of time, I vacated vanity of childish thinking in pursuit of a new awakened journey in the path of faith."*

When time takes its bow at the dimming of our lamps, it ceases releasing its carryings infinitely into the paradise of eternity. With receipts of a completed life, our lives are dispensed into a vacuum of no end losing its material value with no calculated returns. Without measurable boundaries, we drift waiting to connect with a cloud of witnesses for the day when we all shall reappear. We will be seen again; the day when the dead shall rise with those still waiting in the wings of faith; waiting for their redemption to draw nigh.

Initiated in our beginnings, the revolving seasons of time introduced us into the cycle of faith; a cycle with invested dreams and hope fulfilling the expectations of life. We emerged captured by its power struggling to intersect with the light of day. From beginning to end, burden with a cross to bear and Light of God's Spirit shining upon our destiny; instigated a measurement of time dedicated for completion for the proving of faith.

Time turns into seasons as a novelty of change passing from one generation to the next. Insecurities of love centered in dependency of the soft spoken words of a child to maturity of a beholder of faith, we struggle to apprehend truth in search of life's destiny. Time is the most precious possession that is attached to our humanity holding the vault of our beginnings. It is a reservoir of safety preserving the *"Key of Life"*. There aren't any substitutes for the experiences of life we can interject that can compare to our tribulations, sorrows and even joys of our successes. Life is to be lived in its entirety; from beginning to end. Actualization of our lives to the extent we have fulfilled our journey after completing the call of faith; only then will rest come to our weary souls. It will be a welcomed ending of our journey; dying in hope of a redeeming promise.

True North

> *And take heed, lest you lift your eyes to heaven, and when you see the sun, the moon, and the stars, all the host of heaven, you feel driven to worship them and serve them, which "the LORD your God has given to all the peoples under the whole heaven as a heritage.* **Deut 4:19 NKJV**

Years ago, I was presented with a special gift. It was a certificate of a star; *"Aries RA 3h17m10sD29'5"* with the signature of my name. With scanning eyes in the darkness of night searching for its light, the stars of heaven all appeared the same. Where it is, I do not know but this I know; stars are not eternal. They come and go; the same pilgrimage of man, here today; gone tomorrow. For every star that dies a new one is being born. There are no two days the same only the eternity of Heaven exist in fixation of the same day of time; morphing dimensionally in a never-ending conclusion of its expansion.

Our universe is populated with billions of stars with no conceivable end to their existence. Where they end would only be a beginning in our efforts to understand the envelope of darkness and its hidden treasures. We are only claimants to things that we see. The celestial arrangements populating our heavens belong to us all as a heritage to those who set their sights above. Our visualizations are limited by the boundary of light with no conceiving end of the expanse of darkness.

Stars occupy a temporary space in our heavens. As lords of heaven, they twinkle with sparkling eyes as a testament of creation with an existence preceding our reality. If we could acquire their knowledge, they would tell us they were there in the beginning as a witness when the greatest energy the universe has ever known created a vacuum of light for our existence.

By the Word of Faith, *"the exposing Light of God"* invigorated the seams of darkness initiating discovery of all seen realities. Darkness without light exists in *"Perpetuum"*; meaning it is a never ending cycle void of conclusion. In the darkened light of eternity there are dimensions which have not yet met exposure to what God's Light can reveal. It is all part of the creative mystery of creation. Within the range of exposure darkness is dispelled by light. Take the shining of a flashlight on a specific target; darkness still exist as a circumference differentiating light from the darkened canvas allowing us to see existence of things negated in the dark by exposure of detecting light.

In the beginning of creation God made two great lights; one brighter than the other. The greater light ruled the day; the lesser light ruled the night. Their existence emerged when the concession of darkness was crumbled by a superior performance of Light. The greater light is our sun; the lesser light is our moon. Colored in florescent white, the light of the moon is the light of a false star reflecting light in the likeness of a star. Whatever happened to the moon's energy that it refuses to shine on its own? Why does it now require reflective light from the sun to be seen?

> *The sun shall be turned into darkness, and the moon into blood, before the great and terrible day of the LORD come.* [1]

Scripture teaches the day will come when the sun that is fueling our existence will exhaust its nuclear power and reach the same fate as the moon. I won't be around and neither will you to witness completion of a Prophetic Word spoken well into the future of human occupation on Earth. The moon will reflect the color of blood due to diminished return of the sun's energy. In the day darkness arrives, the image of the sun and moon's appearance will no longer be seen. They will be black stars hidden in darkness of the heavens. A star is a star. They all share the same properties of stars that preceded them. A run to Mars won't help; it will be black as well. It already received its fate. By the way, it's a six month ride; one way! Even though the sun will refuse to shine and the moon darkened with no reflected light; the stars will still be shining. They have a power of their own. The sun is our star fueling our solar system dependent on no other light. Our sun is not the only nuclear fused energy in our universe; there are others too far away to discern their existence.

The fate of man waiting until the Lord comes will be full of catastrophic events. How frightening a thought to consider? Bear with me a moment; I can envision the day when man will create his own sun suspended above the atmospheric dominion of Earth fueled by nuclear energy. Yet still it's only a temporary solution until Earth itself succumbs to its own power.

When I was a kid, I watched *"Futurist"* interludes of the *"Jetsons"* cartoon episodes. It was an envisioning of man colonizing the heavens. Have you forgotten about the *"Space Station"* and its experimentations? The Hubble Telescope remains suspended in the void of space peering into the constellations in search of extraterrestrial life in our celestial hemisphere.

Remember *"Star Wars"*? Want to go to Mars? Think twice; it's a one way voyage into the unknown. Do you remember *"Dick Tracy"*? It was theater at the time which appealed more realistically than the unfiltered exaggerations of my imagination, but look at where we are today; cinematic watches that can talk, facsimile technology reaching far into distant space with live streaming videography of undiscovered worlds; cellular phones connecting to satellite transmissions beaming from above. Our advancements have been very prolific but understanding the balance of why things are meant to be eludes our judgment stemming from our inordinate motivations centered in exploitation and greed. But what's our next move? Our exaggerations are now leading us to *"mining the moon"*. Remarkable!

Embedded deep like a burgeoning seed planted in the subconscious of every human being is the ticking clock of our mortality. Some of you may think I am being fictitious what I am about to say; meaning the thought of it is so far removed from your reality you may consider it laughable and stash it away in that *"vault"* you may consider as unbelievable. Despite my seemingly obscured perceptions, time will bear witness but believe in God's prophecies. Have you heard of the *"Black Hole"*? Did you know our universe is imploding from within! All materiality of our darkened universe lies in waiting when darkness again will extinguish all conceivable light. Still don't believe me?

> *And I saw a new heaven and a new earth: for the first heaven and the first earth were passed away and there was no more sea. And I John saw the holy city, new Jerusalem, coming down from God out of heaven, prepared as a bride adorned for her husband.*
>
> **Revelations 21:1-2 KJV**

So now tell me; do you know where the heavens and Earth disappeared to? Can you answer it? Where is the immeasurable dimension of the seas being stored? It will be gone; non-retrievable. God gave us a window into the sequences of time. If you can project that far, it's not very difficult through the imaging of faith to conclude we will be back to the beginning of Genesis; a new creation prepared for our habitation. It already has a name; *"New Jerusalem"*.

Stardust

Stars exist in the far reaching corridors of space as a recorder of time. They are invisible to the light of day and dormant in the presence of a brighter star. Deep into the heavens is an exhibition of electrifying colors pulsating with intensity far greater than the aurora of the *"Northern Lights"* which become nonexistent in comparison. Stars are arrayed in multi-dimensional colors varying in degrees of brilliance. New stars shine in refined splendor as older ones pulsate in diminished glory as faded stars of the ages.

Stars give date to our heavens, even our sun stands as a witness to time of its creation. There was a time that existed before our time that is absent from our present day reality. It existed with the same trajectory compared to our own mortality.

God made man from the dust of exploding stars that pilfered the Earth. The scattered remains of dust from the cosmos gave man universal identity of his humanity. We all share the same dust; born of the same thought with only uniqueness defined in our purpose. Our flesh is no more than *"stardust"* that's being held together by fragile cords extending from our soul. Dust alone has no life; it relinquished its power traveling from the heavens to Earth as fallen stars shattering upon impact into particles void of light.

Dust indicates formation of man's physical matter, an empty house void of occupancy. Life without breath to power our empty chambers is the same as having a car commissioned for an unknown journey without a battery to power it. Our bodies have the same generic value as a star that has lost its power without fuel to sustain its existence. God deposited His breath into Adam's cavity and we became a living soul and have been breathing every since. Without His breath, the adjoining of our molecular structure would wither only to be reclaimed by dust from whence we came. We are always one breath away from borrowed time that has dictated its conclusion to our remaining days.

From God's repository of faith, every soul born of His breath bears uniqueness of life with the choice of framing their destiny. Even our dreams have life if only for fleeting moments that surface in our imaginations. Faith extends our imagination as an action of our belief to restore vision to our sight. What we discovered in the passing of night will surface in the light of day as rays of hope empowering us with sight to see.

The Man from Eden   *4*

You asked,"Who is this that obscures my plans without knowledge?' Surely I spoke of things I did not understand, things too wonderful for me to know." [1]

Just as a child cuddled in security of his father's arms with the protection of love embarking on an unknown journey; Adam was carried from the fields of Earth; a place called *"Eden"* and implanted conditionally in a sheltered garden of beauty waiting in readiness to receive the completed gift of God's desire. From the womb of Earth that procured the dust of man and by Heaven's invitation, Adam was carried by the arms of faith and placed into a resort, a paradise of peace with the *"Sacred Flame of Life"* centered in the heart of God's Garden; *"The Garden of Eden"*.

> *"And the* L<small>ORD</small> *God planted a garden eastward in Eden; and there he '**put**' the man whom he had formed."* **Genesis 2:8 KJV**

The man from Eden is the only known sourcing of life existing in reality of our human experience. It is settled in our DNA in the life of every human being born of this Earth. The Breath of God was His Breath. It was His Life that brought Adam's soul into being before he was taken away from his place of birthing anticipating discovery that would define his purpose. Out of God's envisioning, He chartered off a new path for him. Only after his readiness to take the reins was he given authority to complete his journey.

> *"God can take you from the place where he formed you and put you into the center of His vision purposed for your destiny."*

The place of your formation where you received His Anointed Breath doesn't necessarily give indication of your ending. *"What's required of you is what you are instructed to do."* God's vision purposed for our destiny should never be perceived as peripheral but centered in passion at the core of our existence. This is an area where I see so many Believers miss their mark; sitting on the sideline, watching from afar as spectators in denial of God's trust for their lives.

Enamoring of Faith

Youthfulness is filled with enamoring. I am certain after Adam embraced his awakening in the Garden he was overwhelmed beyond words to describe. I can just imagine the exhilaration of joy exuding as he surveyed the majesty and beauty surrounding him. It was a breathtaking moment; waters surfacing from beneath the Earth flowing as a river of life; mist falling from above as healing vapors forming into morning drops of dew; flowering blossoms of concentric colors releasing a nectar of sweetness filling the air; the fowl of the air in defiance of gravity serenading in a symphony of melodies as they drift effortless in a celebrated dance embracing the wind; reflective streams mirroring the heavens above with glistering clearness as a diamond sparking in the light; penetrating towering mountains peaking into the clouds above the valleys below, rivers gushing beneath releasing its power in a waterfall of rainbow misting sprays; and the sacred peace of the lamb with no enemy to be found without knowledge of the sacrifice waiting at its door. The innocence of God's Garden was bound in harmony void of conflict, chaos and confusion. It was simply a *"Valley of Peace"*.

As a child learning to speak, capturing words as a figment of his imagination, Adam's first words were naming of animals. It sounds rather elementary the limitations of his vocabulary. It was the only life he knew of his obedience to faith with the command of authority that delivered power to his words. Adam was learning creativity by the spoken word of faith; *"The power of his words to become a continual product of God's improvisations of fruitfulness"*.

The word of faith is creative. Whatever is actualized in our belief, we have the ability to transform every thought formulated in our imagination into an image conceived in our minds eye. Belief gives sight to our imaginations and dreams to fulfill the aspirations of faith as we contend with challenges laid in our path.

"Hope is an aspiration filled with expectation." The beating heart of an eagle begins to race when his eye is locked in on its prey; the expectations of a woman imprisoned with agonizing pains of labor in search of

deliverance for the emergence of life concealed in her womb both personify the expectations of faith. Simply put; the expectation of faith is *"hope"*. It is a pregnancy of our belief with shared participation of our gifts and the investment of the Holy Spirit's ability in delivering evidence of our response to faith."

Belief legitimizes hope meaning what we believe is the foundation for things we hope for. Without it, we are merely wishing and we all know to the extent of its usefulness. Hope is an affirmation of belief structured as a connection to our gifting for the motivation of faith. Minimally, it's not enough just to believe but the requirement of hope centers the actions of our faith. Hope exist as a means of exchange carrying our vision from things we believe to the portals of faith. Mirroring of hope and faith when woven together can transform the spoken Word of Faith into a dynamic source of power with visible results of our actions.

Training Ground

God gave Adam the breath of soul still pulsating in continuum. The existence of one's life is a miracle unto itself. Every human being is here by the given breath of God to fulfill the season of their lives. We're not here just for the sake of being here but we all have God's unique signature as a consignment for our existence.

Conception of life is filled with a quiver of seeds to be planted and harvested throughout the journey of life. My seed is not your seed; you cannot do what I do neither is it meant for me to do what you do. Each one of us has a predetermined path to complete the calling of life. But we need more than God's breath and quiver of seeds; we need added value to produce beyond the limitations of what flesh alone can do. We need God's direction to guide us into the straight and narrow path with provisions essential for completion of our journey. With a measure of faith already seeded in the life of every man, we are well equipped for decisions ahead.

Conceivable, a measure is not the whole of faith; it remains minimized until activated by conveyance of the Holy Spirit's *"Gift of Faith"*. Even more so for the finishing of faith; *"We Need God's Authority"*. Faith has to be targeted for authority to exist which authorizes us to perform in the arena designated for our faith.

From the Field to the Garden

In my study of Adam's initial authority given *"prior"* to his assignment in the Garden, I took note that there were five entities of God's instructions of authority; *"fruitfulness, multiplicity, replenishment, subduing and dominion-ship"*. In the day of Adam's creation, the day of his consciousness, the designated protocol of his authority covered the length and breadth of the fields of *"Eden"*. But this would change with a newly defined purpose waiting for his arrival in the Garden of Eden.

Adam received his new commission on the day of his transitioning from the *"fields to the Garden"*. When he arrived in the Garden, I took special note of God's declaration of authority given to Adam which was quite different than the commission occupying in the fields of Eden. The field and the Garden were two separate realities where one was intended for the labor of man; the *"field of Earth"*; the other was specifically created for Adam's tenancy as a steward presiding over God's creative invention of the Garden of Eden. Adam was created in the *"field"* from dust of the Earth before he procured his residency in the *"Garden"*. He would have had knowledge of the existence of both worlds for after all dust of the Earth was part of his constitution.

What was the transitional time between Adam's tenure in the field before being taken into the Garden? Was it *"presto like popcorn"* the day he was created or was it a move with the speed of the *"creep of nature"*? With his jurisdiction of authority now changed was he relieved of his responsibility replenishing the fields of Eden? Could he come and go from the Garden as he pleased; subduing the fields at night while tending the Garden during the day? Was his new authority like the *"Rod of Moses"* with power to subvert the winds or to dictate movement of the seas? Could he control the force of a volcano's eruption? No he couldn't!

Then what was the reach of Adam's authority? Did his authority in the Garden carry over into the fields? Adam's instructions were never meant to subdue the Garden but tend and guard; maintain and dress it. It was already subdued under God's authority with the Tree of Life as the center of attraction. Do you think God delegated authority to Adam to have dominion over the Tree of Life with access to the Tree of Good and Evil to eat whenever he chose? How ridiculous a thought is that? *"That ain't happening"!* That is the reason he got kicked out after sinning so he would not eat of the Tree of Life and live forever. I am on God's side with that one; even though I know He does not need my approval and neither yours.

> *And God said, Behold, I have given you every herb bearing seed, which is upon the face of all the earth and every tree in which is the fruit of a tree yielding seed; to you it shall be **for meat**. And to every beast of the earth, and to every fowl of the air, and to everything that creepeth upon the earth, wherein there is life, I have given every green herb for meat: and it was so.* [1]

Do you like rabbit food? Just kidding! In the *"field"* of the Earth man had the commission to labor for his food by planting seed from the herb and fruit of the trees he ate. Man's diet was intended to be a continual production from his labor securing his survival. The herb yielding seed and tree yielding fruit whose seed was in *"itself"* were considered meat for the diet of man. Meat is sustainment; earned investments from the fields of labor even from our labor of faith that's substantiated through the grace of God which has rewards of its own. The provisions of grace in the life of every Believer is our daily bread; meat earned from our work of faith, labor of love and patience of hope in our Lord Jesus Christ as *"Jehovah Jireh; Our Provider"*.

Adam had only two options; be a faithful steward in the Garden or return to labor in the fields by the sweat of his brow. In the Garden, it didn't require labor for his survival as it would be laboring in the uncultivated fields of Eden. But soon, he would find out on the day of his eviction after losing tenancy due to his rebellion. It would be an excursion back to the same field where God had made him; from the dust of the Earth.

> *The Lord God planted a Garden eastward in Eden and there He **put** the man whom He had formed.* [1]

As a result of God's envisioning, Adam was created and equipped for a designated purpose. Everything He envisions is an implemented thought of His identity that's destined for our lives. *"God thoughts are unique visualizations of His intentions."* He conceptualized our existence by the power of His creativity long before our arrival on Earth. Every life born of man is created as an adaptation for His purpose. Even in the barrenness of the bewildered fields of Earth, God was complete in His preparations for our arrival including sustenance for our survival with food to eat, water to drink; caves as shelters for protection and rest; a measure of faith for creativity to sustain our survival. He even provided Adam with a *"Starter Kit"* made from the seeds of Earth. But God did not provide man with *"clothes"*. He was already clothed in a fabric of skin with the flesh of humanity. More significantly than anything else; God blessed Adam with authority to rule in the Earth. When he was taken from the field and placed in the Garden, his subsidies were now dependent on God.

> *And out of the ground made the LORD God to grow every tree that is pleasant to the sight, and good for food;*[1] *And the LORD God commanded the man, saying, Of every tree of the garden thou mayest freely eat: But of the tree of the knowledge of good and evil, thou shalt not eat of it: for in the day that thou eatest thereof thou shalt surely die.*[2]
> **Genesis 2:9**[1]**, 16-17 KJV**[2]

God's instructions to Adam were not just centered on what he could eat but most decisively; what not to eat. Adam had free rein to eat from any tree God grew from the ground that was pleasant to the sight and good for food. His diet was not restricted to just eating herb with seed and trees with seed but anything God grew out of the ground. In the field, he would plant his own seed but in the Garden, whatever he needed God provided with the exception of one tree; it was the *"Tree of Good and Evil"*.

In understanding the patterns of faith; our lives seemingly may be perfect; doing all the right things, making the right decisions but in truth there is always something purposed to test our obedience to faith. It's a tree with deep roots of familiarity bearing seeds that if consumed, who knows the extent of its reach?

When God gives you food, *"It is good; it's Organic"*! No chemicals, pesticides or other artificial agents, it's just that good! It's the pure *"Bread of Life"* growing in my own vineyard; away from contaminated hands of man. In the intimacy of prayer, God breaks bread with us in true fellowship with new mercies being born each day of our lives. It is an everyday excursion; gathering of His Bread as He shares His life with us to make *"It"* our own. We are commanded to break bread together sharing His love in communion with each other.

Adam's commission was quite simple not needing interpretation; *"Tend and Guard"*. His instructions were now specialized away from any consideration of labor in the field. In the field he could eat anything but in the Garden he was instructed not to eat from the *"Tree of Good and Evil"*. Despite his restrictions, he was brought into a rest free from arduous labor of harvesting seed amongst thorns in the thicket of the field. I can imagine, his view of the terrains of Earth were very compelling and perhaps intimidating without consideration that one day that would be his home.

Let Us Reason Together

Adam's focus shifted unidirectional accommodating his new assignment. This was a novel experience that mandated something never before required of him. In a sense, it proved to be an exploratory event highlighting his ability to *"reason"* specific to the request of God's instructions. Our interpretations, comprehension and judgments derived from our perceptions either from what we see, hear or feel but more discriminately what we think are attributing factors that affect our ability to reason. Reasoning is a presumptive determination of our judgments developed from our biases that forms our ideas and opinions as we battle with arguments to bring clarity to our thoughts.

Materiality has its identity and is easily identified, but spiritual matter has an identification of its own evolving from the invisible impressions of faith into a recognizable image correlated with our understanding. Spirit matter is invisible to our senses; discoverable by the consequences it produces. God's presentation of the animals brought before Adam was proving of his ability to reason by translating God given things for an inherent identification our senses could handle. It was latitude given to test his faith. God's discovery of our intentions is validated by design of His presentations introduced into our faith to expose our motivations.

Motivations highlight convergence of our thoughts and even our dreams justifying what we are inclined to do. The proving of faith is necessary for determination of obedience that will expose our intentions. Time and chance happens to us all but at its vertex we do not always recognize its originality why things just appear. It's an opportunity to bring definition to our faith.

Everything encompassing our reality is defined by a name; people, events, places or things; everything has a name symbolic of an identity defining its purpose. Even if it's a test that enters our lives, it too has a name. God brought before Adam every beast of the *"field"* and fowl of the air to name; some two legged with wings others four legged all within the realm of his influence. In order for him to have named them he must have identified their purpose. Purpose validates God's intentions. Everything that walks on four legs is not a cow; a cow is not a horse. Neither is a sparrow a duck; neither is a duck an eagle born as a predator searching for prey. God presents us with the same challenges just as Adam of accurately identifying the purpose of everything He delivers into our lives.

All living things have a purpose attached to their existence; if it doesn't have a purpose, it cannot share space in our reality. Visually, there is nothing in our hemisphere which cannot be identified. Our reality is framed by definition of our perceptions of things we see. All visualizations conceptualized in our thoughts are assigned a degree of associated value. Without an accurate account defining the meaning of things we see, our response will be without intent of its purpose.

Animals and birds as Adam concluded were not his counterpart. They have reasoning capabilities which are instinctive but unlike ours, their nature lacks the prowess of our human adaptation. But, the burden of faith was delegated to him to *"Name It"*. Conceivably, Adam recognized their right of existence but there was none comparable to him. Clothed in his right mind, He knew he couldn't procreate with an animal or a bird or mammals of the oceans; his nature would not allow it. We as humans have an unique identity embedded in DNA that differs from the nature of our lesser species.

> *And out of the ground the* LORD *God formed every beast of the field, and every fowl of the air; and brought them unto Adam to see what he would call them: and whatsoever Adam called every living creature, that was the name thereof.* **Genesis 2:19 KJV**

God oversees actions of our faith to *"See"* whether we are abiding by instructions He gives us. Just as God brought animals before Adam to name, from the *"field from which he came"*, He will take things from our past for a new performance of faith. Periodically, He allows circumstances to enter into our lives for measurement of our faith. Take patience for example; it is something we are all in need of. If God determines our patience is in further need of development, then we can expect a test for the maturing of patience. If we accept His decisions and not fight against them He will position us for discovery of greater things yet to come. *"We will be tested by faith for the proving of faith."* It is an effort to validate the quality of our character and judgment of our response exhibited in our executions. To have faith is one thing but performance of faith is the determining factor that measures our obedience.

Take the case of Moses when he came down from the mountain; he broke the tablets in pieces! He was *"moved by the things he saw"*. After such a mighty encounter on top of Mount Sinai he was faced with a test; *"to determine the value of what God had given him"*. The broken tablets represent the value we assign to the precious things God entrust us with. It is a test of our faithfulness to see whether our steps are in line with His. We often find ourselves at times in situations mesmerized and distracted on things interjected in our faith. Believe it or not; we can get distracted on things that come as answers to our prayers if we are not able to ascertain lawful recognition of God's appropriations.

In a profound way Moses demonstrated arrogance in his character when he threw down the tablets on his return from the mountain. It is quite clear that he had some anger management issues that went awry after being tested by the infidelities of the people under his authority. After making the effort to ascend on top of Mount Sinai to receive God's revelations, I would have thought he would cherish that rare moment of fellowship with all of his being; the privilege of knowing things never before revealed. He was the chosen one of all mankind to hold the *"repository of knowledge"* of creation. God favored Moses with an experience we should all long for; a one on one encounter in His Presence. We can hypothesize all day long but nothing surmounts to an experience in the Presence of God.

The impact of such an encounter like Moses is life changing. I know in fact it will radicalize everything about you by an overwhelming power connecting with your faith. To fully understand Moses, really, you had to have been Moses. It's like when the Spirit of God fell on the disciples when they were praying in the Upper Room. They all were radicalized in the power of faith inspired by the Holy Spirit's movements; prophesying, healing and launching a proverbial expansion of the Kingdom of Christ. We all should aspire to know God beyond where our faith has settled searching deeper in prayer; seeking to know Him in a level of intimacy purposed to deliver a performance in His Likeness. It is the same Likeness of the Holy Spirit demonstrating the power of God's Creativity.

Believe it or not; others have since encountered similarity of faith in their experiences; but something happened. Quite simply it was *"A Test"* that brought conclusion to their assignment of faith. Ask Jonah; he will tell you of his frustrations when he challenged God concerning His judgments of Nineveh. It's a warning! You could very well end up like him sitting under a tree with augmentations of God's motivations. We all know how that ended; *"Thank you for your service"!*

What was the reason Moses destroyed the tablets of stone? Was his motivation intended to forfeit the good God intended after such a mighty revelation on Sinai? *"Now the tablets were the work of God and the writing was the writing of God, engraved on tablets made by the hand of God".* [1] Moses waited patiently for God to complete His visitation. We have the same choices; we can give our undivided attention to Him or surrender our energies to the affairs of man. If it is the latter, I can assure you it is a disappointing path. The children of Israel were impatient with Moses when he failed to come down from the mountain after forty days atop Sinai. To accurately obtain results of faith requires patience. The actions of faith are not always delivered in whole at the time of its execution but more likely than not it sequences through a progression of time needing patience for its completion. For Believers, this is an area that presents our most challenges indicative of the multiple trips of Moses ascending atop Mount Sinai waiting until completing the cycle of faith. Just as Moses in our walk of faith; we will be contested!

> *Go down, because your people, whom you brought up out of Egypt, have become corrupt. They have been **quick to turn away** from what I commanded them and have made themselves an idol cast in the shape of a calf. They have bowed down to it and sacrificed to it and have said, 'These are your gods, Israel, who brought you up out of Egypt.* **Exodus 32:7-8 NIV**

This reminds me so much of what I see across the landscape of our country, particularly frequenting our Christian community. How quick were we to turn away pursuing agendas not connected with the call of faith. Corruption seems to be the call of the day throughout our culture. From *"house to house; corner to street";* we have fallen prey to seductive influences mired in corruptive behavior of men. That's indicative of how far we have fallen. We can recover! However, time is not on our side. There is no guarantee what tomorrow will bring. But while we do have time, we can implement the solutions for our recovery.

> *If my people which I called by name will humble themselves and pray; seek my face and turn from their wicked ways, then will I hear from Heaven and will forgive their sin and I will heal their land.* [1]

We are unresponsive no different than the Israelites whom God delivered from the bondage of Egypt. Even though we have witnessed a mighty exhibition of His power, we quickly forgot the old landmarks of faith. Has our success become a burden to our faith? I truly believe it may be the case. The success of materiality has turned into an imprisonment appealing as a non-burdensome attraction keeping us occupied away from the resolution of prayer. What's the difference between the performance of yesterday and where we are now? Are we able to identify the hindrances keeping us away from the threshold of faith?

Predictability of our journey parallels the excursion of the Israelites departure from bondage. We need to be mindful of the bountifulness of God. It should never escape our remembrance when He lends His approval of our sacrifices. *"Lend is conditional";* meaning if we are found to be non-gratuitous after success of God intervening in our affairs, there undoubtedly will be a greater complication of faith we would have to unravel. The journey of the Israelites is no different than our journey. From the time of signs and wonders in the deserts sands of Egypt to miracles by the hands of healers of America, our impatience has created a stumbling block redirecting our attention away from the closet of faith. God's expediency isn't linked to our impatience neither was it linked to impatience of the children of Israel in their inability to wait on Moses.

I am cautious of people trafficking in and out of my life. They are there as a provocation sometime to steal life taking away the most precious thing God has given to me. God allocates time for purpose and it is to be revered as a precious gift that can't be replaced. It took time for Moses to repeatedly go up and come down Mount Sinai. It takes time waiting in patience for God to reveal Himself. Revelation is progressive and time sensitive requiring patience to advance into the deeper dimensions of faith.

God judges our perception to see whether things He introduces into our path duplicates His intentions. Replication is the standard of His Word mirroring His Reflection in the eye of faith; to see as He sees and do specific to instructions of His Word. It's been said that facts are stubborn things and they can get in the way of faith. If I may admonish you; *"Speak truth to power, Call it what it is. Don't let boldness of faith shame you"*. Truth is truth and a lie is a lie. In case you don't know; a prevaricator is a liar; one prone with a consciousness of deception. *"Don't get it twisted"*. Even Adam had sense enough to realize the descriptive images of the animals he named were purposed as God intended. It's *"Common Sense"!* But where have our senses gone wrong? Did we lose perspective of God's standards? Truth is not to be arbitrated or commingled with man's deceptive intentions. Truth is what it is! God's wisdom exposes knowledge lying beneath His objectives for an accurate portrayal to enrich our understanding.

The exercising of Adam's authority was evidenced by the animals he named and even the woman made from the rib of his body. But his greatest asset you and I still possess that has lasted throughout the ages is the genius of free will spirit. By divine selection, the rightful decisions we make that are consistent with God's objectives will convey His authority securing a performance of His infallible promises.

An individual action in the execution of faith gives no indication of its completion. The stepping stones of faith are *"gapped"* for a reason. It could be a gap of years sequestered as Prophet Elijah discovered while he waited by the Brook Cherith for fulfillment of his season; dieting on bread and meat with ravens as his only company. Circumstances of life can leave you in hiding for the arrival of faith to complete its call.

Measurement of the success of faith is reflected in our obedience. Apostle Paul said; *"I have fought the good fight, I have finished the race, I have kept the faith"*.[1] Success of faith is the completed word; when our faith is rendered in fullness of what was originally intended. It's not a matter of dotting *"I's"* and crossing of every *"T"*; faith has an allowance for forgiveness due to the dispensation of grace we now live in.

Kryptonite of Faith

Adam's *"helper"* who was compromised in deceit by a beguiling serpent offered him a cancerous fruit filled with eternal seeds of condemnation. It was kryptonite to this giant of faith disabling his judgment of truth. Supplanting of truth induced by the failings of others does not have to be consequential of our own failures, only if we accept them as our truth. Adam was not compelled to ask the question we may have wanted to ask; *"Why did you do this",* but accepted her offerings without excuse. If he had taken a moment to reflect on how perfect the state of affairs was in the Garden, he may have reconsidered. Perfect is perfect!

Perfect does not need any validation. Adam should have considered the cost associated with disobedience. His faith could have rendered a different result if he had remained faithful. Historically, eternity would still exist as a flame of fire in the center of God's Creation. *"The Fire of God needs rekindling in the heart of man."* But for Adam it was too late to reconsider; his senses had awakened and indeed they did!

The propensity to error in judgment is enhanced by seductive influences of impassive silence, subtle in their attempt to disarm our obedience. The unbroken quietness of Adam's unwavering soul encountered a persuasion offered as a choice; *"To choose life and live forever or accept the consequences of someone else's disobedience and make it his own"*. Did Adam have the presence of faith to believe God would again make another woman to satisfy his loneliness? Did he think he would again be left alone even after God determined it was not a good thing to reside in solitude?"

You may want to excuse Adam because he was in a deep sleep at the time God made the woman from a rib taken from his body. But he knew of her creation by his declaration of the attachment of his bone to the bone and flesh of his wife. Have you considered there is a difference between Adam's creation and that of the woman? Adam was made from the dust of Earth but the woman; from heredity of man; *"A Rib"*. The process of heredity has continued ever since by the driving forces of genetic energy. As a molecular generator, physicality of God's engineering still pulsates.

Never again will man be made from the scratch of *"dust"*. God ended that process. We are all made from the same bone taken from Adam clothed in the same flesh of his disobedience. It was Adam's bone and flesh that demonstrated a reluctance adhering to the voice of God's instructions. Ultimately, he made a decision rooted in his insecurities when he was confronted with a persuasion greater than his belief. Catastrophically, it ended in a serious disappointment of faith though he had the ability to call it what it was; *"Name it Sin! Disobedience is Sin"*. But unfortunately sin was named in his own action of disobedience and not the one whom he attempted to transfer the blame.

Consequences of Adam's sin await all of us at the end of our journey, a journey of no recourse to correct our choices. By circumventing God's authority, Adam violated God's trust severing his allegiance in a violent act of betrayal. As a result, he created by *"his"* actions the *"Word of Sin"* unraveling the seams of eternal life fastened to his life.

Sin has a consistent footprint rooted in disloyalty. Seeded in *"euphemism"*, the attraction of sin is always directed to the appealing good of our natural sight. Just like the glitter of Judas Iscariot's stolen silver and the enticing aroma emanating from the forbidden tree both were pleasantly tempting; exuding desire of the eye for fulfillment. The unpleasantries of the offerings of sin are often masked in euphemism. Euphemism is an expression which loses its literal meaning referring to something else to hide its unpleasantness.

Theoretically, euphemism bears an analogy to sin; always hiding in the shadows shaded in a garment of deception. The changing faces of sin and fraudulent perpetrations can be mesmerizing. The presentation of hidden agendas introduced into our path invariably migrates towards our gullibility. Decision to do good in support of faith or to do evil in opposition to truth are choices we all must consider.

Seeing Through the Eyes of Another

> *The LORD God said, "It is not good for the man to be alone. I will make a helper suitable for him."* [1]
>
> *So the LORD God caused the man to fall into a deep sleep; and while he was sleeping, he took one of the man's ribs and then **closed up the place with flesh.*** [2]
>
> *Then the LORD God made a woman from the rib he had taken out of the man, and he brought her to the man. The man said, "This is now bone of my bones and flesh of my flesh; she shall be called 'woman,' for she was taken out of man." That is why a man leaves his father and mother and is united to his wife, and **they shall become one flesh**.* [3]

Adam realized this was *"one"* of his bones and flesh of his flesh. His rib was still his rib! He discovered; *"Flesh made of flesh is a mirror unto itself."* The value of flesh is no greater than its own reflection. What we see in others we see in ourselves; judgment of one is judgment of all. We have the same genetic beginnings.

God extracted flesh from Adam's flesh while he was anesthetized. With the wound of extraction closed and no point of reentry to *"remake"* a process that He had completed; flesh was sealed with flesh. This would end the process of God's production of life. The reins of continual production were now given to Adam with the command; *"Be fruitful and multiply"*. After Adam's sin, God could have made another Adam; but He didn't; He could have made another woman, still He didn't. That was not His plan; *"flesh was finished"*!

It is not my attempt to absolve Adam of his choices. He was clearly given instructions he did not keep while knowing the consequences that would befall him. But I sincerely believe he had predetermined; whatever the cost, he already had a made up mind! It was evidenced in his confession; *"I will cleave"*. He did in fact express a willingness deeply rooted in his entangled emotions that swayed decisions of his heart;

> *"Therefore a man shall **leave** his father and mother and be joined to his wife, and **they shall become one flesh**."* [1]

These were Adam's words which sound so familiar to something we would say; *"she was taken out of me"*. Little did he know, conceivably by his own words, he was creating a self-fulfilling prophecy; *"I will leave"*. Self-awarding of our actions is a declaration of our *"self-righteousness"*. It is in violation of the principles of faith. God is the only one who sets boundaries for our obedience. It is something we cannot determine on our own. Adam projected a willingness to sacrifice whatever consequence would befall him even unto death; *"cleaving; uniting with flesh of his own flesh"!* He considered it of greater value to unite to the image that proceeded from him than remain connected to the life that sustained him. Simply put; it is a form of idolatry when we worship the creature more than our Creator.

By uniting conspiratorially to become one flesh; *"Their collective choice rendered a decision judged as a single thought; the thought of one flesh joining together as one".* This would prove to be a fatal allegiance with irrevocable consequences. Their actions were the same but judgment of one who had authority has caused so many souls to get lost in the wilderness of life. Some will make it and some won't! I can't blame Adam solely on this. We have a mission to reclaim as many souls still in search of the hope of life; the same redemptive hope we discovered on our road to Damascus. It's a road of encounter that truly delivers sight to the blind.

> *So when that the tree was good for food and it was pleasant to the eyes, and a tree desirable to make one wise, she took of its fruit and ate. She also gave to her husband* ***with her****, and he ate.* [1]

Greedy; Greedy; Greedy! What a monumental error of judgment! God grew the Garden; wasn't it sufficient enough for their sustainment? Why do we continue to cry out for more; never satisfied with daily provisions of God's grace? That sounds too familiar! Why do we perceive something is good when we know in our hearts it is not right? When we take God's grace for granted, it can cost you and it will!

After God has released His blessings into our lives and has given us unlimited access to enjoy the fruit of *"His labor"* by sufficiency of His grace; we tend to give more credence to the created thing than gratitude for the Creator Himself. We celebrate the blessing more than rendering a response of gratitude and humility for the *"One"* providing the blessing. Human nature has not changed and never will but we question why God doesn't give us everything we ask for. Remember, *"Father Knows Best"* and it's His prerogative.

It was God's desire to provide Adam with a helper, a facilitator; someone comparable bearing the same DNA. Adam named her *"Woman";* an image made of his very own flesh and bones. I can imagine the joy and exhilaration he may have felt? Maybe he did not realize the power he inherited; the power of his words that would become the product of his imagination. Attachment to the words we speak will evolve to be the life we live. Who we say we are is reflected in the image of our words. Creativity of Adam's words produced long-lasting impressions of his service in the Garden and his tenure in the fields of Eden.

Truth be told, Adam even named the serpent; an inescapable species residing in both land and water. Masked in a persona of cunningness the serpent didn't meet the compatibility test despite standing upright with the ability to articulate; *"It was not the one".*

I believe Adam envisioned the image taken out of him was not his equal; not equal in the sense, she was never given authority. Subjectively, evidence is in the name he gave her; *"Woman"*. As an extension of him sharing the same genetic life she proved she had enough persuasive power to conclude his assignment in the Garden; *"She took of the fruit thereof, and did eat, and gave also unto **her husband with her and he did eat**"*.[1] Adam was complicit with silence; agreeable to her offerings as he watched his wife consummate *"her own authority"* that violated God's imperative to not eat of the forbidden tree. The Bible does not record their conversations; in the grand scheme of things, it's not that important. It was their actions that counted. However, the Bible does record the dialogue between the woman and the serpent. It's a testimony we can apply to our own battles when truth is being swayed amidst our indecisions.

> *For whatsoever things were written aforetime were **written for our learning**, that we through patience and comfort of the scriptures might have hope.* [2]

In pursuit of pleasing ourselves, we could suffer the same fate as Adam by not fully realizing the value of obedience. Scripture says; *"We then that are strong ought to bear infirmities of the weak; not to please ourselves. Let every one of us please his neighbor for his good to edification".* [3] Clearly this indicates what Adam should have considered prior to entering a persuasion that compromised his survival. Faith is a three-way portal; *"faith in God; in ourselves and faith in others"*. We have the ability to empower those who continue to struggle; lifting them up in shared participation of life through edification. When we apply our strength to the infirmities of others, we can transform their weakness into strength. As a matter of principle any infirmity can be radicalized through the power of faith. But if our motivations are not seeded appropriately in faith, weakness can overpower any efforts of compassion.

Recognizing the Difference

> *For even Christ pleased not himself; but, as it is written, The reproaches of them that reproached thee fell on me.* [1]

Even after being told of the consequences, Adam vacated his senses for a mutual participation in a fate that would be shared by both. What happened to his wife also would happen to him. Jesus came with a purpose to undo what Adam did. He took upon the Cross the reproaches of sin and bore them for our redemption. He was commissioned, evidenced by His obedience fulfilling the Word of Faith. But Adam took upon himself the reproach of sin out of his elective will without a cross to bear.

> *Then the man said, "The woman You gave to be with me, she gave me of the tree, and I ate." And the LORD God said to the woman, "What is this you have done?" The woman said, "The serpent deceived me, and I ate"* [2]

It should've been the end of the story with nothing else said; *"Let the woman eat by herself"*. Adam got the whole thing twisted! She was a helper; one whom was made to help facilitate his destiny. Being truthful, he could have named her something else with a different descriptive of her existence other than Woman. Or he could have just named her Adam; after all that was the name God gave them; *"Male and female created he them; and blessed them, and called **their name Adam** in the day they were created"*.[1] Adam had the presence of faith to name all living things upon the Earth.

When we apply our obedience to the instructions of faith, it is without excuse. There is no turning back without suffering consequences; only repentance for any exceptions of faith. The works we do authenticate the purpose of faith. Without being proved our labor in the fields of harvest will be exhausting with no profit.

Soul Ties

Adam's wife was created from a rib from his body. Scripture testifies of it. When I was a child going to Sunday School with my parents, I was taught because a rib was taken from man; a woman had one extra rib. Due to deductive reasoning you would think so. No She Don't! That's a fable and Eve didn't eat an apple! The things people say are the same things people do. *"Dig a Little Deeper!"* Old time religion was a good thing that established principles and character building as a foundation that launched me into the future as well as keeping me out of the streets. For that; I am grateful.

After the rib was taken from Adam God sealed the sum of His creation by closing the area of extraction of Adam's body with flesh. The wound of his flesh was an irreversibly procedure providing a onetime solution to his dilemma of residing alone by a process God would not repeat.

> *"While he was sleeping, God took one of the man's ribs and then* **closed up the place with flesh.** **Genesis 2:21 NIV**

Adam's disobedience was a result of an inner battle taking place between his soul and conscience. He had nothing in his repertoire of experiences to rely on. He was presented with two choices; *"obedience to God's commandment vs. mutual agreement of his soul bound to his declaration to cleave to his wife"*. When Adam's wife was delivered to him, by his own admission said; *"What God separated from me, must be rejoined; the process of becoming one flesh"*. The desire of becoming one flesh demanded unity. They were unified in their actions but even greater; they were unified in their disobedience casting judgment upon them both.

It was an agreement of having walked together and sharing the same life blood as the other. Together, they drew life from the invisible streams of love attached to their souls united under one expression of unity. I readily understand the untenable situation Adam put himself in. Projection of loneliness being detached from the *"river of love"* flowing in his soul was unbearable; a consequence he was not willing to face. To be noted;

there is a caution to rivers; they have the potential to overflow without measurement of their strength. There are times decisions before us overflow with adversity driven by the rivers of our emotions. As our spirit is being drawn upward to God; lateral movement of our soul controlling the activity of our conscience moves in an opposite direction.

The rivers of our soul have their own magnetism; yearning, projecting its will to a connective stream of shared life as a mutual attraction with each other. A river, analogous to love, flows with power thrusting through every tributary it can reach even the streams of faith woven into our fabric. Conversely; still waters run deep drawn from a well of settled peace even in the midst of provocations. Still waters are indicative of the positional attitude of faith always consistent and never changing. It is anchored between the variable elements above and migrating life flowing beneath its surface. Secluded unto itself liken to the curvature of a self-reflecting mirror, still waters are self-fulfilling in uniqueness of its own desire. Just as a crystalline lake is captivated by its own confinement; it harbors faith in a consensus of stillness.

Bad choices can be made in any given moment of time without having a bad conscience. Our souls are bound by the blood it is attached to. In the heat of passion it is extremely difficult to provide an accurate interpretation of our values and perceptions. Adam's acceptance of the offerings from his counterpart was a consummation ultimately exposing their nakedness.

They were naked to themselves in new found shame but also naked before God in disappointment of faith. It was a moment of discovery of their awakened senses as they realized their wretched state; a moment of shared passion to be regretted. Togetherness is good but it can be a liability if the overflow is not contained. The most agonizing prayer of any Believer is in our disobedience when God fastens the Heavens to our prayers. It is no different than the agonizing pleadings of David in the Book of Psalm;

> "Cast me not away from thy Presence; and take not thy Holy Spirit from me." [1]

Our souls are the fueling center of our conscience submitted under subordination to God's Spirit. By submitting to the Holy Spirit's ruling authority as the established government of God's Kingdom, structure of our inner life will bear witness of His Kingdom living within. The Holy Spirit illuminates from within with triumphant power across the face of our darkened conscience exposing the path of faith as guidance in our labor of love. He rules with dominance regulating our swaying souls and spiraling inclinations with an authority of supernatural power to reinforce our faith.

The soul of man is imperishable even when it is withdrawn from our lives. It bears our conscience as an informational database of our works and labor of love. When the dust of stars cease to shine as the habitation of life within relinquishes its power, eternity of God's breath will be recalled unto Himself. It is a never-ending cycle of reproductive life advancing from one generation to the next. Transitioning of our lives from life to the graves of Earth with the sting of death abated; we will be liberated from the *"fields of Eden"* for occupation in God's *"Heavenly Tabernacle"*. It is a welcomed embrace, but this time with the breath of eternal life pulsating within our souls.

"Can two walk together unless they are agreed?"[1] Togetherness is precedence of becoming one in spirit when our souls are joined together in a consecration of oneness. *"Soul Ties"* draw strength from each other bound together in mutual dependency reciprocating the same life blood as the other as a reward for the bonds of friendship. It can't be exemplified any better than the relationship Jonathan had with David; *"The soul of Jonathan was knit with the soul of David and Jonathan loved him as his own soul"*.[2] The process of knitting is strategic, careful mending the seams of faith into an ovum of strength. The soul of man is very powerful in its assertions. It comes with a quiver of domineering persuasions casting shadows of influence over activity of our conscience, emotions, thoughts and powerful enough to affect our vision. Extension of its tentacles has a reach that can seriously impact the lives of others. Most hurt that occurs in our human experience takes place deep down in the soul. The wounds of hurt are very profound and will assess your ability for tolerance. Arguably it is the most painful experience one can have. Deliverance alone is its only antidote that can deliver you from its clutching hold.

Life is in the Blood

Adam was first conceived as a created thought. It's a love story of Heaven and Earth coalescing giving birth to the greatest wonder of creation. Creation of man was the supreme thought of God! The depthness of His love even after Adam violated his stewardship; God still gave us an opportunity for imperishable life by the redeeming grace of Christ.

Adam was made on the sixth day from artifacts of all physical matter left over from five days of creation. *"Yes, your flesh is leftovers!"* It is not that important to consider it more than it is. God envisioned man as the object of His creative genius but needed substance to fashion him into an image of His Likeness. From the chemical dust of stars, mineral life of plants and the waters of Earth; God made man from all the physical elements of our universe.

Water is the major element comprising our anatomy which constitutes nearly two-thirds of our existence but it is the *"blood"* that sustains life. *"Life is in the Blood, the living organism of life."* It is not the blood of animals but God's molecular engine that continuously pulsates through the life of every living soul born of man. Blood is the element of atonement attached to our soul always compensating and maintaining the flow of life. Without it our lives would cease to be!

> **For the life of the flesh is in the blood**, and I have given it to you upon the altar to make atonement for your souls; for it is the blood that makes atonement for the soul. [1]

God Turned Water into Blood

Early one morning in my meditations, with my ears perked in readiness and fingers postured as a ready writer; I began to write as I pondered on Adam in the day of his creation. A stream of interpretation began to flow as I surmised my own existence. The Bible says that Adam was first made from dust of the Earth; *"From dust we were made and dust we shall return"*. Dust alone has no resiliency; it is only powder that succumbs to environmental elements of the wind, rain and sun. Left to itself, it will disappear before your eyes without any resemblance of what was conceived in your mind. Dust does not have the ability of fusing to itself but with added elasticity of a fluid element it will bind itself into a pliable formation.

In my pondering, it led me to consider the artistry of a potter; tools and mixtures he uses to hold things together. Pottery is handcrafted from clay which comes from the ground, usually in areas where streams or rivers once flowed. It is made of minerals, plant life, and animals; all the ingredients of soil constituting the existence of man's chemical composition.

Clay minerals are composed essentially of sodium, calcium, phosphorus, magnesium, potassium, iron and **"water"**. The intricacies of our anatomy dictate we maintain a balance of mineral nutrients necessary for our survival. We are dependent on the cohesion of minerals existing in our bodies. Take for example; I frequently have low potassium requiring supplements to compensate for fluctuations that may occur. It is very important that I remain vigilant in maintaining the proper threshold. If not, I could face compromising circumstances putting my health at risk.

The human body contains 55% to 78% water which is the main component of our mineral structure. The only variability of the amount of water from one person to the next is dependent on our body size. Nevertheless consumption of water is vital for all known forms of life existing on Earth. If you do not believe me; get thirsty! You will be drinking something! The first inclination of a man stuck in a desert is to find water. Although food is essential, it takes water to survive.

Dust and water mixed forms into clay. Clay is a malleable structure that can be shaped and molded into an image of one's imagination. A *"potter"* with a container of clay fashions an image embedded in his mind. He uses a wheel, *"potter's wheel"* to shape the image by removing excess clay after it is hardened. The wheel trims, sculpturing the image emphasizing the minutest detail. Any imperfection the potter finds after the ceramic is hardened results in the process being repeated until the image is completed in the likeness of an impression conceived of his original depiction.

It is no different than how God is fashioning our lives; *"He is the potter; we are the clay being shaped into an Image of His design"*. As the potter, the more He increases speed of the wheel to shape us into His fashion, more water is added into our lives. From a spiritual perspective water is the anointing. It is what He uses to increase His Presence in shaping our lives.

God's creativity is unlimited. From the makings of dust and water, God made Adam as a product formed from *"leftovers"* of Earth's creation. As the breath of soul was breathed into his nostrils, blood began to flow and Adam became a living being. Because of my inquisitive nature, it gave cause for me to dig a little deeper to consider; *"Where did the blood come from"?* As I pondered, I could not escape an evolving thought; *"Life of the body is in the blood"*. Then, it was as if I had an epiphany. I started blinking! I guess I am still blinking! I began to reflect on the miracle of Jesus; *"Turning Water into Wine"*. It was a conversion process; *"Coalescing the provisions of Earth with transforming power from Heaven above"*. The makings of our bodies were already here but it took the Breath of God to transform dead things of creation into resemblance of His objective. The combination of breath and soul caused blood to flow from *"Water turned into blood by a single breath from His existence"*. It was enough to produce nearly 1.5 gallons in every human being.

I discovered while reading in the Book of Exodus, testimony of *"The First Plague"* where God did in fact turn water into blood.

The First Plague: Waters Become Blood

The LORD *spoke to Moses, "Tell Aaron, Take your staff and stretch out your hand over the waters of Egypt over the streams, and canals, over the ponds and all the reservoirs and they will turn to* **blood***; blood will be everywhere in Egypt, even in vessels of wood and stone.* **Exodus 7:19 NIV**

The miracle of Jesus turning water into wine replicates a process indicative of the miracle of man's creation. God saved the best for last creating man in His Image, a *"living being"* with the nexus of Heaven and Earth.

OH, the Blood

Blood is a cleanser; an atonement for imperfections seeded in our soul. Blood flowing through our veins never depletes itself; it replicates continuously. With a built in homeostatic control which simply means it replenishes our red blood cells on the average every 120 days. Our hemostat monitors the production of balancing leukocytes which are white blood cells that is needed for internal defense to ward off infections. Retained in the nucleus of blood is the DNA of our human existence with our unique footprint passed on since the beginning of time. In our DNA lie the genetic codes of humanity broadcasting from a distant land all the way back to *"originality of the blood of Adam"*. There is but one blood; the blood of humanity.

Blood is a commodity precious as life itself. It is not a generic gift of creation. It does not flow as streams of water cascading from peaks of mountains or harvested from the depths of oceans. It has a life unique in its own making bearing seeds of all existing life. Blood had its beginnings only retraceable in its origin. If we knew of its secrets, we would have no need for blood banks to replenish provisions of life that only blood can provide. We could simply; *"Turn Water into Blood like Jesus Turned Water into Wine"*.

Years ago, my mother contracted a life concluding blood disease. It was anemia, not just any anemia but Aplastic Anemia (AA). It is not a cancer but it might as well be; the results are the same. Aplastic Anemia is a deficiency in the bone marrow's inability to produce blood cells because of damage to the stem cells.

Because of our lack of stewardship to protect and nourish our environment, chemicals and poisons have compromised our water and even the food we eat with a myriad of toxins. Even, pharmaceutical companies have gone so far as to incorporate threatening poisons into our medicines. The consequences are enormous! Beware of benzene; it is a killer that will attack your entire immune system beyond your ability to recovery! If we continue to violate the laws of nature, we will succumb to the elements of our betrayal.

The most recognizable place in our hemisphere is our home; *"Earth"*. It's time we start acting like we do in fact live here. Earth is a living organism; it weeps with tears of neglect and will respond with vengeance inflicting pain upon us if we refuse accountability for our disrespect. For the damage we've already inflicted, the retaliatory consequence of our neglect is inevitable; Earth-shattering earthquakes, epic floods swallowing our cities, unmanageable fires sweeping across our terrain, hurricanes with forces never before recorded; obliterating tornadoes with un-measureable width. Earth is not a trash heap; it is our house; the place where we live, move and have our being. Stop being nonsensical because of politics; *"Stop the bleeding"!*

5

Can Trees Talk

Then the LORD God called to Adam and said to him, "Where are you?" So he said, "I heard Your voice in the garden, and I was afraid because I was naked; and I hid myself." And He said, **"Who told you that you were naked? Have you eaten from the tree of which I commanded you that you should not eat?"** [1]

Where are you? Why are you hiding from God? Have your discretions driven you in fear of your predicament? In your hiding were you recognizable while promenading in translucent leaves of palm? The thought of that is discontenting; to a greater extent frightening considering being estranged from communion with God's Presence. Beware, there is a *"Talking Tree consenting to your demise"*.

It amazes me Adam never answered God's question; *"Who told you that you were naked"?* [2] He should have answered; *"The tree told me; not the serpent but the tree"!* Excuse after excuse. *"Could it be Adam had a lapse of memory? Did his eyes fail him? Was the fruit so appealing he could not resist?"* Regardless, something happened! Obviously it was an attraction so great overriding his judgment that he could not smell the stench of death decaying from the forbidden fruit.

Where did the tree acquire its knowledge? Was it a predated harbinger from another world before Adam's arrival in the Garden? The tree on its own was not the knowledge but possessed the knowledge **"OF"** good and evil. Was it the result of a prior occupation before Adam's arrival in the Garden? Could it have been *"Revelation Knowledge"* of times past God did not want introduced into His new endeavor? Was it knowledge of Heaven the Framers of Creation did not want Adam to dissimulate until the revelations of Peter? Was it residual from the war between good and evil waged in the original Earth before this new Earth materialized? It may be all inclusive. But truth remains;

> *Then the Lord God said, "Behold, the man* **has become like one of Us,** *to know good and evil. And now, lest he put out his hand and take also of the tree of life, and eat, and live forever."* [1]

"Has become" denotes it definitely did happen even in a moment of dissent. But which one did Adam become like with knowledge that was so consequential to his disobedience? Did Adam have time to execute the knowledge he had acquired before God discovered him hiding in a thicket draped in translucent leaves? To satisfy the depth of my curiosity I need to know; was it the good one or the evil one?

God is *"Trinity"* unified in the Likeness of His Own Existence. There is no separation of the Father, Son and Holy Ghost; they're *"One"* equal in representation of God's Eternal Existence! God is *"Good"* however we perceive Him to be. His Existence is absolved from evil. So still the question remains; which One of You did Adam become like? If I may offer an answer; at first glance I would say the Holy Ghost! Characteristically, He embodies knowledge of good and evil. He exists as *"God's Leadership";* One empowered to lead and guide us into all truth; truth of good with full knowledge of the patterns of evil. When the *"Trifold Assembly"* of God's hierarchy convened, the Holy Ghost was present when they decided to fashion man into the Likeness of God. It was a visionary creation of the Father, Son and Holy Ghost; *"vision of the Father, built by the Son, implemented by Holy Ghost".*

My suspicion of the culprit also committed an act of treason. It is very conclusive Adam's disobedience was a betrayal of trust the same as Lucifer usurping God's authority. What knowledge did God want to keep away from Adam? Shared knowledge of good is a good thing but knowledge of evil is a cataclysmic invocation for the worst of humanity to embrace.

Was it knowledge Adam acquired more concerning to God of his actions or was it his inability to handle it? What would he do with the reins of power to know good and evil other than demolish the vision of God's intentions? By superimposing his will exceeding God's instructions, Adam solidified his fate with the same likeness as the corruption of Lucifer; *"subverting good for sake of evil".* It is indicative of what we see in our world today of man's inability to handle the powers of good and evil. Under no circumstance is man able to maintain God's Righteousness in the midst of so much evil. God didn't do it; it definitely was not His plan. It was all Adam's invention.

Sin was activated not necessarily in the knowledge Adam received; that was secondary even though when we acquire things not permissive of God's will, it truly is sin. But primarily, God's issue with Adam was of paramount concern; *"Usurping His Authority"*. There is no recanting; *"Sin is sin regardless of its attractions"*. If God does not want you to have something, well then stay away from it! It is not that important in the grand scheme of His plan for your life. You could end up in a situation as Adam in what you may have thought was a small thing; consuming what God has forbidden but now it is a full blown action of your betrayal. After acquiring *"knowledge"* through the forbidden channels of temptation; progressively, you will *"discover the full strength of your decision"*. If persisted long enough; it will become part of your constitution. What a deadly combination; evilness of knowledge and the strength and determination to act on it.

Adam would soon discover in such a dreaded way how painful disobedience can be. Jealousy, murder; likes of which he couldn't fathom the depth of the meaning of sorrow. It came as a whirlwind from flesh born of his flesh; his son Abel murdered by the hands of his jealous brother Cain. I weep from just the thought; brother killing brother. The actions of sin can create horrors in our lives and so overpowering we may never get over it.

"Knowledge is the precursor to actually knowing." It takes the experience of wisdom for the proving of knowledge. If I know something then why do I need more knowledge to discover what I already know? What does it profit me aspiring to apprehend head expansion of knowledge but never using it? Inclining and inclining but never arriving as I see in the lives of so many Believers! It reminds me of the paradigm of the tabernacle; from the outer court to the inner court consuming knowledge but never attaining that level of communion in the Most Holy Place. The highest level of fellowship communing in our secret compartment of faith is the experience of a one on one encounter in the Presence of our Heavenly Father.

God had determined that man had become like one of them with knowledge to know good and evil". Why didn't He just say; *"like Us rather than One of Us"*? It didn't matter, Adam had to leave and leave he did; sent out without a way back in. Adam didn't have the opportunity of repentance as we have today. His tragic decision was without the grace of God's forgiveness.

Adam acquired *"keys"* by his disobedience; a key to the fields of Earth; the other, a key that would take him to his grave. God did not take them away from him. They were his earned through his disobedience. But the key to the self locking door of the Garden was now under strict security by a host of Cheribum.

> *I am the Living One; I was dead, and now look, I am alive forever and ever! And I hold the* **keys** *of death and Hades.* [1]

Consumption of the Tree of Good and Evil voided any further choices Adam could make in the Garden. With a temporary coat of skin as Earth's first atoning sacrifice for sin and the inherited *"key"* earned from his disobedience Adam authenticated entrance into portals of a new world he would now occupy activating the discretionary key of good and evil. With equal access by his choices to the door of good which would extend his life and the door of evil subtracting years from his tenure as an early departure into the vault of Earth; the certainty of death waited for his arrival. Without a spare key to use to prolong his life beyond conclusion of his choices, the generational key covered the span of his life never to be used again spawning new meaning of life's expectancy.

The question remains; which door would Adam choose? The choice of obedience he learned during his tenure in the Garden to the extent it would yield or make a speedy exit with no more choices to consider? The choice was his and his alone but now without God's directive. God did not take away the essence of *"A Free Will Spirit"* from Adam but allowed pursuit of his own destiny relegated by his choices. But sweat and labor in the fields of Earth activated by knowledge of good and evil created a burden for his decisions.

The key to faith is anchored in belief providing us with the same opportunities as Adam; to do good if we choose and it is never a given that we will. But the actions of evil are an ever present contradiction with probabilities lurking in the shadows to void our faith.

The premise of faith is based on truth which has its own motivations. Just as fuel is injected in the engine of a car causing a flow of power, synonymously as the fueling center of our choices, our motivations exist as propellants of faith. They reflect the passion of our hearts burning desires. Faith is motivated towards the beacon of achievement constantly surveilling portals to our destiny. While we still exist in the light of day it is encumbered upon us to consider our choices; for darkness is soon to come and we will exist no more. So which door will you choose?

Adam's consumption of the tree allowed him to gain a level of familiarity of how God does what He does. God is the only righteous judge who can discriminate truth judging good and evil. It becomes clearer why Adam's tenure was prohibited to proceed any further; *"The tree of life was a forever tree guaranteeing life to do whatever his choices would lead him to do."* With the knowledge Adam acquired; knowing too much was a death sentence. His actions were plagiaristic when you consider the level of familiarity introduced in his consciousness to become like one of them. *"Knowledge of God's authority with freedom to exercise his free will over it"* was knowledge Lucifer attained before his fall. God gave Adam every opportunity for continual life as long as his obedience prevailed but he chose to go his own way. He bore the same penalty as Lucifer banned from His Presence. One would expect, this was entirely too much authority beyond Adam's ability to handle. The same power corrupted Lucifer and he began a reign of terror in Heaven because of his familiarity with God's operations. If you recall, his discontent was that he wanted power exceeding the Throne of God. But he was to be denied; denied indeed! This reminds me of what I see in our churches today; a lust for power!

Consumption of the Tree of Life was sustaining with the same lifespan as the Angels of Heaven who forever exist in God's Eternal Presence. Adam's tenure of time in God's Garden was a life of permanence as long as he stayed true to the call of faith. But he changed his jurisdiction failing to complete his assignment. Now he must subdue the Earth with the commission to be fruitful and multiply. And multiply he did with an expansion in continuum; 7.5 billion and still counting. But the window of opportunity was notably shortened with the looming eyes of death monitoring every step of his progression; each step towards journey's end.

Punishment for disobedience is a consequence that puts limitations on the amount of time we need for the harvesting of faith. With our lamps dim and wick shorten; time creates a differential to the vision of faith because of Adam's betrayal. It's been said *"time is not on your side"* but it can be by our obedience to faith. The difficulty of labor indicates that we must operate with expediency to complete the call assigned to our visions and dreams while perpetual movement of the ticking clock continues and it is impossible to stop. Expectations for expansion of time have been severely compromised dictated by one man's decision limiting time as a conclusion for his actions. However, there is a greater promise of faith; God knows the plans set before us. His desire is that we prosper with no harm with hope of an abiding future. With the watch of death looming, as long as it is day *"we must do the works of Him who sent us";* for night is coming when no man can work.

In the cool of the day blending in amongst trees just as a chameleon changes its color for protection, the searching eyes of God passing in the night will come upon us with the sound of His footsteps coming closer to our fears. An awakened conscience of disobedience will cause you to shiver in fear filled with regret and dejection of what is to come upon you. Those footsteps you thought you heard, you are not kidding; I heard them too! The Sound of footsteps were wearing on his conscience; it is now time for God to ease the pain by calling Adam front and center; *"Where are you"?* It is not a clever game of hide and seek as an action of deception but the time has now come to fully disclose his reasons for hiding.

Adam left us in a very precarious situation torn amid our choices seduced by preference of our lower angels committed to our demise. Quite often, along the way on our journey circumstances will arise that are so compelling instigating God to deal with us in a very unusual way. Hearing footsteps in the night is not the place where we want to be. Those footsteps solicit an immediate response for our actions. Accountability can be intimidating amplifying our fears as we stand before God with a presentation to mediate our misgivings.

Adam presented himself before God along with his co-conspirators; *"his wife and the serpent"*. As he stood before God, he adjudicated his position with a new tool of defense by implicating his wife; transferring responsibility upon anyone but himself; *"The Woman You gave to me; she is the one and not me"*! If I were in God's shoes I would ask Adam; *"Did it taste good"?* Kidding aside, I'm glad God didn't have to chase him. By now He was not up to playing anymore games. It is the games people play always baffling you with a ruse of truth to disarm you before exacting their plans against you while hiding behind their disguises.

It is now time for Adam to account for his actions; *"who told you"?* There was nothing he could say; not even to change the mind of God. He was resolute! God immediately expelled them back into the world they came from. I guess Adam felt betrayed and changed his wife's name; *"And Adam called his wife's name Eve; because she was the mother of all living"*.[1] Stop It; not so fast! Why the name Eve? What are you implying? What happened to *"Woman; my wife bone of my bones, flesh of my flesh"?* What's the motivation? Suggestively are you saying; *"The mother of all living is the cause of sin and I blame you"*! Is it vindictiveness? Last time I checked, the only living beings were the two of you. But what about you Adam; you're the son of sin born from Lucifer's original sin! When I last looked at God's charging indictment He blamed you who was complicit in silence and not the one that was with you. Those footsteps you heard they were coming for you dude!

Now the blaming; first the woman now the serpent; from the serpent to the last man standing; it's all about you Adam! All of you are in trouble. When God comes to clean house believe it; He is going to clean house! As a reward for their labor, Adam and his wife received wearable trophies; coats of skin as garments to clothe them in the barrenness of their new world.

Adam had no consciousness of the night darkness would come upon him. Originally, his reign in the Garden existed in the *"completed light of day"*; not in part but full wonderment of God's majesty on display illuminating every corridor of his conscience. Moving from light to a life perplexed with darkness, Adam now had a new covering. He had never before experienced trepidation of darkness and how intimidating night could be; *"with footsteps heard in the darkness of night while shivering in fear; dressed for warmth with the hide of an animal to cover his nakedness"*. The time for accountability had come and gone leaving behind his only defender, *"a weaponized consciousness of guilt"*.

My original intent of identifying God's imperative for Adam's departure is now made clear. *"Now man has migrated from the **'likeness'** of God to become **'like'** one of us."* Which one of you did the actions of Adam emulate? Which one did he become like? It's apparent; *"It was the one who was missing from the conversation, Lucifer"*. Like One of us means *"The Fallen One"*! You remember him don't you; the usurper! A name never to be forgotten; Lucifer the menace of corruption Adam became like; the one who initiated a revolt in Heaven.

As *"The fallen Arch Angel of Light"* who was the highest of all angels with wings stretched across the heavens; He was the one made with splendor with knowledge of good with perversion of evil consumed in his existence.

Characteristically, Adam adorned an image in the likeness of Lucifer; not the good guys but the bad one. It wasn't the Father who brought light out of darkness nor His Son Jesus commissioned to take on the sins of Adam neither was it the reflected image of God's Spirit, *"The Holy Ghost"* who brooded upon the waters of the deep. It was the one fallen from the grace of God.

Adam made a power move with similarity to the likeness of Lucifer's usurping. God deals with that kind of stuff very seriously. You can't touch what He has forbidden you to touch or eat what He prohibits. You may want to reconsider the next time you stretch forth your hand to touch the Anointed of God. Touch meaning; in any way to inflict harm or intentions of malice. God was concerned if Adam remained and ate from the Tree of Life he would live forever in his fallen state contaminating everything within his reach.

A Choice of Trees

One more lingering question; why did God have the Tree of Good and Evil there in the first place? Why not just the one tree; *"The Tree of Life"* that would have avoided conflict of Adam's *"freewill"* to exercise his own choices? God has choices, His angels have choices and so do we. The closer we are to His Presence makes our decisions much easier to make. Even though God bestowed a multitude of blessings upon Adam; it is significant to note He only gave him *"One Promise; the Promise of Death for Eating of the Forbidden Tree"*. Authorship of God's promises is authoritarian meaning that He knows consequence of the beginning and end of our decisions.

Adam discovered the Tree of the Knowledge of Good and Evil had a greater power than the influence of the beguiling serpent. After his eviction into a world filled with so many uncertainties, he had nothing but the *"consciousness of good"* to guide him through his choices as his only reliance. But standing alone, good of his intentions proved to be no match combating the spiritual forces his generation would encounter. He would discover he truly had an enemy; the knowledge of evil seeking to retain supremacy interacting with the affairs of men. Prior to then during his tenure in the Garden, it was never his battle as long as he stayed true to the center of God's attraction; the Tree of Life.

The repository of God's knowledge of good and evil was not meant to be tampered with. It was more than Adam could handle. The reservoir of flesh is incapable to accommodate the full knowledge of God's Existence. But the Holy Spirit can! He is the reason why we need His operation in all of our affairs. He knows what God knows and orders our steps to see what God sees. He exhibited His power participating in the war in Heaven when Lucifer initiated his revolt. The Holy Spirit is the testament of performance of God's power with proven credentials defying any other power in existence.

Adam discovered trees can talk discernible by their movements. At times they will tell you things you may not want to hear. Don't blame the tree; it tried to help you. Adorned with a borrowed apron of leaves to cover his nakedness directed by a tree now consuming his conscience, they both spoke to Adam's fears raging in every corridor of his being of his frantic attempts to hide. It was a meaningful lesson however troubling the consequences that were still echoing in his conscious; *"You don't have enough to cover your nakedness"*. From inside out; Adam was covered with trees. Despite hiding he still was exposed! Footsteps of God rumbling through the trees gave warning; *"He is coming"*.

The first use of forbidden knowledge Adam received convinced him to hide. That alone is indication you have lost the battle by exposure of your actions. What you do does matter. Your actions will expose the inner workings of your heart bearing nakedness as a witness of truth. Adam made a provocative attempt in defense of forbidden knowledge he received. Like you and I, he thought he could hide in disguise of a tree. Maneuvers; maneuvers and more maneuvers! It is time to be true to thine self! No more capitulations and exaggerations. God already knows before He ask; *"Did you"!* So try not to get too clever! You know what you did.

Your *"did you"* moment might not be the same as mine, but as my mother would say, *"you shall have a moment; if not today just keep on living"*. As humans in making our decisions, whether overtly or accomplished covertly, I can guarantee you will at some point eat from the tree of *"I told you not to even touch"*. Whether camouflaged with leaves or not; you can run and it doesn't matter how fast, your nakedness will still be exposed with your skirt lifted up for the world to see.

Disobedience does have a voice and a conscience as Adam discovered. It will speak to you silently with a transmission of guilt. With neon signs attracting as an appealing good, disobedience has a deceptive power that will overwhelm your senses. Coexisting powers of good and evil both are of the same tree. They are in a continual battle for rightful access of our choices. Though they share the same root and fruit may taste the same, the value of their consumption bifurcate producing life and death by the power of our decisions.

Good can yield the same results as evil if the good of our intentions is in opposition to God's instructions. A good thing does not necessarily mean it is the right thing. So many of us consume our time doing good deeds when it is very clear what God has instructed us to do. You can't do both. It's a distraction to invest our energy opposite the will of God. Apostle Paul viewed faith as an urgent demand to fulfill its requirements after having committed years of his life in pursuit of vain agendas. We expense a lot of our time focusing our energy away from our priorities participating in transitional matters that invariably change from one day to the next. If we are not discerning of our steps we can permit theft of our most precious treasure; *"Our time"*. We can't appropriate our own time not even stop it. What we've been given is not to be wasted.

Gluttony of Faith

Adam had only one choice to consider in exercising his free will that gave cause for accountability. He was given latitude of independence using his free will with every right to his expressions but legalistically every expression did not legitimize his choices.

Adam had the consciousness of God woven into his fabric at the moment of his conception. He had a free will not bound by constraints limiting his ability to function autonomously. A free will allows expansion of our thoughts and motivations for development of our visions and dreams. We all have choices loaded with unlimited possibilities. But the choices we make must be in sync with God's objectives even though He will never violate our right to be. With added instructions to shepherd our faith, He requires our obedience.

Adam may have thought he was left alone to do as he pleased but in the cool of the day; time did arrive. *"Answerably; time to give an account for his actions"*. It's no different than *"time"* coming for you and me. Faith is accountable! There are parameters varying from faith to faith (*your faith-my faith*) that are unique with an array of possibilities attached in pursuit of our destiny. What I am instructed to do perhaps may be different than your instructions of faith. Judgment of our choices will be weighed on the balanced scales of obedience. We all can recognize; if God has to ask as He did with Adam *"where are you"* that we may very well be in trouble. In our nakedness, transparent to Him, we have no place to hide.

It is one thing to be asked where are you; why are you not on your assignment but then to be asked; *"Who told you were naked"* bears a greater degree of gravity. Who have you been talking to? Why are you taking counsel outside of the instructions given for your success? Some of the things that I hear people say can be quite elevating that I have to ask myself; *"Who told you that? Where did it come from"?* A voice of persuasion can take you from where you are now to a destination not conceived in your faith. Faith is to be approached with caution. There are penalties levied for taking a *"sideways"* view to the perceptions of faith. Faith's destination is intended to be a straight line; from point A to point B but typically, it never happens that way due to distractions laid in the path before us.

Faith is not debatable! In our interactions dealing with *"human beings"*, we often encounter opposition to our walk of faith. In all honesty, it is purposed for something greater; to validate your resolve. You hear it all the time; *"Did God Really Say"?* [1] You better make sure you know that you know! There are many voices in the Earth but the voice of the Holy Spirit speaking into your ear should be recognizable.

From beginning to end, the revealing voice of the Holy Spirit is unmistakable. He is the true Voice of God's interpretations. Having to debate the surety of God's Word should tell you something concerning your motivations. Faith needs no justification and should never be debated. We have a tendency to step aside from our priorities as Adam did entertaining things that can be injurious to our faith. There can be dire consequences to bear. *"Faith is self referencing"* by the Word of Truth like a compass pointing true north. It mirrors reflection of God's intentions to take you from where you are now to the place He intended you to be.

Adam sacrificed his sovereign rule of occupation in the Garden by creating distrust in the mind of God. By severing the lines of connectivity, he trusted his senses influenced by a persuasion targeted to compromise his faith. To be fair, it was only one sense that awakened all of his senses; his sense of taste. By now we all know; *"He had very bad taste"!* Have you sampled your tasting recently? Be careful! It is not a smorgasbord. Think twice before you bite twice!

Adam's sense of taste was an exaggeration. It was accomplished enough exploiting every sense laying dormant in his un-awakened conscience. He was quick to discover his nakedness. Sin is quick with its own speed of acceleration. Prior to then, Adam's perception was limited within the perimeter of faith. His ears were attuned to visitation of God's approaching footsteps in the cool of evening and like a dove the Voice of Peace embraced his surrender. But something happened! The footsteps of God were pounding like *"Bigfoot"* walking amongst the trees. What he heard was the sound of fear; a fear he had never experienced before.

Before Adam's creative escapade of experimentation with sin, fear was an unrecognizable word populated in his vocabulary. What is fear to one who has never known fear? It is called terror! I can tell you from my experience on the battlefields in Vietnam. It introduced me to the horror of fear! I didn't know that fear had a conscience powerful enough to override my senses to the extent my body failed to respond. Adam found out; hiding in fear to footsteps echoing in his conscience!

By no means did Adam ever fear his wife and not even the serpent but what he feared the most was the terror of God descending upon him. Who wants pain when they have no pain; tears when they have no tears; burdens when there is not a burden to bear? Obviously somebody did! Don't judge Adam; judge yourself! That's a familiar cry we all tend to circumvent when truth appears at our doors. Testimonies are for winners not losers dodging in shame to conceal their pride. Sin is reluctant to transparency with exposure as its greatest enemy. When sin is uncovered; do something about it; learn from the error of your ways.

Adam would need his newly awakened senses in a world ready to embrace his arrival. From dust he came and dust he returned. For his survival there would be only so much time allocated for his explorations. It was time for Adam to dream his own dreams; create his own vision after refusing to accept God's imprint authenticating His Reality designated for mankind. Left to man alone there are no limits to his imaginings.

Man's extremism; a life embolden from one extreme to the next, continues to be encumbered with thoughts of his inferior deterioration. Realizing limitations of his time there is a rush to exploit every evil way he can imagine; salivating with pride for power even at the cost of his own dehumanization. Dissident thoughts of man are one giant *"Ferris Wheel"* in perpetual motion; from thought to thought; around and around with no conceiving end to his ever evolving imaginations.

> *And God saw the wickedness of man was great in the Earth, and that every imagination of the thoughts of his heart was only evil continually. And it repented the LORD he had made man on the Earth grieving His Heart.* [1]

Natural tendencies of man are subversive in pursuit of his wayward nature to create his own rendition of the definition of life. Problematically, his exaggeration continues as an affront to God. In the heart of man; he continues tailor making his reality bundled in iniquity. Saddled with an altered perception compensating for the void created by Adam's sedition; man's aspirations remain aloof as he struggles to re-imprint *"purpose"* originally assigned by divine declaration concerning his future. One day it will all end likened to the days of Noah but this time with fire and brimstone collapsing upon him. It is God's prerogative of satisfying His own judgment of grievance against man which regrettably is irrevocable. But man continues to obstruct God's plan purposed for humanity with his evasive actions.

Attributes of humanity have not changed; lying, perversions, greediness and idolatry the likes of which will continue as a testament against us validating the reasons for our destruction. Somehow if I could think through the mind of God, I can readily understand the pain of rejection of an out of control reality that was never meant to be. Yet we continue exaggerating our individuality as an exception to His vision. When will we mature and disavow romanticizing our flesh?

> *And the Lord said, "My spirit shall not always strive with man, for that he also is flesh: yet his days shall be* **an hundred and twenty years**". [1]

One hundred twenty years by God's designation and we are counting our years toward an end that is soon to come! Not threescore and ten and by reason of strength fourscore as David enumerated in the Book of Psalm which he died at the age of 70. For Adam it was *"930 years"!* I can imagine he is looking down on us saying; *"what happened"?* Why is it that our years are cut so short? We are very quick to criticize him but what about us? He got more out of this life than any of us. Despite disobedience that terminated his tenure, Adam's life was closer to the Garden than ours today. The Tree of Life still extended his days 930 years well beyond anything we could imagine. Presentation of our lives relative to time is but a blur in consideration of God's allocation.

Adam's life after expulsion from the Garden of Eden was no more than a seed deposited in the fields of Earth for expansion to fulfill the vision of God. With an incubation covering the span of thousands of years, he was the engine sourcing all life we see today. There is nothing new in the Earth. *"Everything visible in the physical realm of Earth since Adam entered the fields is an imagination born of the creative thoughts of man."*

Everything in our realm of visibility is an extension of the actions of Adam. From the days of Noah and the Great Flood when God repented for having created man to the exterminating views of today that have infiltrated his consciousness; man's nature remains antagonistic to the principles of faith. His subversive perceptions of God's reality equates to insubordination in his efforts to undermine the true impressions of God's creation. With a saturated mind burdened with ungratefulness of the privilege of life; man has evolved in his consciousness denying *"purpose"* of his creation contrasting the image when God first made him. In his confusion, man has accepted an image of his own making priding the absence of power that created him.

The yearning of dust seeking to reclaim itself is a compulsion of the destiny of man seeking reunification to the source from whence he came. However, the *"Warning of Dust"* is a curse of the ground warning not to be reclaimed just as sin is a warning of the curse of death. Dust has no life neither does the life of sin. It is the terminal end of our choices if we choose not to accept the pleadings of the Cross for our salvation. For indeed; *"We came from dust; we shall return to dust."* When Christ comes again, our lives will be changed reflective of His life bound for *"eternity with no end"*.

> *To Adam he said, because you listened to your wife and ate fruit from the tree about which I commanded you, you must not eat from it; "Cursed is the ground because of you; through painful toil you will eat food from it all the days of your life."* **Genesis 3:17 NIV**

Adam's new dwelling place was amongst the cursed emanating from the ground. There was nothing he could touch that was separate from the judgment he received not even the ground he walked upon as a penalty for the wages of sin. Generally, an indictment is a suspicion indicating there is probable cause but a judgment is the proven action of our behavior. With the litany of details in the sentencing phase for his disobedience; Adam's penalty committed him to the fields of Earth. Without a doubt; I firmly believe he had major skepticism adjusting to his new environment. Swirling in the midst of confusion; deliberating the battles of good and evil, decisions of the flesh would now become his new *"administrator"*. His awakened senses amplified his trepidations; *"Ears alerted as a coyote listening for prey; smell of dust of the Earth drawing him nearer to conclusion of his days; pain from the stress of labor toiling for survival with no fertility from the curse of the ground for the planting of seed."*
The overwhelming power of Adam's fears was stronger than the force of the sun's enticement of Earth in time of its rising. His new found sensitivity seeded in his emotions was recognition of suffering as he looked back with tears of remorse at vaporization of a dream.

Why did he choose to eat more than God allowed? That's called gluttony. *"Gluttony of Faith"* can lead you into some strange places where obedience is overruled by zeal questing for things outside the boundaries of God's guidance. I have been there and so have you. It has taken me across oceans and continents only to discover what I was seeking; I already had! I did not need *"borrowing"* from any man; not that I can't learn from others. Gratefully, the mantle upon my life is not one to be indicted retracing the steps of others.

God created a path for me in the wilderness; to go where faith is assigned to take me where I am still camped out at the doors of expectations. So much of our energy at times is wasted spring boarding on the success of others. That's called franchising! If your spirit is colluded it has a tendency to mimic attributes and inflections that are indistinguishable from others. Adoption of characteristics not reflective of your own mannerism is plagiaristic to the extent you begin to look like them; sound like them but more dangerously is to act as they have acted. Be unique; stay unique and maintain your peculiarity in the vision of God.

We all have forbidden fruit ever before us. God may give us instructions but more often than not; we will go out of our way to do the direct opposite of what we should do. *"Woeful creatures we are!"* Adam should have taken full ownership of his actions and so should we! As a result, faith was instigated with metrics; first rule of law but now a more perfected way; law of grace.

Trees

Trees have an attachment existing well beneath its surface. Hidden away from our sight and disguised by a protective cover of its true life exist the organ of fluid return; *"the root"*. Penetrating deep below the surface of the Earth, roots maintain a stature of straightness as an anchor against any variability challenging its strength to survive. Roots bear no leaves but supply nutrients harvested out of soil to produce what is needed for a tree's growth. On any given day trees may produce good fruit or bad fruit; good leaves and leaves weltered by drought, sun and wind but they are never to be judged in an instant of observation. Though the winds of time may cause chatter at the changing of seasons, leaves remain predictive always fluctuating in appearance from barrenness to bloom by the elements of any given season.

Every tree purposed to bear fruit is recognizable by its production. At times, their leaves may appear to be promising but in the season for their fruit to bear, there is no guarantee of their yield. While some trees may be in the early stages of budding, the season for their production hasn't arrived to yield fruit indicative of their labor. Seasons are perpetual moving from cycle to cycle but time is a constant for events of change. There is a purpose for everything residing beneath the sun. It's been given a time that's uniquely allocated for exhibition of *"what is to be"* and *"what is to do"*. Time of seasons is a window of opportunity measured for the performance of faith. Jesus used the parable of the fig tree as an illustration of discernment of seasons.

> *Now learn this lesson from the fig tree: As soon as its twigs get tender and its leaves come out, you know that summer is near. Even so, when you see all these things, you know that it is near, right at the door.* [1]

Each tree appearing to be wise may not be wise; everything that looks good is not necessarily so. With the wisdom of God as the candle of our conscience, the Holy Spirit will illuminate any discrepancy laid in our path. When we enter into compromise violating God's lawfulness set apart for the intended good of our lives by consuming what He has forbidden, it will respond with consequence. Without discernment, inadvertently we could call good evil and evil good and suffer the same consequence as Adam's wife being baffled by the subtleties of the serpent; *"But God did say?"* [1]

Faith has its own instinct. Words that are spoken into the inlet of our hearing must be filtered. We have to be very careful in our dissimulation of words. As an inspiration to faith, the words we hear discriminately will *"increase our faith to the degree by what we hear"*.

The purpose of faith is not meant for argumentative presumptions we have concluded. Unambiguously, the arguments of faith are *"skepticisms"* originating from misunderstandings and ignorance as derivatives of confusion. As Believers, we have a tendency of being *"headstrong"* exalting our opinions and interpretations of God's Word rather than leaving it to the Holy Spirit for His interpretations. The arguments of faith are not just limited to what is good versus what is evil but expanded to compromising what we truly believe.

The burning flame of God's Righteousness is tested in the fires of our conscience for the proving of faith; to burn away the dross to accurately portray God's vision as He has instructed.

Refreshing Springs

Now the LORD God had planted a garden in the east, in Eden; and there he put the man he had formed. The LORD God made all kinds of trees grow out of the ground trees that were pleasing to the eye and good for food. In the middle of the garden were the tree of life and the tree of the knowledge of good and evil.

A river watering the garden flowed from Eden; from there it was separated into four headwaters. The name of the first is the Pishon; it winds through the entire land of Havilah, where there is gold. The gold of that land is good; aromatic resin and onyx are also there. The name of the second river is the Gihon; it winds through the entire land of Cush. The name of the third river is the Tigris; it runs along the east side of Ashur. And the fourth river is the Euphrates.

Genesis 2:8-14 NIV

Four Rivers of God's Divide

"*What is* **mind** *without an engine of conversion to dissimulate our thoughts; what is* **body** *without a tabernacle to exercise the gifts of God's empowerment; what is* **soul** *without conscience to reason and what is* **spirit** *without a vessel of habitation for God's Abiding Presence.*"

Rivers 6

But Streams came up from the earth and watered the whole surface of the ground. Then the LORD God formed a man from the dust of the ground and breathed into his nostrils the breath of life, and he became a living being.[1]

In the vineyard of God, He made a variety of trees to grow out of the ground; trees that were pleasing to the eye and good for food. God's majesty can be observed in every living thing even in the beauty of trees in their blooming splendor. Some paint a scenic background of flowering blossoms while others portray their brilliance in electrifying colors at seasonal change of the harvest of autumn. Their cycle is our cycle; from fall to winter; from spring to summer, redundancy of their seasons defines the boundaries of our existence in a continual repetition of change.

Without trees there would be no life; not even air to breathe to sustain the breath of creation. We both share dependent life joined in continual exchange of breath concealed in an atmosphere of oxidizing vapors. From one to the other, we both give life to each other; from barrenness to hope; from hope to fertility yielding the fruits of life.

We can visibly see trees in their outward glory but they maintain a hidden life expanding growth beneath their surface not discerning to our sight. Buried in the depths below, their roots penetrate deep into the dark connecting to a vibrant stream of interior life flowing in the waters below. *"Still waters"* do run deep from a wellspring replenishing life to every root.

Water Cycles

God created streams surfacing from the Earth as a perpetual water cycle. Only the subliminal dew misting upon the Earth reflects the same evidential cycle of completeness. Out of abundance, rivers were formed channeling power from the headwaters of Eden as four rivers of refreshing springs. Flowing from the aromatic streams of Pishon to deifying waters of the Euphrates, rivers continues to flow rising from the ebb of tide as a testament of God's creation.

From the beginning of God's creation even until now, water cycles are perpetually moving above and below the surface of the Earth. They change states whether liquid, vapor or ice as the Earth continues its evolution. Even though the balance of water remains fairly constant over the course of time, it moves from one reservoir to another, from river to ocean, from ocean to the atmosphere via the physical processes of condensation, precipitation, or evaporation.

Evaporating power of the sun is an exchange of heat energy exerting influence on our climate which leads to temperature changes. As long as there is a sun, the balance of God's creation will continue to cycle the path of our beginnings. Every law follows the path of fulfilling an obedient end. *"Even the tiniest dewdrop obeys a law and fulfills its eternal purpose."*

During the process of evaporation, water takes up energy from the atmosphere cooling the environment. Conversely, in condensation, water releases energy to warm the environment at times creating fog obscuring our view. Even the morning dew refreshes the Earth despite the restraint of rain from the heavens above. It was evaporation of dew condensed in the Garden of Eden for until then the world knew no rain.

Water cycles figure significantly in the maintenance of life and ecosystems on Earth. Transferring water from one reservoir to another replenishes the land with freshwater and transports minerals to different parts of the globe. Rising air currents take the vapor into the atmosphere where cooler temperatures cause it to condense into clouds creating precipitation. It may fall as snow, hail or sleet accumulating as ice caps and glaciers which can store frozen water for thousands of years. Over time, frozen water returns to the ocean, streams and rivers where our water cycle began.

Man in his neglect of God's creation has managed to pollute our oceans, streams and rivers. Our oceans are dumping grounds filled with deadly contaminates; mercury, uranium, pesticides and even radioactive waste. *"Nuclear energy belongs in the heavens from where it came that has room to absorb its power and not in the trust and confinement of our planet."*

Our fish are dying at an alarming rate and over harvested primarily for the sake of greed disturbing the balance and provisions God intended for our survival. As populations increase around the world, which are expanding at a prolific rate, a contentious battle for Earth's resources is brewing in our midst. Wars for oil, food and fresh water have already laid claim to the lives of millions with no resolve in sight. The time of reckoning is fast approaching with an accountability of dire consequences. We still have time to address the issues concerning our environment but do we have the will to apply our faith as redeeming agents of God's command to *"Tend and Guard."*

The River of Eden

> *A river watering the garden flowed from Eden; from there it was separated into four headwaters.* [1]

In the day of Adam's creation, there was a river that pre-dated the waters flowing from the Garden of Eden. Unsurprisingly, God can take natural elements of His creation and turn them into a spiritual component of His expectation. Just as the River of Eden supplied the diverging waters in a quadrilateral flow, God can take whatever is in our possession and turn it into a greater production to achieve His directives.

Life can't be sustained without a continued supply of water. Not just any kind of water, but fresh water. The mineral balance in fresh water replenishes every cell of our bodies for without it, we would succumb to dehydration or even the possibility of death. Supply of fresh water free of poisonous contaminants is rapidly declining in the Earth without resiliency to recover. Even our coral reefs are disappearing and as reported; 90% annihilation within thirty years if the inevitable consequence of inflicting more harm to our planet is not circumvented.

Water is our inheritance God gave for our survival but because of negligence, it's being rationed as share value to the highest bidder as a commodity on the opened market. How ridiculous we have become by continuing to disregard life's necessities. What could possibly be our motivation other than profit and greed? For all of our actions and inactions as stewards of our home Earth, there is a price to pay with dire consequences we will soon discover in our betrayal.

Historically, wars have been instigated disputing over water rights. Damming of one river inadvertently can cripple an economy; starving the land of nutrients needed for its production but can increase the value and wealth of the one who controls its flow. The same analogy can be applied to our spiritual lives; who is controlling the flow of your river?

Eden's River

Eden can be described as utopia; a place where our imagination would reach the point of exhaustion if we tried to comprehend its reality. While flipping through the patterns of faith in all of my deliberations, there was nothing remotely comparable in my interrogations

I could apply to my visualizations. In truth, Eden did exist in our far distant past and remained guarded by a host of celestial Cherubim.

The River of Eden branched dividing the outflow emerging from its center with replenishing power to supply every branch connected to its source. Just as the four rivers were divided from the River of Eden; the Pishon, Gihon, Tigris and Euphrates, there are four channels of our spiritual lives in constant need of God's renewal; *"mind, body, soul and spirit"*. But their greatest value is realized in synergy which is God's binding expression of *"Unity"*.

The combination of love and unity interweaves the passion of faith into a living dynamo of invincibility. Love personifies the total expression of God's Existence shared in the hearts of all humanity. In the heart of our inner man there is a yearning for harmony for the full representation of God's Presence to occupy our lives. His Presence is the nucleus of love unifying our hearts to the desire of faith.

Sovereignty of mind, body, soul and spirit each have their defining character but superiority of their independence is no greater than the other; not even our thoughts. As our thoughts are conceptualized they should conform to the spiritual consciousness of our Creator. The unified waters of the Garden flowed in a distributive stream that supplied each tributary with enough virtue to finish its designated course. Each tributary flowed uninterruptedly from Eden with a purpose as a reservoir of power in search of its ending.

The Power of Singleness

Singleness is austerity of God's conscience. It came with a breath into Adam's nostrils as the generator for all life known to man. The substance of one breath has fueled our physical existence since time beginning. It was not a breath of resuscitation but the breath of a dynamo of evolving life. Adam's life was seeded as an engine of conversion, converting God's energy into an Image born of His Conscience. God will not breathe another breath into the nostril of man. When He rested He gave authority to man for expansion of His breath that has lasted since the beginning of creation. We are without visualization to see God's breath but evidence is in the breath of life that continues to sustain us.

Jesus appeared as an agent of restoration creating a path of intervention capable of reuniting our lives to His Father's originality. In His arsenal, He distributed love and love's productivity which is the Gift of Faith as our greatest asset. It is intended to counter the natural influences and powers that have hindered the establishment of His Kingdom.

The single breath of God's Existence continues to breathe in the heart of man. It exudes with a love so great to unify our hearts into the singleness of faith. Conceptually, singleness is a projection of harnessed power that can radicalize the actions of faith into greater productivity. When our hearts are woven in singleness with the Holy Spirit's abiding Presence, it brings Heaven within our reach with His greatness in us greater than those in the world.

Rule of the Spirit

Our soul and mind are *"idiosyncratic"*; unique with a conscience of their own. If allowed existence apart from governance by the Holy Spirit, arrogantly we will succumb to rebellion. Any decisions alienated from the Holy Spirit's guidance are calculated steps vying for independence to live our lives as we so choose. The natural man's inclinations are defiant to the operating principles of God's Spirit resulting in justification of pride. To enter into the world of rule where the Holy Spirit has dominant influence empowering our lives, we must accept *"His Reality as God's Authority"*.

The Holy Spirit is the revealer of the Kingdom of Christ in our inner most being. He is a unifier existing as the only true source of connectivity to the center of faith. As subjects to His authority, He equips us with greater exposure of compassion needed to fuel our *"gifting"* for the performance of faith. Oneness of God's Spirit instigates toward an end to accomplish faith through the compassion of love. Love is transcending; unconditionally performing beyond our reasoning and sensibilities to unify our hearts to God's desire. God's desire for unity is accomplished by surrendering our agendas; relinquishing all for the sake of Christ.

Just like a security blanket provides comfort from unsettled elements of our insecurities, the Holy Spirit covers our inner man as a *"blanket of peace"*. On the day of Jesus crucifixion while prostrated on the Cross of no return; His Spirit was willing but His flesh was not as compliant. Sufferings are intended to bring a level of realism to faith balancing our expectations and motivations. We can't deny, the sufferings of the flesh are hurting and depleting but for the resolved of faith; there is no surrendering when faced with persecutions. Sufferings are not meant to be kind; not break you but make you; not punish you but teach you; transposing as a blessing if we are able to identify its purpose.

In the accepted heart of faith, the inward nature of obedience displays an outward conformity of surrender to attain the acceptable and perfect will of God. Truth is; the Eternal Word of God has a soul of its own. With our lives in unity with the Holy Spirit, God's Word forms a conscience of guiding light searching through the channels of faith for revelation of His wisdom.

Steadfastness of faith is compressing; condensing to the point of being unshakable; solid as a rock which cannot be moved. The possibility still exist where we can move with greater distinction into dimensions we have not yet realized if we remain committed and trusting of faith. However, it is going to take a resolve, a genuine press greater than anything you have ever experienced. It requires a conviction beyond the reach of compromise. Apostle Paul's conviction of faith is an imprint we all should aspire to;

> *Nay, in all these things we are more than conquerors through Him that loved us. I am persuaded, neither death, nor life, nor angels, nor principalities, nor powers, nor things present, nor things to come, nor height, nor depth, nor any other creature, shall be able to separate us from the love of God which is in Christ Jesus our Lord.* [1]

"Faith is trust of our will to submit." Submission is absolute providing rest required to enter into the peace of God and experience the love Christ sheds abroad in our hearts. At the Cross, joining of love and suffering, divinity and humanity; Heaven and Earth released its power to complete its call for unity. With our hearts unified, we have the ability to achieve great things in the Earth. What better way to represent the Body of Christ than a performance that can testify of God's power that *"they too may believe"*.

> *"That they all may be one, as You, Father, are in Me, and I in You; that they also may be one in Us, that the world may believe that **You sent Me**."* **John 17:21 NKJV**

Lord, send me and exhibit your power that the world may believe *"You sent me"!* Are you ready? It will cost you but be willing to put some skin in the game. Skin is the expense of dying to your flesh. Despite the pain, discomfort and inconvenience, *"your extraversion must conform to the inward appeal of the Holy Spirit"*. If not, God can take large chunks out of your hide in an appearance of your pretentiousness.

> *Oneness of the Cross of Christ is the character of undivided love personifying unity of the Father, Son and Holy Spirit. "Christ is in search of our lives that we may be one in* **THEM**.*"*

Love is the tangible expression of faith identifiable by our actions. Immersed deep in the bellows of faith with tentacles attached to our soul, love was made perfect from the moment of conception! Pure love is flawless. It is more than a feeling, the *"Eros of Man"*; it is a spiritual power acting as a governor that controls the heart of man. Love is reflective of the character and integrity of God. With the promise of faith, seeds of love were sown throughout His plans for mankind. God knew in advance what it would take to hold things together. Without love; where would we be? Anarchy would exist to the likes the world has never seen. We would be savages in search of the last man standing!

"God is love; the essence of all life." He governs our lives through the power of love. The key to compassion is love and its ability to impact our world to advance God's Kingdom. As a subsequent deterioration of faith, our greatest hindrance has been in our denial of the influence the Holy Spirit brings into our lives sharing God's love in our hearts from Heaven above.

What we visualize through the eyes of God's Spirit brings an understanding to the realities formed in the conscience mind of faith. The conscience of faith lives and breathes; pulsating in our imagination centered in the vision of God. Imaginations of faith are variable, constantly framing new expectations. They are limited only by our ability to retain God's impressions. What's required is singleness of faith as verdict of proof that our lives are indeed ordered to His expectations. With oneness in Christ truly as Christ is in God, *"Heaven's Embodiment of the Holy Spirit is evidence of eternity living within our hearts that keeps Heaven within our reach."* The reach of Heaven bridges the gaps of faith.

The work we are commissioned to do is far greater than our separations with our faith apart from each other. For so long now, we have believed in a surrogate teaching of materialism, knowledge (*mind power*) and exploitation of wisdom to make one wise which is in error of the true intent of God for our lives. We are on a journey and it is a mission of faith. The faith of one is the faith of all that we may be one. that the world may believe in the presentation of Christ as the sent One of God. *"He is the Hope of Glory."*

Boundaries-Power of Separatism

It has been said; *"A thought is never separated from its thinker."* Might I suggest to you, babblings of our tongue does not always give indication of truth existing at the core of our being. Babblings are disguises of trouble brewing beneath the surface of our portrayals. They exist as incoherent images of vexation forming in our spirit. It gives an indication that our senses are conflicting with our spirit in response to motivations formed in our imagination. If we don't address them they will emanate as thoughts of confusion.

Throughout our daily endeavors, there are times we struggle grasping for meaning, justification and even vindication that can be quite evading. It is a source of our babblings where our words become meaningless drifting from one thought to the next as we try to make sense of things surrounding our lives. If we are not careful, out of our hearts discontent, words of fear and discouragement will bring corruption into our faith.

The doorway of our lips will falsify our confessions with our hearts inclined to thoughts of evil. As our thoughts struggle for sensibility, negativity stemmed from our babblings will result in erratic behavior that will override any achievement of self-discipline.

> *Set a watch, O Lord before my mouth; keep the door of my lips. Incline not my heart to any evil thing, to practice wicked works with men that work iniquity: and let me not eat of their* **dainties. Psalm 141:3-4 KJV**

Dainties are seductive influences; always preying upon the gullible who migrate towards the offerings of men. If you are not careful, you could easily end up entrapped with their enticements. What looks good on the outside is not always a true indicator of what lies beneath. The wicked are extremely clever appealing to your sensibilities. Overtly but mostly with disguised intentions the subtle nature of their searching eyes will capture your imagination. Embedded in the toolkit of the wicked you will discover their treasure; *"A quiver of lies masquerading in distractions to blind you from truth with their dainties"*. Sharing the fruit of their pleasure undoubtedly is an agreement to practice wicked works with men who do the work of iniquity.

The purview of our landscape today lends credence to the wicked practices of men and their iniquity. We all must ask God to keep a watch over things we say even before we speak. There have been times in my zest and probably in yours, when I've opened the door of my lips without consideration of how it may have impacted someone else and have regretted every word. At times, it was too late to apologize. The damage was done; sadly irrevocably.

We are in a perpetual struggle of becoming one with the words we speak. Blessings and cursing proceed from the same mouth of our unruly tongue. As a living embodiment of a creative word, we became an entity of God's expression; *"A Word that became flesh by the spoken Word of Faith"*. The word is a conduit; a vital connection of inseparability that keeps our lives joined to His. As a result; we will render an accountability of our mastery of the battles of *"Good and Evil"*. The words we speak gives indication of the condition of our heart representative of what's written upon the tablets of our conscience.

Pattern of Iniquity

The Garden of Eden was overflowing with streams of life exuding from the Presence of God; whether food, water or shelter, provisions for man's occupation were complete by God's sustainment. The inhabitants of the Garden were only allowed to maintain occupancy as long as they preserved their integrity in the likeness of the image in the day God created them; an image of perfection without blemish. When iniquity was found, it perpetuated an imperfection marred by sin denying cohabitation of God's perfection with the rebellion of man unveiled by his disobedience.

> *Son of man, take up a lamentation for the King of Tyre, and say to him, thus say the Lord God; "You were the seal of perfection full of wisdom and perfect in beauty. You were in Eden, the Garden of God. Every precious stone was your covering: The sardius, topaz, and diamond, Beryl, onyx, and jasper, Sapphire, turquoise, and emerald with gold. The workmanship of your timbrels and pipes was prepared for you on the day you were created. "You were the anointed cherub who covers; I established you; You were on the holy mountain of God; You walked back and forth in the midst of fiery stones.* **Ezekiel 28:12-14 NKJV**

Iniquity is not easily discernible. Scripture indicates it takes time for exposure. It does not occur over the course of a day's journey but through the progression of time usually measurable at the pinnacle of faith. Perfection can be maintained for a period of time until tried by fiery stones sent to test our faith. Even though we may have golden pipes serenading with a melody of soothing tones, flattering words of wisdom parlayed in effervescence to flirtations of the hearing ear; disguised garments with ornamental stones of splendor; they all lend their energy to pride entangled in our descending thoughts as time unravels our deceptions. It is then iniquity emerges as a separating power exposing the imperfections that entered our faith.

God is the Creator of all life; He is the Father of Lights of every breathing soul. There is no life lived outside of His exception and no life given He has not fathered in the mind of His Creativity; not even Lucifer.

> *"You were perfect in your ways from the day you were created, Till iniquity was found in you."* **Ezekiel 28:15 NKJV**

Our beginning point does not necessarily exercise permanence of where we will end. It all depends on our obedience. How often have I seen the blemishing of the mantle of faith? I've experienced it and so have you. The Holy Spirit is leading us one way but we choose to go entirely in a different direction. When our lives are submitted under the cover of the Holy Spirit, He will lead and guide us in the way of truth. The Anointed covering over our lives is precious greater than the precious stones of Lucifer's covering. We have the true covering of God Himself by Presence of the Holy Spirit as our shield; *"The Shield of Faith"*.

Often we take for granted *"Pride of His Presence"* and internalize it to be something never conceived of our faith thinking of ourselves more highly than we ought. God has a specific plan with a designated path laid before us. Any perversions of His intentions can come to a destructive end. Our aspirations can lead us away from the concourse of victory, pursuing our own agendas rendering a judgment beyond our ability to recover. Most frequently it is pride.

Pride is unyielding and relentless, always reluctant to let go. It will never surrender on its own palpitating as a beating heart for dominance for the rule of the flesh. In denial of the Holy Spirit's power to rule, the inclination of pride will have a commanding presence exalting above our God given measure.

Evil Intentions

Systemically, evil is the perversion of truth. Without an association attached to the conscience of man, evil has no room to exhibit its intentions. The attributes of evil are representative of attributes we see in all of human nature. As an amendment to my envisioning of the *"Three Monkey Syndrome; seeing evil; doing evil; speaking evil; things we see, things we do and things we say";* every negative connotation has its roots entangled with evil. As a benchmark, our thoughts are the instigating point effectuating all of our actions; just *"as a man thinketh so is he"*. The Word of God is an antidote for suppression of evil. It renews our thoughts as a defender against every evil intention trying to take root in our conscience. Evil takes the good of things and uses it for purposes never intended. We witness on a daily basis the harm inflicted by the use of guns; murder, pain and maiming in total disregard of life. Is this where we have settled because of our fears? We're panicking from fear; fear of government taking control of our lives, fear of intrusions by a *"Boogey Man"* we can't see! We're waning in our trust of God!

Hoe Your Own Row

The maneuvers of faith exist within boundaries for a myriad of reasons. Obedience is the only guarantee qualifying our actions that they are indeed consistent with the will of God. For some, they have expressed a reluctance to launch out for fear of failure induced from their insecurities. For others, they may have been compromised in their faith and can't see their way out. A reminder to all of us; the journey of life is to the end of faith. Though there may be abbreviations due to our trials impeding the destination of faith, it is never over until we have completed our course.

We are bound to the constraints of faith secured in our preparations. Boundaries are a defense; a source of protection defying *"The Law of Interchangeability"*. I remember as a child while working the fields of my grandfather's farm, we routinely had to *"de-weed"* the gardens so the wild weeds didn't overtake the crops. The only tool we had was a *"Hoe"*. It was hard arduous work in the baking sun and I would often hijack a shorter row to lessen the burden of my labor. One day my grandfather's piercing eyes uncovered my ploy as He came to me with a word of correction to this day I still remember; *"Hoe your own row!"* We all have a row to hoe bearing uniqueness of our destiny. Whatever provisions are necessary to achieve success are found within the boundaries separated for our labor. With a willingness to accept God's instructions assigned for the performance of our faith, it will produce a harvest of His plans for our lives. If Adam had been satisfied with his own bread, *"hoed his own row"*, I dare to think he would have had an erosion of judgment in search of something beyond God's provision.

> *"We are not to tend to evil but discern its deception in its departure from truth."*

Isle of Patmos

7

I, John, both your brother and companion in the tribulation and kingdom and patience of Jesus Christ, was on the island that is called Patmos for the word of God and testimony of Jesus Christ. [1]

The Isle of Patmos is a refuge of meditation; a settlement of peace waiting in the patient streams of faith. Just as the monks of old lived out their lives hidden in a mountain of retreat, Patmos represents a strategic withdrawal into isolation, separated under a covering of humility for birthing of discovery and revelation. Discovery is the result of the query of faith, an exploration beyond the beaten path where others have resolved and settled in their expectations. The pioneers of old who chartered out voyaging into the unknown in an unsettled pursuit of faith were led to discover new lands where no one had channeled before.

Without the advantage of modern day technology Google maps, radar and satellites, in the early days of human exploration, seafaring explorers embarked on the most exciting expeditions without a predetermined destination. They made some of the most phenomenal discoveries in history beyond their preconceptions of what was believed to be true. Our understanding is limited to knowledge and does not know the depth of wisdom beyond its boundaries. If the pioneers were settled in their aspirations, we may still be thinking the Earth is flat or the moon shines by power of its own light or never have known boundaries of oceans.

Revelation

Revelation is conception of the thoughts of God. God is holistic which means He is a theocracy of the *"Father, Son and Holy Ghost"* unified as one divine commission. Revelation represents completeness of God's intent which is all inclusive through one action of His Word; *"Let There Be Light."* It was revelation of Himself, the Father of Lights; a Son born as the Image of His Light and Spirit demonstrating the power of His Light. From the time of Moses encounter when he received revelation of creation to John isolated on the Isle of Patmos with revelation of the end of days; it is but one completed thought in the mind of our Creator.

> *And I fell at His feet to worship Him. But He said to me, See that you do not do that! I am your fellow servant, and of your brethren who have the testimony of Jesus. Worship God!* ***For the testimony of Jesus is the spirit of prophecy.* Rev. 19:10 NKJV**

Prophecy is the vehicle of revelation authenticating the testimony of Jesus. Prophecy of today is forward looking as a recorder of what is yet to come during the cycle of the humanity of man. John in his writings of Revelation bore testimony of the Word of God through prophecy of the testimony of Jesus Christ recorded all things he saw while sequestered on Patmos. During his isolation he penetrated deep behind the veil to *"show us things that must soon come to pass"*. As a fulfilling testimony of the prophets that preceded him, they all participated in compiling one testament old and new; *"The Bible"*. From Isaiah, Jeremiah, Ezekiel, Daniel, and Zechariah they all were synergetic in their prophecies of God's interaction with mankind.

From the Book of Genesis to Revelation, prophets recorded revelations of the structure of God's Kingdom as books of patterns revealing the divinity of Christ. *"His Divinity is Trinity";* a threefold expression of His power and authority. Prophet John recorded in his manifest revelation of the Kingdom of Christ and the future glorification of His Church as fulfillment of all prophecies of ages gone by and ages to come. As a prophetic instrument chosen to speak on behalf God; the voice of men; *"Holy Men"* paved way for interaction of our lives with God through Words of His intentions.

> *For the prophecy came not in **old time** by the will of man but holy men of God spake as they were moved by the Holy Ghost.*
> **2 Peter 1:21 KJV**
>
> *Wherefore I will not be negligent to put you always in remembrance of these things, though ye know them, and be established in the **present truth**.* **2 Peter 1:12 KJV**

Apostle Peter said *"prophecy of old time"* came by men appointed to be the voice of God's Prophecies who were moved by the Holy Ghost. But he also brings us into a compelling truth; *"Present Truth"*. Present truth is no different than truth of yesterday. Both coalesce to speak the same of God's purpose. No greater or lesser but equal in their calling as a witness of truth.

Apostle Peter knew of his demise that was soon to come and even spoke of it to the community of faith:

> *Knowing that shortly I must put off this my tabernacle, even as our Lord Jesus Christ hath shewed me. Moreover I will endeavour that ye may be able after my decease to have these things always in remembrance.*
> **2 Peter 1:14-15 KJV**

There is a remarkability associated with faith and it's called *"suffering"*. For some, it could be suffering unto death as a witness of Christ. As a commitment to faith, if you knew the time of your departure before hand at the expense of such a horrific death could you handle it; would you be ready or would you accept it as being an inconvenient truth? Would your obedience lead you to accept martyrdom; crucified upside down on a cross *"on the far side"* of foreseeable pain?

Apostle Peter spoke of the imperative of faith. To achieve the Revelation of Christ it is mandated we will have to pick up our own cross. It is not just a onetime thing but a daily occupation to endure sufferings for the sake of Christ. Scripture teaches; *"offer up spiritual sacrifices, acceptable to God by Jesus Christ."*[1] As our lives are prostrated on the altar of submission, our sacrifices will bring us closer to the redeeming nature of the Cross of Christ. There is a reward achieved in our sufferings awarded through faith;

> *That the trial of your faith, being much more precious than of gold that perisheth, though it be tried with fire, might be found unto praise and honour and glory at the appearing of Jesus Christ.* [1]

> *For even hereunto were ye called: because Christ also suffered for us, leaving us an example, that ye should follow his steps.* [2]

Christ left us His example indicative of a life we should aspire to. We don't often hear it broadcasting from our pulpits; *"The greatest of faith is no greater than we suffer"*. Sufferings are intended to bring us closer to our own *"Gethsemane"*. It will certainly drive you deeper into the trenches of prayer, seeking and beholding God's promises as never before. Sufferings can be painful but they are a necessary part of our spiritual development. Scripture teaches; *"for after you have suffered awhile perfect, establish, strengthen and settle you"*.[3] Sufferings teach humility unveiling grace needed for our battles.

Revelation Knowledge

Revelation knowledge is a relational experience with the Holy Spirit as He reveals things hidden from our sight. It is definitely not a gift of our senses; that's called spiritualizing. It is a gift actualized by the faith of prayer in our search for a more dynamic expression of faith. If we are able to access power centered in the heart of God's Spirit, we would come to know things beyond what is conceived in our imagination.

Quite often in our search exploring the secrecy of God's Heart, we will encounter truth beyond what we were searching for. Unbeknown to us, as our spiritual senses are mobilized, they will expose deceptions and delusions that have encumbered our faith.

Revelation knowledge removes the scales from our spiritual eyes exposing influences and emergence of false ideas opposing the Principality of Christ. With actions of the Holy Spirit working through the gift of faith, we will be able to deliver solutions in the lives of those seeking answers to life's dilemma. When we say we received a Word from God, we are simply saying we have acquired knowledge from His Spirit.

Discovery of God's heart is not an ordinary routine common to our faith. It requires an incomparable level of intimacy developed from the depths of prayer. At times our search for truth is not always achieved out of our elective will but a greater depth of revelation will surface when we are forced into withdrawal; just as John on Patmos. To hear God's Clarion Voice requires solitude; separation from all theoretical influences and imaginations flooding our arena of faith.

There are times we need to hear away from human persuasions that can easily become distracting in our search for that place of solitude. Solitude constitutes an availability of faith for activation of our gifts with an inspired sense of purpose. The ability to hear and see is not a generic gift of our senses. However, in prayer faith invigorates our spiritual sensitivities to acquire revelations of God's Prophetic Word.

Prayer is the garment of faith; a recognizable action of our surrender. *"Humility of faith"* brings visibility to things we believe. The Bible says we have not because we ask not. But we must not ask amiss, only in faith believing to see answers to our prayers. Through our submission to faith's surrender, our eyes and ears become instruments empowered to see and hear the Holy Spirit's Revelations. They will unfold truth as a new discovery in our search for genuineness of faith.

Collectivism

The idea of *"Collectivism"* is quite troubling. It is a closed system of denominations that are collected unto themselves maintaining production and distribution of their own controlling interest. They are restraining in the form as schisms separate from each other. Unlike the Isles of Patmos; a place of spiritual separation purposed for a deeper revelation in the things of God for a clearer indication of God's intentions, collectivism is an inbreeding of man's natural persuasions that's in violation of God's order instigating the call for unity.

Collectivism is built consensually upon revelations of days gone by; previous concepts and dogmas that never changes. It's the benchmark for establishment of the pillars of denominationalism. Collectivism exhibits as a hardened heart resistant to rule of the Holy Spirit as God's authorized agent who brings recognition of unity of the *"Threefold Assembly of God; Father, Son and Holy Ghost existing as one authority for Revelation of Christ and His Kingdom to be revealed."*

Characteristically collectivism perfectly exemplifies some of our churches separated into denominations. They exist in disunity of faith disregarding the basic principle of love Christ commanded of His Church. How can you love God whom you have not seen but continue to put up walls further dividing the Church of Christ? Did we forget; at His return, He will seek out a unified Church flowing intricately as one expression of His love? There are no subsets of Believers; either you are a Believer by acceptance of the *"Full Gospel"* or you have resigned to accept the doctrines of men.

Seducing spirits have led many to believe we can love God but resist love for our brother. We are one body distinguishable by the degree of our love for one another. What is knowledge if it is not shared? If we come into a greater light; share it. Allow the patience to bring others into a deeper persuasion of truth.

Dependent on our commitment to faith, perhaps, we may differ to the degree of our level of response to God's revelations. We are reminded to continue to pray for the thirsting souls still camped out at water's edge with an invocation for God to reveal Himself with a greater level of empowerment. Our spiritual life should be reflective of the presence of faith summoning those away from the shadows by the Light of our candle.

> *The cup of blessing which we bless, is it not the communion of the blood of Christ? The bread which we break, is it not the communion of the body of Christ?* [1]

Bound by constraints of ideology and practices, we are drifting aimlessly in the dark a far cry from unity Christ requires of His Church. On any given Sunday morning, just pick one and you will see evidence of a house divided on full display. From corner to corner, we see franchising of one ideology to another. We all say we love Jesus but choose our own way to get there. Unity of the Church Jesus envisioned will only be accomplished through workings of His Spirit.

The Church is a *"spiritual organism"* of abundant wealth flowing in richness of an Anointing with power to transform doctrines of men into a fluid stream of productive life. But first, deliverance must come to defeat the stronghold of religion that has kept us apart. The calloused heart of man and his religion is resistant to change. With his hardened heart insulated and confined to itself, he has demonstrated no further need for expansion for a greater achievement of faith.

Jesus cleansed the Temple and reestablished the pillars of prayer for communion and fellowship with His Father's Heart. But the convoluted strength of man and his determination to make a kingdom of his own continues as a complication of flesh denying rule of the Holy Spirit. We are dependent on God's gifts and liberating actions of deliverance to respond to forces in defiance of the advancement of His Kingdom.

> *There is **one** body and one Spirit, just as you were called in **one** hope of your calling; **one** Lord, one faith, **one** baptism; **one** God and Father of all, who is above all, and through all, and in you all.* [1]

I am not the sharpest knife in the drawer but what is the difficulty of understanding the concept of *"One"*? Revelation of the Cross of Christ produced unanimity of faith. The physical cross stood temporarily upon a pinnacle as a signpost of God's faithfulness but was never meant to be a choice of idol worship. Go to any Church, *"pick one"* and there you will find the relics of Jesus still hanging on a tree. He is not there!

The Spirit of Christ traveled from Heaven to gain residency in our Earthly tabernacles. The sacrifice of the Cross is the greatest event since the invention of time. The price paid for our redemption is precious but somehow we have managed to misappropriate its *"givings"* into doctrines that shadows truth for the convenience of man. The Cross of Christ came down so we may bear our own before being taken up by its power; caught up in that great day of awakening.

The Holy Spirit is *"Ruler of the Church"* but some of our churches have hijacked the Cross of Christ and perverted it into an image as the golden calf. Practice of idolatry; worshipping the pride of flesh and molten images bearing symbols of divinity, have no power to deliver. Ceremonial jesters and pageantries in our meeting places are not substitutive for devotion and prayer needed for our inspiration.

Some of our theologians, professing to be wise show no indication of a life surrendered to God's Spirit. With hands and feet bound as Lazarus and no discerning eyes to see, their ears lie dormant in deafening silence. Somehow, it seems preferable and convenient for them to accept a god fashioned by their hands than accept the sacrifice rendered on the Cross. There is only One Lord, One Faith and One Baptism. When our lives are immersed in the fire of His baptism, we can scorch the Earth by a power so compelling and evidential.

Revelation Requires Patience

Patience is centered in stillness of waiting. At times God commands us *"to be still to know that He is God"*[1]. We must remain patient and not fret over contrary winds blowing against us. Patience is an acquired peace bringing us closer to exposure of the Cross. The Cross is a place of relinquishing and rest where all of our battles end. Before patience can have its perfect place, the peace of God must be settled in our heart. Absence of settling, the anxiety of patience can cause our faith to waiver even to the point of unbelief. When peace embraces humility, patience invokes a rest in our spirit as reinforcement in defense of faith.

> *We give thanks to God always for you all, making mention of you in our prayers, remembering without ceasing your work of faith, labor of love,* **and patience of hope in our Lord Jesus Christ** *in the sight of our God and Father.* **1 Thess. 1:2-3 NKJV**

Peace is the spiritual seed of love with conquering power over our mind and body in surrender to our spirit and soul. Peace disarms any warring spirit and settles disputes of the heart and flesh.

Patience is recognizable in our sufferings as we bear the burden of others for the experience of Christ in their lives. The labor of love working through our faith is not always an easy thing to do. Scripture says; *"We that are strong ought to bear infirmities of others and not to please ourselves".*[1] But our strength is not always available at a time we need it. Suffering can be compromising while we are in constant pursuit of faith with the added responsibility of carrying others along with us is quite challenging. It would be easier to leave them behind and continue on our way but we need them in this journey in a shared cooperation of faith.

Remembrance of our sacrifices in our work of faith and labor of love are articulated through the prayers of the Saints. Often times, we do not know all of whom are connected to our faith who have a propensity for prayer; praying for the greater good of God to visit our lives as gratitude for our sacrifices. Throughout our journey, we may have touched the lives of thousands because of our faithfulness and dedication to prayer. Our faith alone will never conquer every battle but has a greater strength purposed to conquer the war as we join together in prayer; praying for one another. Our gifts are not purposed for ourselves but for the greater good to affirm faith in the lives of those seeking relief from delusions, suffering and pain.

> *I, John, both your brother and companion in the tribulation and kingdom and patience of Jesus Christ, was on the island that is called Patmos.* **Revelations 1:9 NKJV**

John enumerated he was a brother and companion to our tribulations. As John, I have stood in the gap for others, separated on my own Patmos praying and bearing burdens of others in my secret compartment of faith. There have been quite a few times in this journey I have pondered in my spirit of my own challenges; *"What about me Lord, what about me."* I know how Jeremiah felt when vexation entered his spirit. He cried out to God; *"How long O Lord shall I mourn"?*

The experience of faith at times can seem so distant in bringing resolution to our problems while at the same time our prayers for others bear a greater result. We can see their breakthroughs as the passion of time wears on but struggle in faith when we are required to wait. In some of our greatest battles when we perceive we need God the most, it appears He is nowhere to be found. We search in anguish; still there is no answer. Did the windows of Heaven close up; or did we do something wrong? Have you considered, you could be in a season for an experience with God as never before.

After the baptism of Jesus in the River Jordan, He was led into the wilderness by the Spirit to be tested. It was as Patmos, to discover the anointing waiting at the end of the *"Refiners Fire"*. He didn't know the duration of His season of separation but with willingness and obedience to His Father's instructions, He yielded to the *"patience of hope"*. It was a hope that would release an anointing the world had never known. We do not always know where the path of faith will lead us but in our obedience, we rest in hope and believing in faith; *"God will not take us where He has not already been; He will not lead us where He has not purposed!"* In preparing for a wilderness experience, our submission to prayer equips us for a greater confrontation of faith.

After forty days of preparation in the wilderness as if that was not enough, Jesus was confronted with His greatest battle; *"The battle of the test of temptation; the lust of the flesh, the lust of the eyes and the pride of life."* [1] This is an area where many of our leaders have failed. They never endured the *"forty days"* preparing their strength for the battles they would encounter. Without God's Anointing, the intended good of our gifts will be ineffective when we engage the lives of others.

Motion of Faith

Patience found in darkness is as precious as a pearl secluded in obscurity until its day of awakening. It does not wander to connect with doubt and unbelief but it sanctions God's ability to the cause of our faith. Patience is the developmental stage of our spiritual hearing and sight. Frantic at times in our search for solutions, patience releases a stilling affect ruling over our drifting thoughts with calm as a soothing ointment in the midst of our battles. Patience demands stillness and quieting of our emotions settling our thoughts with peace resting on the mantle of our weary souls.

The image of faith requires patience to develop in our conscience. Often challenges occurring in our daily life are competing with the time set aside for devotion to reconstitute our faith. Patience opens an inquisition for a response from God. In our stillness, the imprint of faith begins to develop; portraying as a static image as concession for our waiting. Waiting, listening and enduring to hear a response validating success of our faith. Just like an altimeter of an airplane determines the altitude of flight, the parallel of patience governs the *"positional attitude of faith"*. The altitude of faith is a direct response to our attitudes of patience.

Static portraits of faith are inscribed as stationary images for our meditations to enter deep into the heart of belief. Portraits of faith are still shots; a focal point defining the intentions of faith. Formation of images in our conscience must be delivered to the mind of faith; *"If we Believe it, we can Receive it! If we can See it, we can Do it!"* Actions of our belief secures the promise of faith; believing to receive through the eyes of faith.

I have been told I am obtuse meaning I don't always think in a straight line. To me that's a good thing! Recognition of my steps of yesterday is retraceable; it's a testimony I willingly share. It indicates where I have been and how I got here. But where I have been does not indicate where I am going. I relate that to being the variability of faith to move with the winds of change and ready myself to accept change in pursuit of faith. It's more challenging to know where I am going when the hint of the past gives no indication what lies in the path ahead. But as God told Abraham in the days of Sodom and Gomorrah; *"Separate Yourself"*. Leave and I will show you. But leave! *"Your obedience will make something great out of you."* To that end, fashioning of my thoughts remains masked until time is ready for its revealing. Be aware; people have a tendency to talk you out of things: *"Did God Really Say"?* [1]

> **Go from** *your country, your people and your father's household to the land* **I will show** *you. "I will make you into a great nation, and* **I will bless you**; *I will make your name great, and you will be a blessing. I will bless those who bless you, and whoever curses you I will curse; and all peoples on earth will be blessed through you.* [2]

As you may have discovered my deliberations often require a greater depth of thought purposed to capture impressions born of my imaginations. It is much easier to articulate something I perceive you already know. However, continual learning of patience necessitates I dig a little deeper; reaching for clarity to make plain the simple; *"Fighting the good fight of faith"*.

Bear with me a moment. I was motivated to write this book by an urgency being born in my spirit. It is an inward journey of bringing expressions to my faith. *"Necessity for Light"* is an inspirational adventure to promote a visionary level of empowerment to recover our stagnating dreams. As a probative exercise, this book is invigorating exploiting a deeper inwardness in convergence of truth and the realm of our imagination to recapture our dreams. It seems we have forgone the dreaming of dreams *"technologized"* by the influence of artificial intelligence systemically droning our culture. Droning is intrusive if not inhibiting. Expression of our gifts and use of our senses are being substituted.

We see by the created word just as Adam when God brought before him every living creature of the field to see what he would name them. It's no different than what we have power to do bringing identity to the words we speak. It's called parables. Jesus used them all the time taking spiritual images forming them into parables intended to activate our senses into a level of comprehension. Parables are *"tempered expressions"* requiring time and deliberation of thought to ascertain words to convey their interpretations.

Imagine this; the image of a dog. Can you visualize the dog running? No! Our minds don't work that way. Try it! Prove me wrong. What was the dog doing? You can see him sitting on the floor and the next thought he is sitting on your lap. What happened in between? Did you see the motion of him suspended in the air before jumping into your lap? I doubted it. You only saw him sitting but the motion in between happened so fast your mind could not keep up with it. Truth is; *"You had thought of the movement but couldn't actually see the movement".* That kind of speed is only realized in your dreams and visions. They are spiritual!

Our thoughts can race but sometimes they can race too fast but not fast enough for our imaginations to be viewed in *"cinema".* The separating barrier of visibility morphs into invisibility at the speed of light which is 186,000 miles per second. Now that's fast! The miracle of our senses is that we can see light but not on the far side of it. You will need an escort in the likeness of an angel that can supersede the speed of light. Spiritual speed has unlimited barriers depending on the time it needs for birthing of revelation to arrive.

Our visualizations are purposed to precede actions of faith. If we can believe it can be predictive. Our faith has the ability to produce cinematic movement but it requires rigorous meditations. So tell me; can you see a dead man rising from the grave; can you visualize him jumping for joy? Jesus did! Lazarus was His name. Jesus told His disciples; *"I am going there to wake him up"*.[1] It's kind of amusing when Thomas said *""Let us also go, that we may die with him."* [2] In other words; wake us up too! After the stone was removed from Lazarus's tomb, he was brought back to life with hands and feet still bound. Jesus told His disciples; *"Loose him, and let him go"*. [3]

The sealed tomb of our faith needs uncovering to demolish thoughts of unbelief and doubt to experience supernatural performances of God. I guess Thomas was disappointed he wasn't loosed from the tomb of his conscience sealed in unbelief. That was his history even after witnessing the supernatural power of Jesus in operation. He could not fathom, even after Jesus rose from the dead, these things were still possible. *"I am the resurrection and the life."* [4] Do you believe it? It is a truth awaiting all of our decisions.

What was the motion in between from the time of Lazarus death to time of his resurrection? Thomas had spent four days with Jesus without gaining perspective of the identity of Christ. Jesus waited patiently for four days for the pattern of faith to emerge that they too may believe. Faith must be targeted; specific of intent and void of "*randoming*" to achieve its highest good.

Jesus said to His disciples; *"And I am glad for your sakes I was not there,* **to the intent ye may believe***; nevertheless let us go unto him"*. [1] Still Thomas failed to understand a critical principle of faith; *"believing and knowing the will of God to execute the actions of faith"*. The life of faith is God's life. If we can ascertain the visualizations of faith; *"what we see we can do"*! Faith spirals from belief to motion specific of its intent. But the lack of belief instigates disputes of faith which falls short of believing to see the dead man rising.

Our natural thoughts are no more than a series of static events formed in our imagination. A natural man is full of exaggerations running wild trying his best to apprehend fleeting moments of thought beyond his grasp. *"To be overzealous is fear of underachievement."* It is a provocation for error believing you are doing something that hasn't been done before. If you are prone to its deceptions, pride will target and you will remain captive in your high minded imaginations.

> *Casting down imaginations and every high thing that exalteth itself against the knowledge of God, and bringing into captivity* **every thought** *to obedience of Christ.*[2]

"The meaning of life is the interaction of our senses responding to every stimulus in our environment." Our thoughts are transient energy of our imagination born with new presentations every single day. Collectivities of moving things are much easier to retain than static images of our past performances. Our achievements of yesterday were purposed to *"shape us"* for movement of tomorrow's dreams to *"make us"*. The movement of faith trains our spirit to view our thoughts in *"cinema"*. However, once cinema is set into motion, it becomes more difficult to stop the continuous loop of portrayals forming in our imagination.

The Holy Spirit brings life to static images formed from the portrait of faith invoking movement towards the end of completion. We can see movement in our dreams. They are cinematic portrayals allowing us to see development in our deliberations even discovering resolution to lingering events passed on from the day before. But we also can be predisposed to encounters yet to come causing the uncertainty of anxiety.

"Faith is intended to do something more than be something." What is faith without the action of it? To be something establishes recognition only; it's your identity. It validates who you are defining the purpose of your existence. But purpose must be translated into action; *"doing"* as justification of its intent. We all desire to make a name for ourselves but how? Actions! *"By the things we do!"* In the beginning *"God Said"* but recognition of Him are by the things *"He did"*. Without His actions none of what we see would ever exist!

The burden of cinema provokes a need for wisdom of God's Revelations to give us understanding of the images of faith. To be productive, enhancement of the Holy Spirit's Anointing delivers power allowing us the ability to perform things revealed. It is not enough just to have an image but the image must be brought to life flowing to see the end of the image of faith. For the natural man, he will never see beyond the imprint of his imagination of Lazarus being raised from the dead for that matter nor what the dog was doing; it could very well have bit him without accurate knowledge of its intentions. With Christ in our lives guided by the revealing light of the Holy Spirit illuminating our path; God reveals His intentions from the beginning to end validating the cause of our faith.

Voice of Patience

> *I have called upon You, for You will hear me, O God; Incline Your ear to me, and hear my speech.* **Psalm 17:6 NKJV**

Patience not only has ears but it also has a voice. It speaks boldly yearning for God to hear our cry. There are times we search in a desperate cry as Ishmael and Hagar when they were excommunicated from the house of Abraham. The thought of her predicament is rather painful when you consider it was not a fault of her own. It was Abraham who got himself in trouble due to his flawed perception of God's intentions. The lack of patience in anticipation of faith will cause you to error moving ahead of what God has promised.

Abraham did what many of us have done when God does not move fast enough after He commits His Word; we then try to do it ourselves compounding a simple solution into an infectious situation affecting lives of everybody around us. Hagar didn't have choices. Her decisions were subordinate to Abraham's. We can be quick in our judgment of others, perhaps not realizing they could be in a compromising situation where their decisions are being made for them. Compromise is a deductive part of our reasoning limiting our choices beyond its original intentions. With nothing left but her tears and an unknown destiny in the road ahead, Hagar left; journeying on to discover Patmos waiting in a wilderness of rejection. It was the only path she could to take. Faith demands decisiveness despite the pain of loneliness and rejection; *"Just Leave"!*

> *Then she went and sat down across from him at a distance of about a bowshot; for she said to herself,* **"Let me not see the death of the boy."** *So she sat opposite him, and lifted her voice and wept.*
>
> **"And God heard the voice of the lad."** *Then the angel of God called to Hagar out of heaven, and said to her, What ails you, Hagar?* **Fear not,** *for God has heard the voice of the lad where he is. Arise, lift up the lad and hold him with your hand, for* **"I will make him a great nation".** *Then God opened her eyes, and she saw a well of water. And she went and filled the skin with water, and gave the lad a drink.*
> **Genesis 21:16-19 NKJV**

Throughout our journey; there are things we have left behind God has purposed for our vision where we have concluded there is no hope of life. You may want to reconsider; for it could be the greatest asset towards facilitating your destiny. At times we may see no hope when our well has run dry but God's determinations are destined to out shine our disappointments. In our fears; what we thought was dead is still crying out for completion yearning to discover the end of a future already planned beyond the point of our surrender. In patience; God's intentions are discoverable if we don't move ahead of Him to create things for ourselves.

Overreaction in a moment of fear, disappointment or anger can silence your voice. Just as Hagar went a distance away from her son, we tend to follow the same path of our inability to cope primarily because of fear. We are to be careful; in our observation of the predicament of others is the same disappointing view of our own demise; *"I am dying and so is he!"* I fully understand Hagar's sufferings and rejection rendered by the hands of Abraham. No one wants to see demise of their children but the experience of rejection should have never been transferred to her son.

As humans, the rule of thumb dictates a tendency to treat people the way we have been treated. However, as a child who experiences rejection, it is an inflexible persuasion to overcome. It will make you bitter and combative alienating you from the necessary things of life. If deliverance doesn't come, most likely it will be very difficult to fully apprehend the gift of life.

The Spirit of Rejection is generational; leapfrogging across ancestral lines. If it runs deep enough it will alter your genetic root. One of the biggest concerns dealing with children in foster care is the influences of rejection. You can easily recognize where love has been missing due to abandonment. Fundamentally, at the root of every inferiority complex, there is a reference to some element of rejection in one's past.

Rejection dims the candle of love and its attracting flames. It smolders in fumes resistant to love. It can lead to disassociation just as Hagar when she left her son to fend for himself. She derived at a place believing there was no further participation of belief and hope beyond where her fears were settled.

With no more power to weep and a yielded voice of surrender, just as Hagar, our faith will squander in the shadow of unbelief. At times in our desperation, God will hear our cry through circumstance of a barren wilderness and open our eyes to see His deliverance all around us. It will be as a well of refreshing water with replenishing strength to restore sight to our vision.

Jesus fasted for forty days and forty nights in a wilderness prepared for His captivity. At the end of His forty days in servitude to the obedience of faith, the angels ministered to him. Obedience always has a spiritual reward if we are faithful to see it through its conclusion. It's not meat or bread as our expectations often lead us to believe, but spiritual empowerment; an Anointing that is not connected to any material substance. I can eat anytime!

To receive God's investment in the way He intended to release it requires completeness of faith. It may not be forty days and forty nights or for that matter forty years but the requirement of faith demands obedience specific to a word designed to bring recognition of God upon our mantle. Our faith has a magnetic appeal to an opposite attraction capable of drawing men to God.

"Faith is attached to our will to believe and do". But without a word of destination, we are left in a barren land as Hagar and her son; wandering without the provisions of grace needed for an unknown journey. The Bible teaches; *"faith without activity of using our gifts is non-accomplishing"*. It's actually dead on arrival if we are not pursuant of what is required of us to do.

It doesn't matter how many good things we do even though it's an admirable achievement but God judges us by our obedience to the *"Word of Faith"*. In a letter to the Romans, Apostle Paul wrote;

> *But none of these things move me, neither count I my life dear unto myself, so I might finish my course with joy and the ministry, which I have received of the Lord Jesus, to testify the gospel of the grace of God.* [1]

We are not to be moved by things! It was the voice of peace that calmed the waters when the disciples were in distress on their journey to *"The Other Side"*. John the Baptist was that voice of one crying in the wilderness while waiting for the promised One. He said; *"There cometh one mightier than I after me."* [2]

A wilderness experience is of greater value in its end than its beginning. What we receive at the end of a season of patience reveals the mystery surrounding our intentions while pursuing faith. We do not always know what the end will speak but I do know; *"God will not fail us when He is perfecting us. In every wilderness encounter; patience always precedes revelation before apprehension of a greater promise."*

Vertical Connected

Do you remember the account when Jesus asked Peter; *"Who do you say that I am"?* Peter answered *"Thou art the Christ; The Son of the Living God"!* [1] For flesh and blood can't reveal that kind of stuff to you! Revelation stemming from the throne of God's power can only be achieved through a relationship of prayer and seeking. Only then will we be given the keys of the Kingdom of Heaven. *"And I will give unto thee the keys* **"OF"** *the Kingdom of Heaven: What we bound on Earth is bound in Heaven; what's loose on Earth is loosed in Heaven."* [1] What a remarkable manifest! Jesus never told Peter I will give you keys *"TO"* the Kingdom of Heaven. You can't come and go as you wish. The keys presented to Peter were conditional! *"OF"* meaning *"the power of it"* if you choose to adhere to its principles!

Adam's keys were keys of authority and a key of his free will to exercise his choices. With a command to tend and guard; multiply and subdue is the same authority given to the life of every Believer with power to *"Bind and Loose"*.

Can I Get Your Attention

When was the last time you heard the voice of the Holy Spirit speaking into your ear? What did you hear and where were you when you heard it? Did it shake you with alarming urgency or did it come with the voice of stillness as Elijah encountered God trying to hide in a cave?

Elijah was a cave dweller and in a time of challenge, he retreated to that place of familiarity; the only place he knew that would provide shelter to his disguise. While escaping in fear from Jezebel who threatened his life, he attempted to hide in a cave and even from the Presence of God. There are times God will awaken us to His Voice with the sound of a rushing wind, an earth shattering earthquake, in the blazing heat of fire or in stillness of a small voice as He spoke with Elijah. Whatever it takes, he will exhaust His options to get our attention. He will go so far as to leave you sitting under a tree as Jonah immersed with complaint of His judgments. It really doesn't matter; He will find you as He did with Adam even as to ask; *"Where are you"!*

A few years ago, I stopped at a restaurant for lunch. I ordered a sandwich and decided I would sit in my car to eat in relaxation, away from the noise of music drowning my ear. Most of the time, I desire being alone to be at peace. I have long since been delivered from the expectations of people with their façade of ideas and vain renderings of reality. I have grown weary of the *"plastic smiles of deceit"*. Smiling faces do have a tendency to tell lies once they have gained your trust.

As I sat in silence, my car began to shake violently with rocking motions from front to rear. Suddenness of this event did not allow time to process my thoughts as to exactly what was happening. My immediate thought was that someone was playing a trick on me. Then I had the flashing thought that since I had just purchased a new car that maybe there was a defect. As my adrenaline continued to increase, I thought for a moment my car was on the verge of blowing up. Suddenly, an overwhelming fear came upon me.

I made haste to get out of the car and as I tried to establish my footing, the ground beneath was shaking. I noticed people began to run out of the buildings as car alarms began serenading in confusion. Then the light switch turned on! How slow I was to discern what was happening? I was *"right smack"* in the middle of an earthquake! I have never experienced anything like that before. It is a rarity for this occurrence to happen in my part of the country. It was an Earth shattering experience but it got my attention.

Sometimes God awakens us rather unexpectedly. At times it can appear to be Earth shaking. Because of His sovereign power, He retains the right to intervene in our affairs with a commanding persuasion to arouse our faith. Through floods, drought, fires, hurricanes and ravaging tornadoes frequenting our land the Spirit of God is speaking in our time delivering justice to awaken the deposit of faith for a performance yet to be realized. But there is a question I must ask you; has He gotten your attention yet? Trust me; *"He will"!*

Sixth Sense of Prayer *8*

"If you being evil know how to give good gifts to your children, how much more shall your Heavenly Father give the Holy Spirit to them that ask Him." [1]

When the veil of the Temple was rent in two at the crucifixion of Jesus; Heaven's Gates were opened. It marked a new beginning into the hidden dimension of faith exposing a newly discovered path back into our Father's Kingdom. From top to bottom, Heaven to Earth; it ushered in a new season towards completion of our Father's Vision. The works of our hands had finished and what was left to be completed was through the spiritual dimensions of faith. We were freed from the responsibility of duty.

With no more workings of flesh, power of the Spirit to perform the works of faith was released. It gave us access directly to the source from which all power stems and released the power of grace to perfect the work the law could not fulfill. No more priests and burning of sacrifice but the sacrifice of our labor of love and commitment to faith.

When the curtain was rent in two, it released the resurrection power of Jesus. That power is still here today. God's Spirit is eternal and His resurrection power still remains. What happened two thousand years ago was the firstfruit of our eternal occupancy into His dwelling place. The rent left an entry way into God's Secret Chambers where we can experience His Presence at the Altar of Faith.

God's hiding place now becomes our hiding place. There we began to live under the shadow of the Most High God and receive revelation that comes from His Presence. It is only in *"This Place"* in our submission we will experience a spiritual makeover reordering our lives to His desire. Our lives will be transformed from a world labored with the weight of visible things into a spiritual world where our faith is now governed by the rule of His Spirit.

A secret rendezvous in the Presence of God will always produce a performance of public power. The secret place is a refined place cultivated out of our obedience. The price is costly and the sacrifice remains to be defined to dwell in His Presence. It is a spiritual mandate which requires an absolute surrender of our will to pursue the divine will of God relinquishing all in our confession; *"If it is Your will take this cup away from me, nevertheless not my will but Yours be done".* [1]

The Saints of the Most High, the Body of Christ are the living Tabernacle of God for His Indwelling to fulfill the mission of faith. Every Anointing where the Glory of God is manifested requires a covering; a shelter of fellowship for communion and prayer to ascertain His power; *"He that dwelleth in the secret place shall abide under the shadow of the Almighty".* [1]

The Protocol of Prayer

> *But thou, when thou prayest, enter into thy closet, and when thou hast shut thy door, pray to thy Father which is in secret; and thy Father which seeth in secret shall reward thee openly.* **Matthew 6:6 KJV**

If we would follow the protocol Jesus initiated for accessing Heaven's Gates; *"Go into your closet, shut the door and begin to pray in secrecy";* all interference to our pursuit of prayer would be minimized. Secrecy of prayer is a labor all of us are not conditioned to do due to the lack of patience to wait on God. Often our busy lives persist as an obstacle to prayer. God sees our heart, our travailings, weaknesses and knows our strengths. We must allow Him to perfect us through patience as we wait for His response to our pleadings.

It's what we do in the dark that bears a greater weight than our pretentious portrayals judged in the eyes of men. We can live out our lives mastering the techniques that are pleasing to men and waste the precious opportunity of communing with God's Spirit.

After Jesus was driven into the wilderness by the Holy Spirit, He emerged from a season of fasting and prayer. Subsequently, He realized John the Baptist had been beheaded. While sequestered, Jesus never had a subscription to the daily newspaper to keep track of world events neither a cellphone to keep in touch with social media. He did not conflict the time committed for prayer. *"The protocol of prayer is to pray in secret while hiding in secret."* Jesus wasn't aware of things going on around him but after receiving His Father's manifest, then and only then did He contend with the affairs of the world.

So often after the Holy Spirit drives us into a place for a divine encounter, we neglect patience of waiting for God to speak. We need His empowerment to do the things He has called us to do. Our culture is filled with so many distractions worrying about things irrelevant to our destiny. We must be vigilant in respect of our stewardship to not let people and circumstances steal our most precious commodity: *"TIME"!*

Public prayer is a necessity as an invocation in our gatherings but to display the power of prayer it must be a continuation of what we accomplish in our secret chambers. It's not about elegance and sophistication mastering the vocabulary of men or formulated generic procedures of prayer but through our humility, we have the ability to coalesce the power of Heaven with our obedience to pray.

Prayer is the precursor to the execution of faith. Belief in prayer derived from our secret rendezvous in the Presence of the Lord can command a performance of the Holy Spirit to deliver what we have achieved through our diligence to pray. But it requires the belief in God that He has already delivered answers to those things we are seeking. We all can bear testimony of the victorious nature of prayer of how it has impacted our lives and those we love. Prayer changes things and every connection to it! Assessment of the production of prayer has unlimited possibilities. However, because of our inconsistencies to pray, we fail to realize it is our only hope for God to hear our petitions.

Usually, we pray out of our circumstances needing immediate solutions more so than anything else. There is a cause to every prayer either being encouraged to pray; out of our affection to attract the Heart of God but mostly it is because of dictating circumstances. We are to pray without ceasing entreating an invitation for a deeper experience into a lifestyle of prayer.

Have you noticed, God's answers are not always spontaneous? You can pray and pray and seemingly nothing happens. More often than not, prayer requires labor. *"God will leave you in prayer until the pattern of prayer is developed in you"*. It's much easier to pray when you consistently pray. Scripture says; for after you have prayed awhile until the fulfillment of prayer; *"Until your word comes to pass"*, you stand to reap a testimony as confirmation of your pleadings.

> *And when He had sent them away, He departed into a mountain to* pray.
> **Mark 6:46 KJV**

Send people away! The power of encroachment is purposed to defeat you as if we don't have enough to contend with. It is quite often; the burdens of others shadowing our faith can be an impediment hindering our own solutions; if we allow it. There are things we need not carry into our secret compartment of faith. The burdens of some will still be the burdens of some. Why do we wrestle with the problems of others when they choose not to pray for themselves but yet they possess the power to seek deliverance on their own? It is not our place! We can't write their testimonies. We would be rendering a disservice to their faith. At some point we all must be resolved to pray.

I remember a song from my youth from the famed showman James Brown: *"I don't want anybody to give me nothing; open up the door and I will get it myself"*. That's the attitude of faith! Through our gifting and talents, we have the ability to accomplish great things if we would recognize the power of our own faith. Don't get me wrong; we need each other as we are compelled to pray for one another.

The prayer of faith has a greater power when we come together in unity. But the mundane occurrences introduced into our lives by the reluctant of faith to pray causes so much unnecessary worry and can be cast as a burden. That's called an intrusion! You should figure things out for yourself. It's an elementary principle; *"The path of least resistance is a straight line"*. Well then; toe the line! It will take you exactly where you need to be and not where someone else wants to take you. My father once told my mother which I found to be quite amusing; *"Let me wind you backwards before I bring you forward"*. The worry of yesterday is yesterday's but every day is a new day.

My Father's Closet

Growing up as a child in my father's house was quite a unique experience. From the outside looking in, it may have appeared we had everything. We did! We had the love of our parents which is irreplaceable; something that is not so recognizable by the standards of today. We had a *"Home"* enclosed with wisdom established upon the principles of faith. It was a faith my father exercised in every waking moment of his life. My siblings and I were liberated with the gift of love my parents acquired through their experiences of faith.

My mother was no different; she was very wise and instructive. She had a love so uncompromising to the likes I have never seen before. Always giving, loving and sharing from a well of experiences. Even after I grew up and left home; upon my return, her love was still there with a greater intensity targeted toward me and my future which was still being weighed in the balance of my decisions. So many times she would wake me up in the early morning hour for an occasion to share life's wisdom. I still hear her voice emanating in my spirit; *"Do you want a cup of coffee?"* I knew what that meant; it was an opportunity to empower her strength into me. I needed it! I had gotten lost in the trafficking of life and clung so desperately to the only source I knew; *"My Mother's Love"*.

My father was a praying man who dedicated his life to prayer. He had seen the miraculous hand of God move on behalf of his sacrifice of fasting and prayer. When dealing with life contentions, so often I would hear him say; *"I know how to turn my plate down!"* When my little brother was a baby and had gotten sick to the point of death, my father fasted and prayed for days until the doctors had determined a miracle had taken place. What a remarkable testimony of faith! He had come into his own believing; *"There is no secret what God can do. What he has done for others he will do for you"*.

My father discovered the secret of prayer in his closet. He had unwavering belief in the principles of faith following the prescription Jesus recommended. It started a revolution! On many occasions from the time I was growing up in his home and even when visiting, I would see him absent from the dining table; separated and isolated in prayer.

Secret Communion

When I received my conversion, I had a reoccurring vision. Every time I went into the prayer closet, I would experience the very same vision. It was a vision where I was bowed down on bended knee at the foot of the Cross of Jesus. Tears were streaming down my face; my hands were cupped, yielding, thirsting; needing so desperately to drink of His blood. The blood came pouring from the wound of His suffering where they pierced Him in His side. They rejected Him, neglected Him and never respected Him. I could feel His pain and hurt in my own body. The cup of my hands began to fill with an unlimited flow of His blood and I began to drink as never before. I was being cleansed by the power of the blood flowing in me; changing me but even more filling me with a metamorphosis of love changing the outside of me to look like the conversion taking place on the inside of me. The love of the Holy Spirit was feeding His life into mine. I began to get so filled with His blood; His life was now becoming my life. The blood that flowed in Him began living in me. I partook of His Presence and shared in His power to sustain my own sufferings. When His Spirit left His body, it entered mine and now the life of Him is living in me. After three days, He rose with power giving me a new name; He called me *"His Disciple; Now Go! Do As I Have Done. They rejected Me, they will reject you"*. Take up this Cross and never leave it! It will testify of Me of the love I have for you. With the power of His Spirit I am now able to carry my own cross.

I started my journey into the unknown not realizing the cost I would have to pay for a love so great, but I was fully persuaded. After the visions discontinued, my mother gave me a *"Word"* concerning my future, but I did not realize how experiential it would become:

> *So Jesus answered and said, Assuredly, I say to you, there is no one who has left house or brothers or sisters or father or mother or wife or children or lands, for My sake and the gospel's, who shall not receive a hundredfold now in this time houses and brothers and sisters and mothers and children and lands,* **with persecutions** *and in the age to come, eternal life.* [1]

Persecution, persecution, persecution! Little did I know the power it possessed; I know now! I refuse to complain. I readily understand after seasons of testing, they are purposed for my humility. But there is a grace that accompanies persecution which has a power of its own. I have learnt and will continue to learn the power of God's sufficiency that sustains me through every battle, every assignment for the sake of righteousness. But you better be right! God forgives ignorance but there is a penalty for disobedience. I remain bound by constraints of my captivity to a desire He has placed in my heart and it will be until the end of faith.

My motivations have moved me into compliance of a predetermined path to fulfill His calling upon my life. It is the path of faith that demands my obedience. My journey from the foot of the Cross led me in search of revelation back to the beginning where the Angels of God are still standing; standing at the gate guarding that which is sacred and eternal; *"The Tree of Life"*. With the blinding light of the flaming sword swirling about, I cannot see inside to know what He knows nor can I find my way to that place of His desire. There is only one way back into the Garden of God; *"purity and singleness of heart through the gate called narrow"*. It is my desire to see Heavenly things for the Revelation of God in our times. My daily prayers are indicative of my desire for God to complete His perfect work in me; praying the Words prophesied into my life; *"Call unto me and I will answer you and show you great and mighty things that you know not"*. [1]

Heavenly things cannot be seen unless God opens our spiritual eyes to instruct us in *"His Way"*. When motivations of our heart are acceptable unto Him, He will flood our spiritual corridors with revelation that comes from an unseen dimension of His grace. He will give us His gifts to discern and His power to perform the works of His destiny. *"Blessed are the pure in heart, for they shall see God."* [1]

A Word of Prophecy

> *And they swirl about, being turned by His guidance, that they may do whatever He commands them On the face of the whole earth. He causes it to come whether for correction or for His land, or for mercy.* [2]

I was in the Spirit and saw tornadoes that would come upon our land bringing destruction and death. It was a vision that still continues to deliver truth to its power. We are living in a world of mass confusion with confused hearts lingering in darkness. Apathy in the Church has led many to adopt the fruits of secularism. Some are bordering on the threshold of unbelief. If we incline our ear to hear God's Spirit, He will pour into our hearts streams of revelation and His wisdom as a defense against deceptions that have led many astray. Unfortunately, our reluctance to engage our gifts has caused unnecessary sufferings permeating within our culture. In search for answers we have to be resolved to reclaim what we have lost. The events of our time demand a response of faith from a Church gone silent.

Perilous Times

We are living in perilous times as my Father always said! Who could have envisioned the level of chaos that's happening in our land today? Where have our Prophets gone; can they not see? Our house is on fire; burning from within with a church gone silent without a voice to buffer the fray! Pestilence, drought, wars and the rumor of wars, pandemics and the insatiable satisfaction of greed woven into the consciousness of greedy men have contributed to the diminished state of our existence. We are on an express lane heading over a cliff. If we do not humble ourselves and pray and seek the face of God, we are destined for a big fall! We can have revival if we would simply come together in prayer; banish our disunity and repent of our fallen ways. We still have a chance to recover and secure the path for generations to follow.

Time is waiting for our obedience to surface and take hold of the reins of power God has delegated for our survival. The choice is ours to make but the enemy of our procrastinations has waged a war inundated with confusion preying on our sensibilities. There is a sense that's common to all of us; *"Common Sense"*. Maybe we can begin there; *"Use It"!* As a nation, our reasoning and judgments have been compromised for the sake of convenience. We have no other choice but to deliver ourselves from mesmerizing influences and persuasions that have sullied our spiritual ambitions. It is a battle we must win. *"Truth is Truth"* and stands singularly upon a pillar of its own.

Fresh Oil

With humility as my pedestal, I make my ascension to my Father's Throne with a cistern of tears and gift of olives pressed out of His love. With my head shaven bare, He anoints my head with *"Fresh Oil From Heaven"* filling my cup overflowing with His love. A river of oil flows upon my crown as the oil descending from Aaron's beard. I drink the Wine of His Offerings to celebrate His Gift; a river of life with waters everlasting. I received strength from His Presence, power from His Spirit; I received His Life to make my own. Sealed with His touch with His Hand upon my head, with *"Fresh Oil From Heaven"* He Anointed me to flow.

9

Open Heaven

When Christ who is your life shall appear then shall ye also appear with Him in Glory. [1]

Heaven exists between a firmament of dividing waters. We often fix our eyes gazing in a distant endless search to consider what lies beyond in the waters above. The covering shield of the firmament limits access into treasures still hidden in secrecy of our Creator. Visibility of creation is evidence by waters gathered around our Earth but there lies a dimension of creation invisible in the distant corridors of our universe. It is a place of spirit bound only by God's Creativity.

Mystique of spirituality is a shroud of invisible life; a supernatural existence with no defining boundaries of its end. God is a Spirit and His Presence is all around us. His life is a consuming life and our lives can never be apart from His. Jesus came that we may discover the abundant life centered in faith. It is by His sacrifices that have bridged the gap between Heaven and Earth. He gave us directions into the path of faith connecting God's Divinity to our humanity by the transferring agent of the *"Cross"*. When the curtain rent in two; Heaven descended amongst us through the victorious obedience of Christ as a testament of His Divinity that we may live as *"One"* joined in eternal trinity with the Father, Son and Holy Ghost.

Look Inside

Take a look within for there you will find Heaven presiding as the ageless Spirit of God that traveled throughout the ages to connect with our destiny. He is God's representative here on Earth with telescopic powers to reveal the past, present and unravel our hopes of the future. Peering into the distant past, God sent His Spirit as a creative force with power to enrich the spectrum of life here on Earth. When the curtains were rent, Jesus temporarily relinquished all Earthly connections and Heaven came to dwell amongst us as *"Revelation of Christ Living Within"*.

The Holy Spirit is the sole representative given as *"revelation of all pre-existing time"*. He is God's Eternal Presence, *"His Morning Wings"* dwelling in our hearts as a connecting power to bring Heaven within our reach. Heaven is dominion-ship of a King reigning in authority who sits upon the throne of our lives. We as Believers; the throne of our conscience rests beneath the Anointing of the Holy Spirit governing the rudder of our soul as we channel through the tributaries of life. The Holy Spirit is the firstfruit occupying our hearts as *"Revelation of Christ Living Within Us"*.

God's Evidence

There is a universal aspect of God embodied in His creation. It can be found at any sector of our planet in any given moment of time. Through our observations our senses can connect to the visible things He created before our existence. Mountains peering into the sky with lakes and valleys resting beneath; trees piercing the firmament of the highest heights; a vault of life swirling in the oceans with fish and mammals resting upon its shores; roaming animals drifting across the terrain in pursuit of their nature; stars sparkling high above exploding into shooting stars racing across the night all evidence of God's appearance before our time.

Rocks and Stones

God's creation of the moon, sun and stars are hard immovable things made of stone formations that can't be displaced. You can't move them if you tried. They will be there until the end of time. Even if the sun explodes; they still will be here as remnants occupying the heavens. They have nowhere else to go. In the vastness of our universe, the advent of discovery can only take you but so far. The further out we go we begin to lose perception at the concluding limits of exploration. Knowledge of existence of other realities and any other form of life comparable to our own is conclusive; *"Earth is God's destination for man"*. There is nothing new to discover in the endlessness of the heavens except rocks and more rocks some shining with light while others are not so bright.

Raindrop

Envision the boundary of our universe, if we could escape that far, there is an existence only known as *"Beyond"*; a place called *"There"*. Scripture reveals it is a place of dividing waters; *"Let there be a firmament in the midst of the waters, and let it divide the waters from the waters"*. [1] Compared to eternity, our universe is no more than a raindrop carved out of water with an immeasurable expansion born of God's creativity. The expansion of light had its limitations of dispersion of fully removing darkness that defined an incalculable ending to the boundaries of our universe.

The light was limited to a thought of God's creative ingenuity. Take for example a raindrop falling in the center of a cup of still water. It creates reverberations expanding outward from its center. If the cup is wide enough to absorb the impact created from the force emitted, it will ripple towards the outer edges until you no longer can see where it ended. The same is with our universe. It's only discoverable to the extent light exist. What lies beyond is unknown existing under a cover of darkness limited only by the preclusion of light.

Symbolism of the Tree

Moses ascended atop Mount Sinai several times with each time learning of the sovereignty of God. God intended to establish a covenant relationship with the children of Israel by instituting laws and ordinances as a measurement of compliance. Just as Moses, Jesus ascended to His Mountain called *"Calvary"* carrying a fashioned tree with a crown of thorns for His Throne. Calvary was a revelation of a new law; the law of grace that superseded all other laws. Softened with tears of humility, His weeping in the *"Garden of Gethsemane"* awaited a betrayal as He journeyed with unrelenting steps to embrace a cross of suffering and pain. It is the same betrayal laid in the path of every Believer. It has a name; *"Judas"*. Jesus sacrificed with an unmitigated will to complete the journey of faith despite opposition to His appointment at Calvary. When all was said and done after completing the call of faith, He uttered His final words; *"It is finished bowing His head giving up the Ghost"*;[1] opening the gates of Heaven for a glimpse into eternity past.

Revelation of *"The Tree"* is metaphoric; from the Garden to the Cross, from blessing to curse. Jesus took upon Himself the judgments of Adam and made them His own that Heaven would again encounter Earth restoring God's order back into His originality. Golgotha's Hill had its accomplishments and so did Jesus. He made it possible to ascend into heights to discover truth from the spiritual dimensions of faith. If by faith actions of God formed the worlds; it will take faith to discover His truths to apply to our existence.

The Openness of Heaven

Proportionally; Heaven continues to evolve with mansions being built everyday for our occupation. Very few have had a vision of its existence. Heaven is the infinite expression of God. We've been given a taste of Heaven's treasure distributed by the Holy Spirit's Presence occupying our hearts. His Anointing is truly experiential; embodied as firstfruits of Heaven living within until possession of our rightful place in our mansion above. He is always ready to intercede on our behalf to demonstrate Heaven's power as He makes concessions for our faith. As Believers we have yet to scratch the surface of Heaven's entitlement God has purposed for our lives.

Heaven is progressive; morphing from eternity to eternity in an ongoing expansion. There is no interlude in Spirit; it is constantly undergoing development for future habitation of a world to come. Our beliefs and perceptions are limited to what we have accepted as truth. Superiority in the consciousness of man is not adapted with the willingness to accept change beyond what he has already extracted from his learning. There are limitations to our assemblage of truth which often are resistive elements of previous conceptualizations. But there is but one truth; God is a Spirit and His Truth supersedes time and makings of its beginnings.

God's character is woven in infinity with no defining expression of a source other than His Light emanating throughout our universe. His name the Great Jehovah; *"I Am that I Am"* is a name above all names! Heaven belongs to Him but is shared in the hearts of every Believer as *"firstfruit"* of His occupying Presence. The Presence and Power of His Spirit that traveled from Heaven found a dwelling place in our yielding hearts as a consummation of *"Heaven Living Within"*.

Heaven is an open arena unto us all as a conduit to discover our Father's heart. Jesus did nothing of His own invention only what *"He saw and heard"* from His Father. Without sight to see the image of faith as God reveals and an ear to hear His interpretations, the works sanctioned for the performance of faith will fall short of His expectations. Without God's Anointing, execution of our gifts with reliance solely on our own energies is a commitment to failure. Any alternative of a God directed life is an inundation of labor by the works of our hands and sweat of our brow with a born enemy in the *"likeness of our defeat"*. Adam's forfeiture of life centered in the appeal of God's attracting beams pulsating from *"The Tree of Life"* held his attention true until he rendered his own exceptions.

Prerequisite of Heaven's power to reveal itself is by an open conduit of prayer. Prayer streams the light of God's enlightenment into our lives as an entitlement through communion and fellowship with His Spirit. Consecration of our togetherness entreats our Father's love to release into our lives sight to see from the heart within. In our cry, *"Lord that I may receive my sight"*; the floodgates of His abundant life will open showering blessings needed for our decisions. What misery it would be without His direction. The journey of faith is not subjugated to chance; it is Spirit directed. How many times have we cried; *"Lord go before us, lead us; never leave us to ourselves."* It's the same cry of Moses entreating his father-in-law, Jethro, for direction to navigate in a barren wilderness in search of a promise.

> *It came to pass Jesus also was baptized; and while **He prayed**, the Heaven was opened. And the Holy Spirit descended in bodily form like a dove upon Him, and a voice came from Heaven saying, You are My beloved Son; in You I am well pleased.* [1]

Exploits of Heaven's power cannot be accessed without precedence of prayer. As Jesus was praying Heaven was opened and like a dove with the wings of faith, the Holy Spirit descended upon Him in a bodily form. The Holy Spirit is God's Anointing and once He comes upon you, His Presence will fully consume you; *"full body possession from head to toe"*. Just like the Holy Spirit descending in a bodily form gave evidence of God's invisibility, He gives form to our prayers as tangible evidence of His acceptance.

Praying to See

The achievements of faith are born in prayer. It is the birthing place for spiritual revelations. The Holy Spirit interprets God's instructions empowering our eyes and ears to implement His conclusions. God is the ultimate sponsor of faith who holds the blueprint. Under the Holy Spirit's leadership, He will lead and guide us through all of His intentions.

By faith God framed the worlds and by faith we can produce evidence of the spoken Word of Faith by things He instructs us to do. *"His Likeness"* is His Word evidenced by the visible things we see. The image of His Word creates an image within the heart of faith mirroring upon our conscience bearing the Image of His Likeness. The power of revelation is catapulting. It connects God's Omnipotence to our faith invigorating our lives for a performance He envisions. We have a unique opportunity to bring into visibility every Word God originally intended through empowerment by the Holy Spirit.

"Where there is no vision the people perish."[1] Absent the rightful perception of the thoughts of God seeded into our conscience, there is a perishing affect left to the interpretation of our senses which are limited to our experiences and areas where our faith is yet to be tested. Without God's thoughts becoming our thoughts reverberations emanating in our movements are quite noisy. Devoid of peace to settle our emotions, our thoughts will roam with warnings as sounding brass or tinkling cymbals; clouds thundering with no rain on a desert in thirst for life.

Our lives are purposed to be a productive source of empowerment; empowering the lives of others more so than ourselves. Without the Holy Spirit's revelations as the guiding influence discerning our needs, our faith is limited. *"Destiny without revelation to understand its intentions have a wandering effect; roaming, moving from place to place outside the boundaries of faith."* To ascertain the true path, the power of Heaven must be harnessed as a torrid river flowing unilaterally within our conscience to carry us in a direction beyond our presumptions. The Holy Spirit's is the bridle of our conscience directing us towards greater achievements.

Power of Let

Agreeably, the most productive word spoken from the mouth of our Creator as evidence of His Creativity is *"Let"*. Let personifies allocation of authority as a permit for creativity to produce evidence of the spoken Word of Faith. It is an expression of power spoken through the channels of faith of invisibility adorning the garment of visibility. Let is God's power mandating darkness as a confirming witness to the revelations of faith that says; *"It was so."*

> *And God said,* **Let** *the waters bring forth abundantly the moving creature that hath life and fowl that may fly above the earth in the open firmament of heaven.*[vs.20] *And God said,* **Let** *the earth bring forth the living creature after his kind, cattle, and creeping things, and beast of the earth after his kind and* ***it was so.***[vs.24] **Genesis 1 KJV**

What an awesome performance of God's power; just one word of authenticity, *"Let"*. The power behind the word produced the same performance from one day to the next, as it was in God's six day creation. Each day had the same command as the day before but with a unique emphasis assigned to His Word. The word *"Let"* is transforming converting invisibility into visibility. Invisibility is just a retainer of stored treasures hidden in secrecy with retention power until a power emerges greater than its ability to retain. As an executor, the tentacles of faith are empowered to bring into reality everything God assigns His Word to accomplish.

The waters, the firmament and the Earth each had the same command, *"Let"*, but with a different result in response to the spoken Word of Faith. While reading the Book of Genesis, I was enlightened to discover what I had not yet considered. I realized everything God created; the sun, moon and stars, cattle, creeping things, beast of the field, birds that could fly, great whales and moving creatures of the sea, all had a source from what He had pre-created. Their birthing place was either from the *"firmament, the water or the Earth"*. I know the source of stars; they had their origin in the firmament, cattle of the field were brought forth from the Earth and fish emerged from the waters. But what about the birds; what was their source?

> *Let the **waters** bring forth abundantly the moving creature that hath **life and fowl** that **may fly** above the Earth in the open firmament of heaven.* **Genesis 1:20 KJV**

From the waters of Earth, moving creatures emerged that produced life and fowl that *"may fly."* They may or may not depend on what they were made to do. All birds need the ground of Earth as a habitation for their nesting. Some can fly like Eagles with wings soaring high in the firmament. But they can't stay up there without coming down. Others have adapted to living along the beaches without flying wings to the likes of penguins residing in Antarctica. But birds are birds; some flying in the firmament while others have resolved with adaptability to just walking.

Why is our physical anatomy 60% water? Does that suggest to you something I don't know? Every cell in our body is made of water; for without it our humanity would not exist. Exactly what's holding our molecular structure together? Water! When we were carried in our mother's womb, we were encased in an ovum of fluid attached to an umbilical to provide nutrients purposed for our development. All life is born in water. Nothing exists outside the waters of creation; not even the stone of Earth.

Characteristically, God's creativity in our physical domain has an evolutionary component suggestive of a process that produced a manifestation of wings upon creatures that could only swim. The seeds of evolution embedded in His creativity produced life and fowl that could fly. The dynamic transformation of our world is ever evolving. New lands are being created by volcanic eruptions; rising sea levels reclaiming land back to the oceans while shifting climates around our planet are causing modifications of our adaptability to survive. Genetic modifications being researched and developed by our scientific society will impact genetic coding of human genes. It can ultimately evolve into something beneficial to our survival or something more sinister.

Have you taken wonder at the metamorphous of the butterfly? The incubated life of the butterfly initially existed as an egg before emerging as a caterpillar. After being restricted to a life of crawling, it urges towards completion of its call. The next cycle of development is concentrated on fortifying a dwelling place; a cocoon until completion of its metamorphous. This is the last cycle in its growth before evolving into its destination in life; a butterfly with *"wings of freedom"* to fly in an atmosphere of vapors. The evolution of the butterfly is indicative of our own human experience; from an egg to the womb to crawling; then walking to running this race towards destiny's end to reach the goals of life's intent. From invisibility morphing into visibility; that within itself is evolutionary! It's not osmosis! How else can you explain it?

Don't let the word evolution send you into a tizzy. Were you there in the beginning when God created the Heaven and the Earth? Do you know how long it took? Where were you when He brought forth light? Did you get blinded by the light? When He divided light from darkness could you stay up day and night evening and morning long enough to see what was going on? Where were you when God hollowed out an expanse for our existence when He created a firmament by separating water from water leaving behind a division of waters which were under the firmament from waters which were above the firmament? Did you get to witness when the Earth was in water and out of water at the same time when the waters under the heaven gathered together unto one place and dry land appeared? Again I ask; where were you when God put the stars in their silvery socket and the sun received its nuclear power? I have an answer; I wasn't there, neither were you! God's processes and solutions are a mystery to our understanding and are by no means predictable.

Evolution simply means; *"Gradual development of something, especially from a simple to a more complex form".* Procreation is an evolutionary component of God's invention clearly defining a process born out of His creativity. From the making of man that began with one sustaining breath inhabited in the soul of every human being that has ever surfaced the face of this planet; there is no other process since that can validate his introduction into our reality. God blessed man with the ability and authority to be fruitful and multiply. How? By a given process; from the sperm of man unionized with the egg of a woman we developed into human beings to bring shape and form to the fruitfulness of God's Word. *"Every life born of man is a product born of God's imagination."*

As in the life of the butterfly, our journey continues in metaphoric stages of development. Ultimately, man must undergo a conversion to obtain his eternal wings of faith that can travel the heavens far above the limits of Earth's confinement. It is a search for treasures stored in the vault of God's wisdom. *"Wisdom is the principal thing, therefore get wisdom and with all thy getting, get understanding."*[1] At the pinnacle of faith, understanding provides sight to see while not being governed by the things we see.

We were born of flesh until the occupying power of God's Spirit retained its rightful ownership; changing our mortal bodies into *"Image of His Likeness"*. We have an awesome task laid before us to complete the mission of faith; transforming the dominion of Earth into a habitation of the *"Kingdom of Christ"*. In every aspect, we are commissioned to reconstruct our arena of faith shaping it into the *"Image of Christ"*. His Image preceded the makings of our reality as a reflection of the purity of love without violation of sin encountered in the disobedience of Adam.

In defiance of gravity, when Jesus returns, we will need those wings. Maybe we should take the lesson of the butterfly and see how he does it. We have a flight to take. With vanishing wings as angels caught up in the magnet of His Glory, there is a celebration waiting that the heavens have never witnessed before. We will be changed, even as life and fowl emerged from the waters below, into the *"Light of His Revelation"*. To be caught up in the heavens when He appears, our faith must be ready to emerge from the waters below for a transitioning into a new heaven when our souls are reclaimed. At the moment of rapture, we will no longer need wings of faith to complete our final destination of a life to come; it will be completed by the Faith of God.

Prophecies of centuries past gave us foreknowledge of the changing dynamics of time and seasons we are living in today. While we continue to distant ourselves from the spiritual impressions of faith, our curiosity of time and its beginning is drawing us much closer to judgment. In our exaltations in search for justification of our elevated presumptions, we have acquired an inordinate thirst for knowledge seemingly by feckless measures in an attempt to bring our own definition of time to validate the purpose in why we are even here.

Resultantly, these measures have allowed structural changes to the fabric of faith. If left to ourselves; the likes of deceit, perversion and corruption will rule our senses without discriminating the order assigned to our humanity. We are struggling to access wisdom of God's uniqueness in an effort to make it our own; not fully aware of deceptions circumventing His rule in our lives. The nature of man is combative defending the rule of his senses and consciously with every effort he suppresses the truth in his unrighteousness.

> *For the wrath of God is revealed from heaven against all ungodliness and unrighteousness of men, who suppress the truth **in** unrighteousness, because what may be known of God is manifest in them, for God has shown it to them. For since the creation of the world **His invisible attributes are clearly seen, being understood by the things that are made,** even His eternal power and Godhead, so that they are without excuse, because, although they knew God, they did not glorify Him as God, nor were thankful, but became futile in their thoughts, and their foolish hearts were darkened. Professing to be wise, they became fools, and changed the glory of the incorruptible God into an image made like corruptible man and birds and four-footed animals and creeping things.* [1]

The dispensational direction of faith is a penciled sketch flexible without the etchings of hardened stone. Its variability embraces forgiveness to the extent we accept the rudiments embedded in its discipline. Faith is the evolutionary component of our belief; always forward looking competing to bring life to the promises of faith. The resolve of faith is to become one with the *"One who sent us"* unified in perfection with His Spirit residing within. The concession of breath deposited in the soul of man created an image in the likeness of Himself that we would be unified in the oneness of Him. Heaven will yield its power when our hearts are united to His Eternal Good. With an open access for discovery into His treasures, it's quite puzzling why we still remain sedentary as the Earth continues evolving towards its end groaning with *"the creep of time"* for completion of its call.

Healing is so needed in our world. As agents of the Cross, we have power to deliver and change everything around us and even change ourselves. But the desire of compassion must be instigated for a performance intended of our faith. Compassion is the burden of faith; the cross we bear for the sake of others. *"Must Jesus bear the cross alone and all the world go free?"* Answer it! *"No! There is a cross for everyone and there is a cross for me."* To see me is to know me; not by name but by testimony of the persecutions that I bear.

Compassion is a dynamo exuding with urgency as a burning flame of fire radiating from the center of faith. Compassion is the monitor of faith searching through the trenches of our wavering desires. As the driving influence for exhibition of God's power, compassion will radicalize our motivations by connecting with the spontaneous impulses of faith. Our spirit man must continually migrate towards the attracting flames of renewal in the burning fires of compassion to elevate joy above sorrow; victory above defeat; faith above fear; hope above dismay. As a sequestered river waiting to release its flow of passion igniting power to fuel our expectations, so does the pining of our hearts yearns for love's connectivity centered in the desire of faith.

Heaven is open to our aspirations but they must be mixed with the subtle dew of the Holy Spirit's giving. God's interaction with our faith is an embedded power of consciousness of His Spirit waiting to implement a performance through our gifts. *"The Holy Spirit is the Glory of God; the Glory of Christ Living Within."* He is the driving influence behind our gifting, desires and motivations with no power given beyond His exception.

Now

THEN

Sankofa

Sankofa symbolizes a mythic bird that flies forward while looking backward with an egg symbolic of the future in its mouth. Sankofa has refinishing seeds to repaint patterns of our dreams and visions deferred from yesterday's sorrows with hope of tomorrow's fulfillment. Our future is embodied in our past laden with sufferings from generations who sacrificed in faith. It's our inheritance; our identity; an investment not so easily recognized amidst the changing winds blowing from centuries past.

"Sankofa" teaches that we must go back to our roots, the place of our beginnings, reaching back to discover the best of what our past has to teach us. In order to achieve our full potential as we move forward, we must never forget the sacrifices of our Elders.

The pathway of our destiny to recover whatever we have lost, forgotten, forgone or been stripped of can be reclaimed, revived, preserved and perpetuated for our future. Time is a filter; a discriminate judge of the choices we make. It is given to us as a gift born from the revelation of God's Creativity.

10
Side-Meat Beans & Biscuits

"Therefore I say to you, do not worry about your life, what you will eat or what you will drink; nor about your body, what you will put on. Is not life more than food and the body more than clothing?" [1]

Side-Meat, Beans and Biscuits? Sounds intriguing particularly for an old country boy like me! Or would you prefer roasted locust and wild honey as you sip sweet nectar of a delicious wine flowing with an aroma of fragrant spices? Beware; aromatic spices flowing through the corridors of your mind do have a tendency to throw your equilibrium off balance and when you stumble, I think you would readily accept my invitation; Side-Meat, Beans and Biscuits. It does have a sobering effect.

Do I have your attention yet? At times, images that surface in my imagination are encumbered with a little humor. Humor embraces as a defense against the abrasive elements of life. The exercise of humor is so missing in our day. We are wound too tight holding on to so many unnecessary things. We tend to discount simplicity of life; simple things that truly reflect the virtuousness intended for our lives which often gets lost in the balancing divide of our daily encounters.

Side-meat

Maybe everyone knows about side-meat. If you like good eating like me; you should. Sorry Vegans! You have my condolences. Side-meat merely is meat taken from the side of a pig allowed to cure over a process of time. It is peppered and salted mixed with herbs and spices found at mostly any store in the form of bacon, fatback and even jerky. Cured, it is used for seasoning adding flavor to greens, beans and a variety of soups.

Side-meat is a connotation for southern style living. It's a place I refer to as *"country"*. To be country has an implicit meaning of being raised on a farm, in a remote setting off the beaten path. It was the place of my birth and early childhood. Born in a house; not a hospital but believe me it was the old fashioned way.

In a moment of reflection secured with a bookmark in my vault of memories; I opened the page stamped with the seal *"Unforgettable"*. As a reflected mirror of time; I began to ponder with much pragmatism with respect to the days of my youth. Experimentally, it was a season when my spiraling imagination seemingly was very difficult to control. With dreams developing, nothing was relatable in my surrounding that gave any indication where the road ahead would take me.

I miss those precious days of innocence; the smell of garlands and the aroma of pollinated wild flowers enraptured in a gentle breeze racing across fields blooming with nectar. I can still hear the songbirds singing in celebrated unity and the static flight of the hummingbird's wings rapidly beating against the wind.

The serene silence and beauty of the butterfly resting upon inviting petals of the *"Honeysucker"* blossom, gave invitation to all to feast from their giving.

During the spring, the creatures of Earth awakened from dormancy of the stillness of winter, wrestling in folly joyous of a new season. It's the time when love keeps on giving; searching for fulfillment; yielding as an agent of healing soothing all wounds. Following the same path of creation from one season to the next, the repeated cycle of love renders a life of refreshing for all of Earth's inhabitants. In an environment constantly changing, the making of new life flourishes with hope, filling the atmosphere with the scent of revival. It is a time of recovery from the offerings of winter to reclaim ownership of the sharing of life.

During my childhood, I enjoyed the simple things of life; interacting with nature, growing things with an expectation of a harvest after a toiling season of labor. I became so fascinated with animals and spent time observing their beauty. I enjoyed the food; okra and tomato with field peas; fresh vegetables, grapes and berries picked from the vine, succulent melons fresh from the field and corn so sweet, you could eat it raw. On Saturday mornings we would load the trailer to take a load of fruits and vegetables to town. It was an opportunity to subsidize more income for the farm. I remember as I rode on the back of the trailer I would always hear my grandfather's cadence bellowing down the streets; *"Watermelon, watermelon red to the rind; get'em right now or they'll all be mine"*. Unforgettable!

I learned how to clean fish when my grandfather would go to the creek returning with a bountiful catch. They had very attractive colors, some adorned with beautiful complexions of blue, red and sparking silver almost reflecting as a mirror. I learned how to clean them but more than that, I ate them with a serving of *"Side-meat, Beans and Biscuits"*. After the washing of every plate, a new spooning of those delicacies was served to my delight leaving nothing but a desire for another bite. Those memorable times sustained me above complaint and humbled me in gratitude for the simple things of life.

When my grandfather harvested pigs it was very fascinating to watch. Pigs and chickens provided other sources of income as well as sustainment throughout the winter. After packaging the different parts of the pig; some to be sold and the rest kept in freezers; nothing was discarded but the dung secluded in its entrails. I even enjoyed blood pies made from blood of the pig. Looking back, I don't know how I pulled that off. The sound of it now is rather repugnant to my senses. I am even cringing at the thought of it but at the same time humbled in revealing my upbringing.

I learnt respect and dignity of the ultimate sacrifice of the blood and soul of animals. That's why we pray over our food when we eat out of benevolence. I would eventually come to realize God made man as a rational spirit with an ability of discerning choices. God's life is evidenced in all of creation and we all share equality in our existence, even that of animals we have subdued.

We have ventured further beyond the point of need for our survival by perverting God's intentions into a sport of trophies hanging on our walls of the ultimate sacrifice of animals. The thirst for blood salivates to no end; not conquering by *"rule to subdue"* but by lust of flesh as an inappropriate exhibition of God's authority.

Comfort of my surroundings was a source of peace, love and hope that provided security for a journey awaiting me. Visions of my dreams revealed a future in disguise with so much uncertainty because of poverty and its feeding streams of entrapment; streams with binding tentacles as an octopus holding onto its victim entangled in a life restraining clutch. The tentacles of poverty has restraining power limiting access to just the fundamentals of life with no apparent escape. However, poverty does have its advantages sensitized with compassion that flows in the bowels of hope. In the channels of compassion is an underlying reservoir of power gained from a life of simplicity.

Life then seemed so precious and never-ending. The concept that it would not last forever did not enter the cavity of my reasoning to consider there would be a conclusion to its time. Often at night, I would lay on the ground with my eyes affixed gazing upward at the celestial display as the fragments of eternity glittered with stars. With only the sound of crickets chirping and the shining light of the moon as a guide in the night, my eyes would scan the heavens searching for an end to its beginning. I often pondered; *"Where did I come from? Why did I arrive for such a time as this"?*

The Narrative of Life

Looking back reflecting upon the day of my entry into this world of visibility; God created an Earth for my habitation with a flourishing garden flowing with rivers exuding from its center. Written upon the scrolls of faith were my instructions; *"Subdue the Earth and fill it with His Image as an expansion of His Kingdom."* As I waited in the patient streams of time; waiting to adorn wings of flight to carry me to my assignment in life, I pondered the meaning of its existence. What is life and purpose that I had to travel so far? Why was there such a demand disturbing my comfort of peace by separating me from my origin to integrate a life of flesh and spirit? Where was I to go and what was I to do? Why would there be pain and so much suffering in this new world filled with hunger, strife and bitterness then dying journeying back to where I began? These are simple questions for the curious but not so simple in unraveling life's intentions. Ascertaining the answer is embedded in the spiritual conscience of our Creator; *"The Wisdom of Ages."* It was He who calculated the time and purpose of my existence for the intended good of His Kingdom.

Before my awakening, He knew me and planted me in the womb of His creativity and assigned His energy to my destiny. Equipped with the essence of life, a measured appropriation was seeded into life's destiny for a journey to be discovered. Shrouded in mystery, His Creative Spirit unveiled my purpose envisioned for a journey far into a distant future immersed in the path of faith. Life is a valued and precious opportunity measured as a temporary investment eternity reclaims at the fulfillment of its purpose.

My travels began as sparkles of light illuminating with a brilliancy of colors surrounding me. They were arrayed as the color of angels in a multi-dimensional display serenading in sound. As I passed through the cosmic prism of time, the purity of light that existed from the beginning separated into many vibrations of colors; from blues of jasper, to the green of jade with clarity of the purest diamond. The color of my vessel was an earth tone of brown with a garment stitched in black. From the dark soil born from the death of stars, I did not know I would bear shame, suffering and pain but born with refined beauty in a garment of darkness most appealing to the light. Light impressing upon darkness is converting changing into recognition of something greater in value.

The *"Angels"* traveled with the speed of light from afar delivering me into a house of preconstruction. It was a house made of clay from cosmic dust sealed with the drippings of dew. When the inspired breath of God filled my hollowed cavity, I began to vibrate to the rhythms of life. Every cell in my body came alive as they began to dance in celebration. Life is movement, always oscillating; from the blood moving through our veins to transient intangibles of thoughts surfacing from our imagination. Life is tuned to vibrations of an invisible array of colors that separates the cycles of our existence defining the light waves of our years.

Traveling from the cosmic heavens to the greenery of Earth, I embraced life with inexpressible joy singing as a song bird embracing the light of day. I readied myself in faith as an eagle pruning its feathers for a flight in the heights above. Earth now has become my dwelling place, far away from the distant land awaiting my return. With a connective voice to call on strength from above, my ears are prompt in readiness to receive transmissions coded in Spirit. Although interruptions may occur; I cry out in anguish in the middle of the night; the pain of separation proven too much to bear.

In night's sabbatical, I retreat to discover mysteries hidden in darkness. Moving stealthily, I escape in the temporary arms of faith for a spiritual journey back to my Father's Kingdom. His Spirit guided me through the night as a pilot searching for a beacon of pulsating light. I discovered; *"To be absent from the body is to be present with the Lord"*.[1] But I must return, forever stricken by the peace and love shared in a moment of retreat. With frequency I make this journey for without it, life would surely cease.

Color and Light

The harvesting of light assembled in the beginning of creation had enough energy monumentally greater in intensity than an atomic detonation billions of times the energy of the sun. For the unbeliever; they call it the *"Big Bang"*. The truth is; *"It Was a Big Bang"*! I do not disagree. But please be informed; the sound you heard was the *"Light of God Banging"* on the doors of darkness that still reverberates in continual expansion of creation for a new habitation populated with a new heaven awaiting our possession.

The harnessed power of light when released upon its target creates fragmentation of the light itself. The Light that detonated darkness after God spoke Light into existence, *"Let There Be"* generated a frequency of colors. Theoretically speaking; the frequency of colors is the frequency of *"electromagnetic visibility of light"* that creates a spectrum of colors. The colors of light are visible sound waves endowed with cosmic energy; the same type of energy God used in creation of our universe. Light has color and it also has a voice. It's like thunder and lightning; you can see the lightning and can hear the thunder. Thunder is the sound of the electromagnetic force of light dispersing its energy bringing light to any darkened cloud.

Existence of light encompasses all visible realities. Without it there would be no colors but the color of darkness waiting in readiness at the interval of time. Darkness is as thought, a wealth of stored treasure waiting for opportunity to lend its power to embrace the light. Light is transparent and revealing. The color of light will amplify every imperfection in its path.

As light exposes darkness, it brings to the surface recognition of materiality. God's dispersion of light is *"His Materiality; recognizable by the things He created"*. Without recognition of our senses there would be no justifying cause linking us to a material existence. What would be the point of it? God's senses are not our senses. He is a Spirit; the forever existence of time and eternity but even then His Existence is endless. We are the product of His *"materiality"* fashioned in the Likeness of His Image. As mortal beings sealed in a circumference of clay, we are endowed with the Light of His Reflection.

Pulverization of materiality dissimilates seeds of life as justification for the purpose of light. Howbeit, as creatures of Light, we were born by the same Light of God's Existence that spoke us all into being. We are not surrogates but true Light bearers with illuminating ability contained within the conscience of every man. The fact that we are seen is visual recognition of the existence of Light having entered into our perception. Being void of that Light has the equivalent value no greater than coffins submerged beneath; housed in the cavities of Earth removed from the Presence of Light.

We are objects of God's intentions of light; created entities with given visibility of sight to see the wonders of His creation. However, just seeing is not enough; it is only a tool to correct our perceptions of the awe of God's wonderment. Life is more than a visual display but it interacts with our gifts and talents to achieve all that He intended including our redemption. Without God's Light beaming upon our conscience recognition of His intentions will remain obscured until the light of discovery illuminates our destiny. After coming into the knowledge of truth, it will mark a new beginning in the journey of faith validating our encounter with the Light of God.

Man's conscience is a living thing; if it is living it has light. Instinctively in his nature in the day of his entry into this world, he is not born with a clean slate; proof of it is in his early *"cries"* for fulfillment. He knows when he is hungry; when he is sick; needing to be changed or comfort of a hug after separating from nine months of incubation; all beckon attention to his instinctive cries for satisfaction as inherent attributes embedded in his conscience. His instincts aren't learnt or taught but genetically ingrained as a natural feature implanted in the consciousness of all humanity. Man's induction into this new reality of human existence has a paramount incentive of the impulse for survival. Over the course of years in his development inundated with the vulnerabilities of learning, negative elements of human nature can creep in creating impressionable differences altering the course of his life.

In a strong sense of encouragement scripture says we are to *"Train up a child in the way he should go and when he is old he will not depart from it"*.[1] Decisions we make; our beliefs, principles and morals integrated in the actions of our lives are dictating to the extent they can be generationally compromising. Enforcement of one's principles upon the developing conscience of a child is incredibly impactful.

A child easily attracts to images. They undoubtedly will mimic in their response to impressions developed in their observations. Their actions are duplications of our example developing in their fragile minds. When images of our behavior are repeated enough in the presence of a child, it is likely they will be incorporated into their own imitation of life. Image of our thoughts; the things we permit and instances where we turn our eyes away from enforcing is an allocation for them to do as they choose. Image this; if a child thinks he is raised up amongst wolves, he will think he is a wolf. He will be howling in the night and you are thinking; *"What's wrong with him"*. There is nothing wrong with him; something is wrong with you; you are the root of the problem! *"The way you view it is the way you do it. Change your view; then change your do!"* He won't be howling in the night and neither will you!

The Finest Wheat and the Blood of Grapes

> *Curds from the cattle, and milk of the flock, With fat of lambs; And rams of the breed of Bashan, and goats, With the choicest wheat; And you drank wine,* **the blood of the grapes.** **Deut. 32:14 NKJV**

The life of seclusion on my grandfather's farm gave me an opportunity to dream and explore possibilities swirling around in my imagination. In the morning hours around the break of dawn; I would wake up only to be surrounded by trees; *"Friends of Morning"* getting comfort from the rising sun. While observing their beauty, I discerned their movement sequestered in the cool of the morning breeze as actions of benevolence as they unfolded their leaves as hands of praise. With leaves as hands lifted high towards the sun reflecting upon their countenance glowing in the Presence of

God filling the air; His vibrating steps could be heard across the fields of harvest giving cause for every tree to tremble. Celebrated in a coronation to the call of morning in the excitement of praise, they all released their fruit with their leaves clapping for joy.

The trees of Earth are instructive as a witness of time even their purpose inscribed in the veins of their leaves. They are indicative of the same patterns from trees as in the days of Adam; *"Provide herbs of plants and the fruit of the tree as a reward for our labor"*. As stewards, we are charged with securing their survival.

Trees are part of the plant kingdom. There is no other place in our universe where they can be found. Their kingdom is a kingdom of silence. It is impossible to hear them speak unless you live amongst the wind to hear their chatter. With shared roots of strength as an anchor securing a foundation for protection and the supplying of life for all to feast upon;

> *They give us shelter from the blazing heat of day and a fire of warmth in the cold of night; they become a leopard's hiding place as he perch disguising in a cover of leaves to ambush his prey; they provide a resting place for the birds of the air to recover strength from their flight; "blood of grapes" taken from the vine as water turned into wine to soothe our soul from the weariness of time; the finest of wheat with the color of gold but more precious in value than money could ever buy; a cavity for bees storing a vault of honey with a nectar of attracting sweetness running rampart filling the air.*

Green Blood and Red Blood

The composition of a plant's existence is a color of green symbolic of the vitality of life. They are made green from *"green blood of chlorophyll"*. Though their species vary in size, shape, form and purpose, they still remain the same color of green. Their blood never changes. Armed in friendliness and beauty, together they exhale; releasing a passion of breath of invisible vapors purified by the morning dew. At the rising of the sun, with leaves migrating toward the repeated path of celebration, they embrace the light reflecting upon their leaves but often go unnoticed *"introvertly"* reaching for fulfillment of their season.

We have reshaped our landscape with buildings made of stone and concrete as a substitute for trees reducing their appearance. We've determined them to be an inconvenience without a rational interpretation for their existence. Cities of stone are competing with the habitation of trees replacing their purpose with a surrogate of umbrellas and awnings for shade. It's all because of the greed of capitalism. Trees instigate life; they breathe; not stones! The green forest will one day be reclaimed when the squandering attempts of man have failed but this time resiliency of the forest will be superimposed upon a foundation of crumpled stone.

Trees and plants are servants to our survival; they are always giving asking for nothing in return. Most plants are made green and at times it is difficult to make distinction from one to the other. But the Tree of Good and Evil in the center of the Garden was highly visible comparable to no other tree but the Tree of Life. Both stood towering in stature competitively appealing to the attractions of man; one pointing vertically into Heaven drawn to the Light of God; the other stretching laterally across the conscience of man adorned with ornaments of seduction.

Of all the real estate on Earth, this one tree, the Tree of Good and Evil, had enough cancerous power *"pandemically"* to destroy all of humanity. It was pleasing to the eye but not so good for food. Pleasures of the eye are seductive influences that prey on our conscience; blurring our vision to the point it becomes challenging distinguishing the rightful animations of the human experience. Do you recall the story after Jesus had laid hands on the blind man; he made a remarkable confession; *"I see men like trees, walking"*.[1] Sounds like to me you need another touch if your vision is so blurred you can't bring distinction to your own perceptions. Men are like trees always moving; trafficking in and out of our lives. We can see them coming but can't discern their blurred intentions and stealthy motivations. May I suggest; *"Get another touch just like the first one you got. Go back to the well; it hasn't run dry"!* Take your eyes off of man and his attractions and look up for your healing draweth nigh! Looking up is an extension of faith connecting you closer to healing than the lateral enticements of man.

> *After that He again put His hands upon his eyes and **made him look up** and he was restored and saw every man clearly.* [2]

A tree's sustainment is by life flowing through its roots. If it detaches itself, it will die separated from its source. Roots of plants penetrate downward; searching for an anchor into the interior of Earth. As humans, we are sojourners roaming the face of Earth without a permanent attachment. Trees and humans share life but unlike trees, our roots are a spiritual extension of Heaven beyond the confinement of Earth.

There is a commonality of our lives and that of the Plant Kingdom; we both share the same dependency of living streams of water Earth provides. Bound within an atmosphere of exchange of air, our contribution to each other sustains our survival. Even though the life blood of trees flow from the Earth, we as Believers are separated unto a life flowing from within; spiritual life of Heaven connecting from above.

In the beginning, there was a season in the Garden when man ate herbs and fruit of the trees. Because of his disobedience, we entered into sweat of labor of the field with profound consequences. It came with a price that now we feast on sacrificial life of animals to eat. *"We are bearing fruit of one man's response to faith changing our diet from green blood of plants to red blood of living creatures."*

Trees never lost their color neither changed blood; they remained the same since the beginning until now. Their life span also has not changed, but the days of our lives are now limited by the breath they breathe filtering carbon dioxide so compromising to our health by purifying the air with the freshness of oxygen.

We as humans have red blood flowing through our veins but maintain no outward distinction except for the color of our skin. The life of soul is in the blood and we share the same consistency of life from one to the other. We all breathe the same air, eat the same food, quench our thirst from the same waters of Earth and even our laughter and tears bears no identity of uniqueness; not even the 100-120 day life span of the blood cells in our bodies.

Despite our colors, God made *"one"* Adam from the variability of dust of the Earth. But He also created a living being through *"one"* sustaining breath into the cavity of man by Heaven's power with an exponential factor of eternity. We are *"one"* humanity existing in commonality bearing the same purpose defined in our creation. We were born as God's praise in the Earth; *"Light bearers of His Countenance as a radiant flame of fire shining from within"*. But the disguising mantle of flesh must be removed for the Light of our lives to be on full display.

Years ago while in my backyard; for no apparent reason, I took hold of an ax and struck an oak tree with a punishing blow of strength. Tears of sap began to flow from the vein of the tree. I humbled in regret to the voice of my son; *"Dad, the tree is bleeding."* It was almost if I had an epiphany. I began to feel its pain and tearing displays exuding through the bark. I felt remorse realizing that God made the tree and it had a purpose existing even before my creation. How vain I was to violate its sovereignty compromising exhibition of the beauty of its intended purpose. The tree is still scarred as a witness of the scarring seared into my conscience. Introspectively, there is greater reflectivity of my actions realizing that the same elements of a tree exist in me. I was made from the Earth with the same constituency of life from everything green; plants, trees and even algae from the oceans. *"God gave life to the tree and life to the tree living in me."*

Adam relinquished the God given life of eternity for a temporary occupation in the fields of Earth no more valuable than the life of a tree. His choice to live amongst trees anchored in the dust that would reclaim him secured his ending. The *"God given life"* is eternal life absolute in its renderings. There are no exceptions.

The purity of God's life flowing in Adam's blood was contaminated by consumption of a forbidden seed that continues to bear fruit of its power. The blood of Jesus sacrificed on a tree at the pinnacle of Mount Calvary fell upon the Earth as a redemptive power cleansing our blood from shame. Cascading from the mountain top covering the depths of every valley, every stream and tributary connected to our lives; the blood of the Lamb resurrected the diminished glory of our fallen countenance with love, joy and peace.

House of Clay

> *Therefore I say to you, do not worry about your life, what you will eat or what you will drink; nor about your body, what you will put on. Is not life more than food and the body more than clothing?* [1]

Life is full of worry sent to rob us of our faith. It causes distractions rather than implementing positive assertions into our faith. Worry surface as a result of our unpreparedness to encounter the events of life. At times, suddenness of overwhelming circumstances will bear consequences seemingly without a predictive end. If we could see outside suppression of worry obscured by clouds of fear, we would discover that trees never worry neither do birds searching for early morning food. Bears secluded in the caves of winter render trust to accumulated fat harvested from a season of labor. Nature exists above worry, reclaiming from cycle to cycle, season to season, never failing in a trusted communion of giving and receiving.

The lack of trust is suppressive existing below the threshold of confidence needed for our battles. Trust is central to our confessions. Resolution to worry while dwelling amidst uncertainties only serves to rob us of peace. Worry doesn't have its own life; it's resuscitated out of our fears as a diminishing light restraining our visions and dreams. Life's magnetism has an appeal for balance; from worry to hope; hope to fulfillment.

Worry is a denial of faith; an unsettled dispute of soul and spirit! As God's eye is on the sparrow that has no need or want but finds food at the doorsteps of faith at the awakening of every day; we should know; *"My God shall supply all your need according to His riches in Glory by Christ Jesus."*[1] The content of our need is stored in Heavenly places where there is no want or shortage. Heaven is rich to discovery of faith!

"Flesh will never apprehend the principle of trust." This is a lesson of spirit. It would be inconsistent with the character of God for us to believe He would create something He does not have power to sustain. In our defeats, we are only to blame not being fully convinced it is our problem and not God's of our refusal to accept *"His Grace"* designated for our solutions. In seasons of worry, we have a tendency to be buffeted by influences that are assigned to keep us away from apprehending the promise of faith. *"Being fully persuaded that what He had promised He was able also to perform."* [1]

Worry indicates our priorities are not in synch with the spiritual expectations of faith. Imbalances of our actions are indications of a spiritual deficit of our hearts not settled in belief. We tend to concentrate on the anxiety of tomorrow (*lack of trust in God's ability*) on foolish things; the clothes we wear, cars we drive, our houses or just obsessing our energy trying to keep up with the *"Joneses"*. By the way; the emergence of technology has altered the way we live. In our rush to keep pace, constantly being updated, the versatility of robotics is taking control of our lives as a distraction. In essence, we have surrendered the governing of our lives to the *"pushing of a button"*.

Outer dominance of flesh with our soul succumbed to fleeting passions of infertility induces imperfections to the cause of error in our spirit man. Flesh instigates as a false balance in settling the stability of faith as we weigh our lives upon the scales of hope. Hope is an idea of fruitfulness born in our spirit. It is spiritual!

Conceivably, our spirit is the only productive agent that can produce the expectation of hope into results centered in faith. If we embrace belief by accepting the God's Word as the unadulterated Truth, His Spirit would energize our gifting radicalizing the performance of faith into greater level of achievement.

Our lives become so unfruitful when our desires for things outside of necessity are conflicting with God's intentions. When we yield our time pursuing vanity, it accomplishes nothing but strenuous labor subtracting years from our vision. Grace is *"freedom of choice"* of our will to accept it. There is no power greater in our humanity than the power of our choices to accept or even deny God's solution for our lives. Faith has its hostilities when we choose the *"works of our hands"*, labor from past dispensations substituting at the expense of the gift of God's free flowing grace.

Dishonorable Motivation of Need

Spiritual discernment is grossly missing in our day. At times, I perceive we are as sheep being led to slaughter just as the slaughter among the people that followed Absalom. Fleecing of the flock is a common phenomenon in our church arena; men hiding under a deceptive cover with tantalizing fruits of prosperity. Some of our leaders, disguising behind spiritual labels, have manipulated the production of faith and turned it into an enterprising business for their gain. I have witnessed where some of them who exist above need satisfy themselves in excess of greed. Leaders who are charged to develop the Body of Christ meticulously in protocols of faith should be by constraint of their gift but with a willingness that is seeded in compassion. It's unfortunate that some have never traveled the way they are trying to lead without a light shining upon their mantle to even show them the way. Their dimly lit lamps are reluctant in power to shepherd the way.

> *Tend (nurture, guard, guide, and fold) the flock of God that is [your responsibility], not by coercion or constraint, but willingly; not dishonorably motivated by the advantages and profits* **[belonging to the office]**, *but eagerly and cheerfully; Not domineering [as arrogant, dictatorial, and overbearing persons] over those in your charge, but being examples (patterns and models of Christian living) to the flock (the congregation).*
> **1 Peter 5:2-3 Amplified Bible (AMPC)**

The advantages and profits belong to the *"office"*. I have witnessed the arrogance and dictatorial practices of some of our leaders who stand with domineering stature which only denies the faith of others. It is a very disturbing pattern and model of Christian life. The worldly practice of materialism is simply idolatry disguised as truth with a garment of flesh hiding itself behind its glitter of accomplishments. For the sake of *"filthy lucre and pride"*, there is no other validation of its cause. The cunningness of man propagates idolatry to sustain power. In truth; ideology centered on the posturing of man is pride; *"A lie against one's self"*. We, the Body of Christ are only to blame.

Apparently, we have made icons and celebrities unwittingly of some who are standing before us whom we have elevated above their measure. Resultantly, we have caused many to error by induction of pride. When the Jews wanted to make Jesus king, He disappeared from amongst them and so should we in fulfilling our Father's will. It is very important to realize; *"Humility is the cornerstone of faith"!* But, it is a path many steer entirely away from because of the sacrifices required.

Some of our leaders rule by separatism; alienated from the ones they are called to serve. They isolate themselves one-dimensionally executing their office without incorporating the full complement of ministry. Authority of the faint of heart is easily threatened. How often have I seen men get uncomfortable in their skin in the presence of other men? Ministry is not about competition. If you are truly called to do what you do there shouldn't be any hindrance to your performance.

This has been going on for quite some time and leaving it to man, he will not change on his own. God's gifts are manifested in the lives of all His people with equal distribution of *"His Callings"*. The degree of our willingness and sacrifices in offering of our gifts is the only thing separating our lives from one to the other in servicing the lives of those who so desperately need it.

"Side-meat, beans and biscuits" are our portion; readily accepted as God's provision for our lives. The raiment we wear or the food we eat bears no indication of the life we live. But live; indeed we shall until it's determined we can live no more.

The Cross

Jesus was crucified upon a Cross with water and blood separating from His body surrendering to Earth that which was born of Earth. The Earth was purified by blood flowing from His veins as an offering of atonement and water from his body as a fountain of life. When the Heavens were rent in two, the Spirit of God descended upon the Earth as reformation for the completion of faith opening a path back into our Father's Kingdom. The blood and water that poured from His body colluded with dust turned into clay but this time breathing the breath of His Spirit Living Within as an expression of His grace. Jesus came to purify the Earth as it was in the beginning taking sin to the Cross defeating the devil of his power. He cleansed the Temple, gave sight to the blind, opened deafened ears and even raised the dead. He restored the order of creation back into the Image of His Father's originality with power given as a legacy to man to fulfill completion of His call.

"Bacco" 11

The Lord has promis'd good to me, His Word my hope secures; He will my shield and portion be, as long as life endures. **John Newton**

Bacco is a shorten expression for *"Tobacco"*. I first heard that expression while working the fields during tobacco harvesting on my grandfather's farm. Tobacco farming is hard strenuous work mostly done in the hot baking sun un-relentless to cries of relief. The cry of *"Bacco"* is a familiar cry of urgency. For some of you who may not have heard this unceremonious expression, *"Bacco"* is an alien interpretation born from the pain of labor.

On my grandfather's farm, those golden leaves of tobacco were the most important source of income we had. What we harvested would be the breadwinning crop, the *"Cash Cow"* for the whole year. Corn, wheat and soybeans would be a second tiered supplement of income along with vegetables and fruit contributing to more wear and tear on my fragile physique. As a child, my father gave me the nickname *"Skinny"*. I had legs as twigs and dreamy eyes with an adventurous spirit full of mischievousness. Looking in the mirror today, Skinny has taken on another dimension, layered in gluttony of time and its consequences. It's remarkable how the movement of time induces so many changes.

At the beginning of tobacco season, my grandfather purchased seedlings and we would transplant them in designated beds of soil and cover them with plastic for protection from frost. They ultimately outgrew their bedding and were now ready to plant. After the fields were plowed, as straight as an artist painting a mosaic of defining lines, we planted the seedlings nurtured with fertilizer and a continual supply of water. As weeds would grow, plowing continued in a display of artistry, manicuring each row, field by field. Rows and rows, acres and acres seemingly that had no defining end. I was convinced my grandfather had the largest farm on the planet!

Grass and weeds coalescing at the tender roots of the tobacco plant loved the same environment. Weeds just as plants will produce a seed of its kind. Where they differ; weeds are born from seeds of confusion. You will never find them growing alone but in a cluster with their roots entangled. Brooding in secrecy of night they thrive on persistency conspiratorially breeding from root to root. Standing alone their survival is quite limited. They have a very prolific growth cycle; growing with haste to claim as much ground as they can. If you leave them unchecked without intervention, they will obscure light from everything in their path. That truly is an analogy to faith; blinders separating you from your faith. Weeds illuminate with a dark light casting dimly lit shadows over our understanding. They love the comfort of crowds as a network of confusion.

Conversely, plants grow from the soil of simplicity; isolated, standing apart at a distance from each other. The lives of plants are dedicated for a specific purpose without the competing interest of weeds compromising their development. Contrarily, wild seeds of weeds are complications of drama. *Drama! Drama! Drama!* Some of us live our lives obsessed with drama. It is a feeding center for negativity, jealousy and discord apparently without cause except to discredit others. Wild seeds planted in untamed fields of man's conscience act as a breeding ground for corruption. Apostle Paul described them as having a *"Fit"*. When was the last time you had one? Did you accurately judge your response or did you leave it for others to whisper in the night?

> *For I am afraid that when I come I may not find you as I want you to be, and you may not find me as you want me to be. I fear that there may be discord, jealousy, **fits** of rage, selfish ambition, slander, **gossip**, arrogance and disorder.*[1]

Plants draw their strength from solitude powered by invisible rays of the sun. Each root has an individual responsibility attached to it. During the growing cycle, their roots broaden at the base for greater strength to sustain their production. Some plants like the tomato need additional support *(a stake)* to maintain their straightness when loaded with fruit.

Have you taken time to notice plants grow vertically reaching towards the sun? But wild weeds grow in a horizontal direction searching to connect with life of their own kind. Weeds, unlike plants do not require our attention for sustainment. They are *"renegades"* existing with a high degree of resiliency. Weeds and thorns are prolific flourishing from the same nutrients as plants. If you don't deal with them early, once they gain their strength, they are very difficult to deal with.

> *"And some seed fell among thorns; and the thorns grew up and choked it, and it yielded no crop."* **Mark 4:7 NKJV**

Just as seeds of plants grow into flowering blooms, *"seeds of faith of the hearing word"* needs continual cultivation, pruning and *"de-thorning"* to replenish the expectations of faith. If given right to exist, weeds and thorns will exist in confusion; choking the word and yield a substitute of their own.

Spiritual weeds are chattering weeds of confusion; un-symphonic distortions vibrating at the root of our understanding. Unlike the symphony of faith, weeds speak with the voice of negativity in opposition to faith. To be clear; some connections we have made exist only as weeds with a competing interest to steal rewards of our faith. They often surface as a thief in the night; whispering, camouflaged in a thicket of distractions with an appearance of truth. Some weeds are adorned with deceptive power, blooming as plants and if you are not discerning, your eyes will fool you.

Our lives exist as dependent life beaming from the love of Christ. With the Word of Faith attached to our destiny, we have a responsibility to tend and guard just as Adam's commission in the Garden. God views our lives as trees for the production of faith for the yielding of fruit extrapolated from our gifting. He has given us receptive ears to maintain connectivity to His vision preserving the channels of transmission by the Word of Faith. As a cultivated Garden, our weeded conscience must be filtered. The cluttering of words symbolic of weeds, if left unfiltered has the propensity to prematurely overtake us in our faith.

> *And he shall be like a tree planted by the rivers of water, that bringeth forth his fruit in his season; his leaf also shall not wither; and whatsoever he doeth shall prosper.*
> **Psalm 1:3 KJV**

Broad Leaf of Faith

After planting the tobacco plants, thorns and weeds would appear with suffocating intentions. It demanded arduous labor which by all means was intense plowing row after row; from sun up to sun down. Between the plants, grass had to be hoed and dirt shaken from their roots exposing them to the sun eliminating any further production. With enough weeds gathered, we set them afire burning every root and seed.

Our thoughts don't always align with God's Word. Just as the burning of wild grass fumigating in the fields obstructs our vision, weeds of our conscience have the same effect arising as a cloud with enough suppressive energy to disrupt our visualizations and ability to reason. Through prayer and renewal of our mind by the *"Word of Faith"*, we can extinguish the wild fires burning in our conscience; destroying the weeds of distraction and vaporize every disruptive seed from taking root.

After hoeing and plowing were no longer necessary, the next course of action, *"topping"* was required. The topping process; clipping the top stem of the plant, made the tobacco plant spread its leaves broadly (*Broad Leaf Tobacco*) and gain a wider body rather than shooting upward. Failing to do so will cause the plant to sprout up prematurely without the support of sustainable roots. That's the same as the lives of some Believers who possess a fragility of head knowledge and not rooted and grounded in faith.

Equally, our faith should have the same topping effect as a tobacco plant. In a triangulated relationship synced with connectivity from above movement of our faith expands laterally touching the lives of others that personifies the principle of the greatest commandment; (*firstly, love God in a vertical relationship and love thy brother horizontally connected by the same standard as we love ourselves).* The promise of faith of things we believe and the investment of our hopes are centered vertically but the application of faith is a horizontal connection of our actions to do the will of God. *"It's not always the things we say but what we say and do that differentiates our obedience to faith."*

The expansion of the broad leaf of faith requires testing. A test is no different than the topping process of a tobacco plant. It will stop you in your tracks and humble your strength for a greater production of faith to evolve. Topping is intended to make good of God's promise that no temptation is allowed to proceed as an impediment to your destiny greater than your ability to handle it. I can speak from experience; your wings will get clipped if you get too high and mighty.

Temptations of life at times are provoking; giving cause to operate in defiance of God's will. Failure to adhere to the principles of faith can be compromising aborting completing our goals. But take comfort to note; you are not original. There is nothing new under the sun; decisions of yesterday are no different than the choices we have of today. They are predicated on three principles that continue as an obstruction; the *"Lust of the flesh, lust of the eyes and the pride of life."* [1]

> *There hath no **temptation** taken you but such as is common to man; but God is faithful who will not suffer you to be tempted above that ye are able; but will with the **temptation** also make a way to escape that ye may be able to bear it.*
> **1 Corinthians 10:13 KJV**

When the tobacco plants grew to about medium height, they began to bloom in blossoms of pink and white. I dreaded their growth and their attraction. You would think I would've been at awe of their concentric colors but fear replaced beauty. Bees and large green tobacco worms appeared; pollen for bees and worms with sapping power draining the plant of its nutrients. We had to pluck them off by hand one by one and they did have a bite!

After the tops were removed, the plants grew with *"suckers"* attached to the stalk. Plowing, planting, bees, worms, spiders, snakes and now suckers! By then, I was convinced I was out of my elements. I was ready to go home! It was quite depressing, pulling hundreds if not thousands of these little out-growths sprouting at each junction of leaf and stalk. This was happening at a time when the tobacco plants were producing a prolific amount of tar. Every part of my body would be covered with a dark bitter substance that had the taste of rejection. If you were not covered head to toe in the depressing heat, it was a challenge to remove the thickened accumulation from your body and clothes. We used diesel oil and old fashioned lava soap to remove the sticky deposits from our skin.

We have spiritual leeches in our churches that would rather drain you of your anointing than render a sacrifice worthy of their own faith. We need to hear God for ourselves without dependency of the gifting of others. Exhortations from others have their limits and were never meant to be a substitute for our sacrifices. If we are not careful ascertaining self reliance of faith, independently acquiring our own decisions; we could suffer consequences that have no productive life. In doing the will of God, our faith must be measured to know the limits of our expectations.

After marinating in blazing heat, the leaves are now ready for harvest. This is a process of weeks if not months depending on the cooperation of weather. At the beginning of harvest and throughout the summer, on any given Saturday morning, we all assembled in unity of faith for the task at hand. Neighbors, aunts, uncles and cousins gathered early in the morning to escape as much heat as our labor allowed. It was a cherished moment of comraderie; shaking of hands, hugs and kisses and laughter as we gathered in a seam of *"one accord"* pursuing a common goal of being our brother's keeper. It was a time of giving, sharing and embracing the bonds of love that kept us united. No egos just sacrifices of the labor of love.

Love has a compass of its own. It is magnetized to respond in one directional flow; *"Outward"*. It is as the river flowing outward from Eden passing through the center of the Garden then dividing into *"four rivers"* with tentacles supplying every outlet connected to its source. The power of love flows intricately streaming as the *"four chambers"* of a beating heart pumps blood to every organ. The *"four rivers flowing out of Eden and the four arterial chambers of the heart"* are strategically positioned responding to every demand put upon it without delay. The heart never stops beating; the river never stops flowing until it has completed its course. The veins of faith distribute life giving nutrients from its chambers continuously. Just as the Brook Cherith sustained Elijah until it dried, so will the brooks of our lives continue to flow until the finishing of our faith.

At the beginning of Saturday morning harvest, we joined together in prayer; praying for God's covenant grace of protection and bountifulness. With beating hearts joined together hand to hand, synergy of our togetherness was woven in faith to believe success waiting at the end of our labor. The bonds of fellowship were strengthened as having a communion of bread and wine being shared over a friendship of memories.

From my earliest recollection, I worked at the barn with the women who were *"stringing"* tobacco on sticks to be hung on tiers in the barn. I did not necessarily enjoy this phase because of the fast pace of *"handing"* clusters of leaves to the ladies. I wanted to be out there where the action was; in the field with the men, who were chewing tobacco, smoking cigars, laughing and telling strange jokes elevated above my understanding. I guess it was their laughter that attracted me.

Some seasons, because of crop rotation, the fields were quite a distance away from the barn which led to gaps that had a tendency to slow down the process. After handing a load of leaves from the field stringing them on sticks for the curing process; with a collective cry ringing through the air; the call for *"Bacco"* began to resonate. Truth is; the ladies were getting very impatient. They were ready to finish so they could get on with their remaining chores. Even when I was old enough to leave the barn and work in the fields, I still heard the unceremonious call whistling across the tree tops; *"Bacco, Bacco, Bacco"!* It initiated a response for immediate action; no more jokes; no more laughter!

As it relates to my faith, Bacco is a call of urgency; an undeniable call demanding an immediate response. It is a place of occupation only patience can occupy. I discovered faith, true faith, will linger in perseverance until its completed end. Perseverance personifies the endurance of waiting with patience in our expectations for the seeds of faith to blossom; *"Pressing"*, living in hope for results of faith. The experience of faith builds character, responsibility and discipline in preparation of a continual production from one season to the next.

> *Not as though I had already attained, either were already perfect: but I follow after, if that I may apprehend that for which also I am apprehended of Christ Jesus. Brethren, I count not myself to have apprehended: but this one thing I do, forgetting those things which are behind, and reaching forth unto those things which are before, I **press** toward the mark for the prize of the high calling of God in Christ Jesus.*
>
> **Philippians 3:12-14 KJV**

Farm Life

Farm life is a self-sufficient life of survival. It is a place of development of trust and simplicity of faith to believe. A farmer's life is shrouded in expectation; from one season to the next not knowing what the planted rows will yield but so is the life of faith. We sow seeds of belief with the nourishment of faith as an extension of our reliance on the promise of God's faithfulness as a reward for our labor. Performance of what He has promised to do in cooperation with our faith develops a trusting relationship. Worry has no place; it is as an *"Achilles Heel"* to faith. Worry is a place of obsession with unpredictability without a guaranteed outcome. The lessons learned from my youth were fortifying to defy worry with a resolve of patience.

For every trial there is a victory, for every sickness there is a cure, for pain and suffering there is joy which releases its hold at the rising of the sun; for poverty, the cure of compassion conquers despair and ignites the *"Everlasting"* flaming fire of love.

> *"The greatness of need is of greater value in search of fulfillment than to have had no need at all. Need is a justification for Faith."*

Need creates an urgent demand of faith. From the womb of expectancy, need accelerates creativity of our greatest thoughts. It fuels our imagination with desire to be fulfilled more than anything else. Every need has its requirements and must be prioritized with hope; initiating faith in our search for fulfillment.

Poverty

I have discovered that poverty is a concept of our perception with exception given for those in dire straits of the most basic needs; food, water, shelter, clothing, security and even love. Though depressed conditions may exist, poverty needs a comparative outside its realm of view to validate itself. As a simply analogy;

> *"The way you view things is the way you do things. You will never know you're in the midst of a forest while existing amongst the trees but stepping back; it will give form that will reshape your perception".*

In the midst of poverty you would never know you were poor unless someone told you but even then you would not be able to fathom the concept. Without clear visualization of an alternative your perceptions would remain the same. As a child, I did not know my life was consumed in poverty. I enjoyed the necessities of life in want of nothing; enjoying the comfort of peace only love can offer. As I grew older and my conscience was awakened, I discovered a level of deprivation in my surrounding; a reality of materialism; consumable things with only the temporary value as a breath of air; here today gone tomorrow.

> *While we do not look at the things which are seen, but at the things which are not seen. For the things which are seen are temporary, but the things which are not seen are eternal.* [1]

Poverty exists at varying levels. Below the median threshold to severest of deprivation, if it is allowed to exist in an isolated state away from light shining on its condition, poverty will accept disparity as a standard not knowing there is a difference. It becomes a mirror of its own reflection. Just as in darkness which has not seen the light of day, poverty can never discern similarity to something not yet revealed.

As I have traveled to many different countries, I have witnessed disparity of poverty but have also seen its contentment; a level of peace and happiness from joys of simplicity. In my discovery, I discerned some cultures had no desire to enter into a world aggregated with complexities of the burdens of materialism. The terrain of poverty has its own opportunities; a desire satisfied in its own contentment or it can invigorate a flux of aspirations seeking a venue of change.

> *Let your conduct be without covetousness; be content with such things as you have. For He Himself has said, "I will never leave you nor forsake you." So we may boldly say: "The LORD is my helper; I will not fear. What can man do to me?* [1]

> *Not that I speak in regard to need, for I have learned in whatever state I am, to be content: I know how to be abased, and I know how to abound. Everywhere and in all things I have learned both to be full and to be hungry, both to abound and to suffer need. I can do all things through Christ who strengthens me.* [2]

The life of poverty has its own speed; never in a hurry but never left behind. It has a conscience of simplicity and sincerity that can move the hands of faith. As Paul reflected, poverty is a learned condition of the heart to accept the good and bad along with the bitter and sweet. The abounding grace of God through Christ Jesus is a catapulting event that can achieve the accomplishment of faith; even our dreams for the fulfilling of life. By accepting the provisions of God's grace is a paradigm change; from dependency of the works of our hands which has no power to deliver to acceptance of faith and all the prophetic promises.

Poverty forces a demand for the highest of faith. It has a level of creativity that can take the ordinary and forgotten things in our surroundings and by faith turn water into wine. Faith lends its power to convert what God has already provided into a performance of our imagination. *"It's not what we need God to supply, but what's already in our possession His Grace provides."* There is a power embedded in our gifting to manifest beyond the point of need. Faith is simple! Existence of poverty in the midst of our aspirations reflects greater expectations we can achieve if our belief is actualized.

Poverty forces an examination of our priorities with true value we assign to the essence of life. Poverty also stands singularly upon a pillar of hope stripped of the burdensome weight of worldly attachments. Bonds of love, family, relationships and gratitude constitute freedom within one's soul from the cuffs of materialism that can become an impediment to our faith.

In a cruel way exhibiting our success of faith, I have seen people stand in judgment of the conditions of the poor as the friends of Job who descended on his demise. We often make the mistake of judging people during a season of their trials. Poverty may appear as an existence of rubble and debris or lives we perceive that has no calculated value. This should never be the determining factor what faith produces. *"Be Careful"!*

Don't judge others while on your way up; you may end up entreating their favor on your way down. Scripture says; *"Time and Chance Happens to Us All"*.

Those in poverty give more out of their need than those with much who tend to want more not given to the gift of sharing. The widow woman with two mites surrendered her whole livelihood, not by mandate but a *"sacrifice"* of greater value than giving out of one's abundance. There is no comparative to whole. Whole means yielding; full allocation and commitment of one's desire for complete comprisal of faith. Whole and absolute are synonymous; with no other recourse to consider anything existing fragmentally.

> *Jesus sat opposite the treasury and saw how the people put money into the treasury. And many who were rich put in much. Then one poor widow came and threw in two mites, which make a quadrans. So He called His disciples to Himself and said to them, "Assuredly, I say to you that this poor widow has put in more than all those who have given to the treasury; for they all put in out of their abundance, but she out of her poverty put in **all** that she had, her whole livelihood."* **Mark 12:41-44 NKJV**

Jesus summoned His Disciples to teach them a valuable lesson on the principle of faith as it relates to giving. It was a profound revelation of the audacity of sacrifice. Giving is the footprint of love when given as a sacrifice surfacing from our need, exemplifying the greatest of faith. There is no one rule that governs one's giving other than to give with an unselfish heart.

As a standard of faith, it is essential that we give to the poor which will always exist amongst us; feed the hungry, take care of our widows, give shelter to the homeless soothing their wounds with an ointment of compassion. It is telling; the rich gave and some gave much but the widow gave abundantly out of her need.

Simplicity of faith teaches that Jesus is closer to the poor and needy than those who exist in excess of need. For the humbled and meek, they cry out for an exposition of God's grace; *"Give us our daily bread!" "The Bread of God is the Bread of Abundance!"* His Bread is inclusive with sufficiency for all of our needs.

Camel People

It wasn't too long ago when the Holy Ghost was on full display in our arena of faith. Healings, miracles, signs and wonders were on exhibition in our churches, tent meetings and even on the streets. Masses were being saved, healed and delivered. It was a peek into treasures of Heaven awaiting the life of the Believer. The Anointing of the Holy Spirit paved a path for many of our elders occupying our churches today who were there to witness manifestation of revival to the likes of which I have not seen since. However, they failed to *"pass the baton"*. Maybe they are holding on to it as a souvenir. For some, the opportunity availed itself to just get out of the cold; taking a seat at the table of salvation. Many are still there, sitting; waiting on the *"by and by"!* I am elated for their deliverance but it was meant to be a beginning and not an ending.

There is a greater testimony awaiting the faith of every Believer. We need to *"Get Our House in Order"*. For some, it will take the powers of Heaven to dislodge them from their seats. They have reached a place of contentment and can't be convinced otherwise. Many traditional churches closed up shop because they lacked spiritual innovation in advocating truth as the benchmark of faith in the changing dynamics of our culture. It's time to transfer the mantle!

Not that long ago; the spiritual atmosphere in our churches shifted in the performance of *"The Anointing"* operating in our midst. It was profound adjustment due to the actions of man. Man in all of his pursuits, always finds a way to *"Mirror the Cross of Christ"* into an image of his own making; even into an image of himself! And he will not let go until Heaven pries it out of his hands. The determination of man's will is a strong force to be reckoned with. With a calloused heart of stone; he is resistant to change.

When the *"Teaching Ministries"* surfaced they began to franchise across the landscape of America. It started a movement but not the kind you think I am talking about. There was a significant decline in the actions of faith. It was a cause for some to settle in; partaking complacency of comfort food our assemblies provided. You may ask what was so wrong with that. To answer; nothing! Then what is the issue? You know as well as I do; *"The Message of Materiality!"* It was a message that hasn't gone any further than itself. Did it lead into deeper dimensions of faith or were you kept on the outskirts basking in the glow of praise? Faith without the workings of our gifts to reach the lost and hurting exist without profit. The Holy Spirit aligns our gifts indispensably to a performance of God's expectations.

After the Church adopted teaching protocols, it only managed to invoke a materialistic approach to the Gospel. They advocated a one dimensional teaching; *"The Principles of Prosperity"* as if God's grace is not sufficient enough. Our churches are inundated with prosperity seekers; seeking blessings of materiality. In lieu of pursuing experiential methods of faith; they have settled. I reference them as *"Camel People"*. It's just a transient thought not meant by any means to be condescending. *"It is easier for a camel to go through the eye of a needle than for a rich man to enter into the Kingdom of God"*[1] It should be a warning indicating that you have more than you need. If you are living in excess saddled with a beast of burden to help carry profits you accomplished in faith; you may consider a nobler cause for the good of your brethren. We have resources to eliminate poverty out of our abundance and address every need of the poor.

Don't get me twisted! There is absolutely nothing wrong with prosperity. I would be a hypocrite if I said I'm not enjoying fruits of a prosperous life. I believe it is how God intended me to live; in peace and uphold accountability of faith to also be my brother's keeper. There is no nobler cause of faith than love as it applies to keeping of our brethren. What I have is my desire for all; peace and love beyond the point of need.

The events of life have a way of shaping our reality, changing from one day to the next. Wisdom acquired from our struggles can alter our perspectives and even approach to faith. Often, we will be forced with difficult choices compelling us to dig deeper in the trenches of meditation and prayer. Our trials are meant to be teachers; things we can learn from and improve our walk of faith. But seemingly, to our detriment, the possibility of heartbreak and pain's persistency will continue to exist in the path of life's presentation.

Exposure of our treasures concealed in our hearts when the trials of life come to test our faith will reveal things we care about the most. The test of faith is an ordinary experience in the life of Believers also anyone desiring to apprehend the mantle. We must prepare ourselves for persecutions which have a tendency to separate us from any material attachment we may possess. It avails us with an opportunity to reprioritize our spiritual commitment.

Faith will challenge you at every step; not faith of materiality but faith existing in confidence of God's trust. We must be convinced in ordering of our steps; *"God will not lead us where He has not already been."* There are circumstances we may encounter specifically designed to bring us into a fuller revelation of God's plans. In truth, I have been there and so have you.

Riches can become a crippling generational power if allowed to exist without a proper understanding of its purpose. Not need; but greed! Need is an essential. Truth is, *"Greed is an obsession with the pride of life".*

"Pride is an exaggeration but greed is an extravagance; lavishing in excess beyond the point of need that can destroy your faith." Pride and greed go hand in hand complimenting each other at any expense to achieve supremacy. They ultimately can lead to a superiority complex exalting oneself beyond their *"given measure"* believing they are somebody they are not. Humility is the antidote of pride that will cause any hardened heart to bow in surrender.

Riches are seductive. They have tentacles that can entice your imagination to the extent it will induce a provocation to pursue things not inclusive in the boundary of one's faith. *"Name it, Claim it."* We've all heard that before. Scripture says many are the plans in man's heart, but only the counsel of the Lord will stand. It is very compromising devoting our energy pursing things framed in our imagination that only serve as distractions. But we must consider this truth; *"The Lord will not lend His energy to things outside the boundaries of what your faith is purposed to achieve."*

We have to ask ourselves as a qualifier of faith; are riches a premise merely to further enrich ourselves? Is it a disguise of pride to stand amongst men raising our stature higher than it already is? Then what is truth of the misgivings of riches? It's simple; *"Not sharing"!* In the distribution channels of faith we are to help those in need significantly, widows. Before my father passed, he spoke of his animate passion to take care of them. Widows are our *"Mothers, the Heart of Family"*. Family life would be decimated without their presence.

I understand we are living in a different day where the institution of family is in the midst of a revolution due to collapse of morality in our culture. Statically, single parent families constitute 16 million households with a 75% majority of women. What a morality shift in our land! Incarcerations of our youth due to broken relationships may very well have been prevented if there was dual participation of a loving mother and caring father. There are no exceptions of faith. The Book of Timothy states; *"Anyone who does not provide for their relatives specially those of his own household; he hath denied the faith and is worse than an infidel"*.[2] Selfish lives living in a community of *"Me Only"* with consideration of others deemed an inconvenience is a selfish exaggeration of pride.

Law of Moses

The Law of Moses instituted harsh penalties for sin particularly for issues of infidelity. You've heard the phrase *"it takes two to tango"*; then why was judgment only for a woman and not for the man as well? Sin is sin if it is not forced against your will. The blame game continued from the Garden of Eden through Moses' Law until fulfillment of the Law of Grace. Grace erases the penalty of sin through the power of repentance. *"The Law of Grace was not an allocation for perfection but removed the penalty for our imperfections."* Sin is sin and can be forgiven but still it is disobedience. But repetition of sin without regard of grace that covers sin is a remarkable denial of the sacrifice paid on the

Cross of Calvary for our remediation. God has not changed and His righteousness still remains the same. *"The law of grace is forgiving; Go and sin no more"*. Do not allow sin to repeat itself.

> *Now Moses in the law commanded us, that such should be stoned: but what sayest thou? This they said, tempting him, that they might have to accuse him.* **But Jesus stooped down, and with his finger wrote on the ground***, as though he heard them not. So when they continued asking him, he lifted up himself, and said unto them, he that is without sin among you, let him first cast a stone at her.* **And again he stooped down, and wrote on the ground***. And they which heard it, being convicted by their own conscience, went out one by one,* **beginning at the eldest, even unto the last***: and Jesus was left alone, and the woman standing in the midst. When Jesus had lifted up himself, and saw none but the woman, He said unto her, Woman, where are those thine accusers? Hath no man condemned thee? She said, No man, Lord. And Jesus said unto her, nor do I condemn thee: go, and* **sin no more***.*
> **John 8:5-11 KJV**

I have always contemplated exactly what did Jesus write on the ground. I believe, He encrypted a new law; saying I forgive you not as the Law of Moses written upon uncompromising tablets of stone. He wrote with *"His Finger"* in the sand of Earth; moveable with no retention power; not to be remembered from the day before. Whether by wind or rain or even the footsteps of man being washed away with the sands of time, we are not to be condemned in our carryings of the faults of yesterday. This new law was forgiving not as the law existed in the days of old adjudicated by judgments of men but it established deliverance from condemnation of the law that was encrypted on tablets of stones and scrolls of papyrus.

The inscription of Jesus writing on the sand was God's signature as a new found template for humanity. From hardness of stone to solubility moving in the heart of man, an accountability and conviction would now be judged in the conscience of man. Even though there is vulnerability in examination of our conscience, we should be truthful to ourselves and of others as not to find fault in our judgment of them. It is easy to point fingers but be reminded; *"We've all fallen short"*.

I recently returned from Las Vegas after attending my nephew's birthday celebration. It was quite an event filled with lasting memories of true fellowship. There was a collegial phrase frequenting the airway; *"What happens in Vegas stays in Vegas"*. It didn't take long to figure out why. Truthfulness and transparency are not the most appealing attributes applied to our human nature. We are full of disguises sheltering our faults somehow make believing we have none. But we must realize, just as Jesus inscribed on the ground; *"What happens in the Earth stays in the Earth with no escape of judgment from God's searching eyes"*.

After there was no one to be found who could cast the first stone, the accused woman was the only one left for a face to face encounter with Jesus. For the second time He made an inscription in the sand again with His Finger. Whatever He wrote; He was definitely not doodling. What's written on stone is permanent but sand is forgiving; soluble enough to disappear with the changing seasons of our lives. Jesus asked the woman who refused to run and hide; *"Where are your accusers? Didn't even one of them condemn you? No, Lord"!* [1] Perhaps she contemplated in answering Jesus questions with a musing thought; *"No! They all left. They had problems too"!* In truth, all of her accusers came in alone but didn't leave alone. They left with their own accuser; *"their conscience"* without a stone to cast. Revelation knowledge is a powerful agent of God's Spirit. In the mind of faith, there is a knowing that occurs in our inner man; *"to know things as God reveals; seeing as He allows us to see".*

There are things buried in our past that will surface demanding accountability. It may not be relevant to anything going on in our present life, but they are still there and people have a tendency to not forget; even though they may have been doing the same thing you were doing. If our hearts are not hardened, just as the accused woman committed actions of infidelity, we can move on delivered from thoughts of condemnation.

I found it to be rather amusing when Jesus waited to see who would cast the first stone; they all left in a generational order; *"from the oldest to the youngest".*

Response of the eldest was quick; the first in line to accept culpability. There is a Vietnamese word I learnt in Vietnam during my tenure in the war I recall using quite a lot. It was an expression when fear hits and you can't say nothing else; *"Didi Mao"* which means; *"Let me get out of here and do it fast"!* We are quick to shy away from scrutiny of the light of day bringing exposure upon us. You may say I am doing all the right things; *"I don't go to bars, I don't go to clubs, I am not running the streets, I go to Church every Sunday, so what's the problem"?* For some of us we fail to realize that it is our attitudes! Unfavorably as some of them can be, we have a tendency to harbor things in our heart not realizing they too have consequences.

The expression of attitudes usually insinuates some type of negative connotation. It's very rare when you hear compliments directed towards you of having a good attitude; that's not how that stuff works. We tend to judge people by looking through two-way mirrors. Which side are you viewing? The one reflecting as a mirror of yourself or the one in disguise of hiding; you can see them but they can't see you? Just because I can't see you in your perpetrations; it doesn't affect my vision. It only indicates success of your camouflage. I can see clearly to the extent I am never to be judged by other people's thoughts. Impressions of negativity can cast shadows upon your faith; if you allow it.

Attitudes are quite discouraging; no better than the judgment of people in how they perceive you to be. They are debasing as a mission of the flesh at every instance attempting to devalue God's investment in our lives. Attitudes are rooted in disloyalty without a commitment of trust. With reluctance, attitudes have a tendency not to embrace the good they see in you while they are masked with their own inferiorities. With a condescending persona exalted in self-pride, attitudes of some believe that their knowledge is by far superior to anything anyone could ever know. That's a clear description of a fool in waiting; waiting for their consequences to arrive.

Attitudes summarize our demeanor; our vibrations. Some refer to them as *"Vibes"*; some good, some bad. Our vibes are defined as tones we project descriptive of our mannerism. The sensitivity level of our vibrations are discernible exposing whether a person is at peace and approachable. Distorted frequencies vibrating in our inner man are quite noisy; vibrating so loud you can hear them coming. Usually we tend to avoid an encounter with them. Vibes are magnetic establishing an *"aura"* around you. We all have an aura suggestive of our character and behavior. It defines why people are attracted to certain things. What may be appealing to you may be offensive to someone else. Attractions are mutually consenting bonded in commonality of a shared interest.

Masking of our inferiorities does indeed affect how we communicate. Jealousy, pride, envy and arrogance just to name a few are identifiable characteristics of a descending attitude. Even resentment reflective of our own shortcomings and expectations are antagonistic towards fulfilling our goals. Stooping to the level of our inferiors is quite condescending. It may not be so easy to adjust our personality but our attitudes can surely change. *"For as he thinketh in his heart so is he"*.[1] If our actions are in violation of God's Word, our hearts will be judged accordingly. Every thought framed in our imagination has suspicious intentions until acted upon; even thoughts emanating from our conscience. Our thoughts and our conscious will be subjected to scrutiny by the Holy Spirit's surveillance. He knows our thoughts before we even act upon them.

Our hearts are no more than *"retention centers"*. As a legislator; whatever is retained in our heart frames the foundation of our conscience which is no different than inscriptions written upon tablets of stone. Heart and stone serve the same purpose but with a different protocol indicative of the process God has chosen to judge our actions. In the dispensation of grace, God's acceptability is no longer determined by itemizations on etchings of granite but by freedom of expressions of our attention to faith. What's written on stones is on stones forever recorded but in the migrating heart of man, obedience is *"judgeable"* by movement of our faith in our efforts to accomplish the will of God.

Choice is freedom and our right to choose based on our perceptions of truth. When truth emerges in our conscience it becomes the standard that governs our morality and hopefully institutes a level of faithfulness to satisfy God's true intentions. Just as the accused woman; whatever we may have done can be remedied without the lasting consequences of guilt just as Jesus told the accused woman when she stood transparent before Him; *"She said, No man, Lord. And Jesus said unto her, neither do I condemn thee; go and sin no more."*[1] But be reminded; God will not be mocked in His correction of us! The skirt of our pretentiousness will be lifted up for the world to see! Although our pride may suffer, He will not allow us to go unchecked.

Yesterday

While reconstructing imaginations of yesterday, I was drawn into a power longing for simplicity. By comparison to today's reality, the life of yesterday may appeared to have been stagnant, void of elation and pleasures compared to the fast changing paradigm of today's society. With paved streets of cement cluttered with cars in a hurry going nowhere fast; flashing lights pulsating at every corner; order and control of the minutest details restricting exhibition of the simplest freedom; impersonal communications from neighbor to neighbor, they all paint a picture of how isolated and artificial our lives have become.

Today's reality has created a demand for faith that's centered in vanity; perishable things that have no redeeming value than a breath of exhaling air. Even though I enjoyed the simple things of yesterday, there was never an indictment of inactivity of my faith. The accumulation of abundance can be compromising, robbing you of a deeper experience in the depths of faith. The burden of materiality is very infectious and prolific enough to sway our hearts from things we truly believe. As the captured *"Breath of God"* spoken from time beginning; faith exhibits the passion of our beliefs stimulated by our affection in seeking the Heart of God for revelation of His judgments only He can provide.

Comparatively, the modernization of today's Church reflects how much our values have changed. The use of technology has supplanted the platform reserved for independence of the Holy Spirit's performance. It is apparent that we've reached the point of resignation of our dependency on the gifts of the Holy Spirit to the extent that we are unable to access power needed for an *"evidential performance secured in our gifts"*.

Faith is the life we live but we are judged by the things we do. The hearing of faith is so necessary but it's only a source of empowerment providing us with the tools to *"Do the work God instructs us to do"*. Work is an occupation; a performance of what we know. The Anointing is ever-present accessible to every Believer but we are failing in our need of a deeper experience of faith accomplished by the abiding influence of the Holy Spirit's Presence. There aren't any exceptions for our reluctance to pursue His power. But be advised; we will be held accountable for our inability to manifest the performance of God's agendas.

Technology was never meant to be a substitute for access to the portals of prayer but it provides a means to deliver what we have secured in prayer. Technology allows us to touch and agree but requirement of our presence is imperative to deliver results implemented by our gifts. Our gifts are beyond recall. We've become very sophisticated moving further away from simplicity of the Gospel. It is not that complicated nor should be considered burdensome. Being truthful, there is much wisdom to be acquired and a deeper understanding in the application of how it empowers our lives. How can you touch my life without a commission of energy to heal the blind, make a lame man walk or open a deaf ear? That power is the *"Holy Spirit's Anointing"* and there will never be a surrogate. His Anointing is the supreme power of God delegated for a performance of every Word proceeded out of the Mouth of God. He is the Helper of our faith to perform the works of God.

Trust is an acquired action attached to our faith. It indicates reliance on the Words God have given us to believe. Existing above what faith alone can produce, trust anchors our belief giving cause for obedience and willingness to accept God's solutions. In the trusted channels of faith, God's integrity is paramount! His thoughts are perfect deliberations of His intentions.

"God's thoughts are superlative!" Attributes of His Existence are reflected in our thoughts conforming to His as an expression of His life living within us. It's a reflection of holiness as the transformational power of the Holy Spirit converts our lives from the dualistic motivations of flesh vs. spirit into a sole subsidiary *"completely comprised of His instructions"*. It is not term life as our decisions may change but whole life founded upon the premise of faith resonating in our belief of every Word God has promised. Holiness is

God's pure conscience incapable of any dissections. He is the completed end of our faith fulfilling His justice and faithfulness to deliver a performance of those things He has said. In the words of my dearly departed father; *"What God has for you is for you. He is your Father and you are His child and He hears the voice of your cry."* It's crying time; we need a touch from above!

In tribute to my mother; I am constantly reminded of a song she would always sing; *"I will trust in the Lord, I will trust in the Lord until the day I die"*. And she did; all the way to her grave and beyond. I always could recognize the season she was in by the songs she would sing. Sometime she would sing because she was happy other times you could hear the flirtations of burdens through her song. Around the house as she was doing her daily chores, she always had a song in her spirit. They were love songs serenaded before the Throne of a King who had dominion over her throne.

Whatever is constituted in our belief will invigorate the patterns of faith that will determine our success. If we believe, truly believe and accept the unadulterated teachings of Christ without the ambiguous appealing of our senses but with full reliance on the Holy Spirit's guidance; we can accomplish all God requires of us to do with a compelling testimony validating His approval of our actions of faith.

Where Healers Fail   12

"For the Word of God is living and powerful, and sharper than any two edged sword, piercing even to the division of soul and spirit, and of joints and marrow, and is a discerner of the thoughts and intents of the heart." [1]

Healing is the children's bread; the bread of redemption. With purchasing power greater in value than the riches of Solomon's gold or Queen of Sheba in all her glamour and fame, healing has power to restore and mend the seams of suffering and pain so often frequenting our lives. Whether our battles are spiritual, natural or whether from a myriad of circumstances emerged from *"the crisis of faith"*; healing is a performing influence that addresses every sphere of our existence.

Healing is so precious if we only had the presence of faith to believe. In the proven strength of God, power of the Holy Spirit is released through the workings of faith turning our defeats into a victorious testimony testifying of His good and perfect will. How many souls would have given all their wealth, fame and fortune for the priceless gift of life healing provides to restore breath yearning to continue?

We are God's healers in the Earth with delegated power to bring everything under our subjection. We have authority as kings with a dominion of governance over a Kingdom dependent on the gifts invested in our faith. Our world is in so much turmoil with an internal cry of desperation yearning for connection to power our presence provides. Cries from waning and pining can be heard emanating from *"the ruins of faith"* for emergence of the *"True Sons of God"* to take their rightful place to avenge wickedness that has seduced our imagination. The stronghold of perversion and transgression in defiance of God's laws has caused our land to withhold its yield. By our permissiveness, we've allowed our walls to decay as we sit perched upon the pillars of compromise in the valley of betwixt opinions.

Healing is God's Solution

Healing is an engagement of our faith to render God's solution for sickness, disease and a multiplicity of afflictions. Along our journey, there will always be encounters greater than our ability to resolve. There will be times we cry out seeking relief only to discover God's judgment has not *"yet"* connected with our faith. If we are patient in our pursuit for answers, we will discover results our faith is purposed to produce.

There is no variance in God neither a shadow of turning. He is the same today as He was yesterday, never changing and always can be found at the same place where we first encountered him; at the Altar *"prostrated in prayer"*. It is the place where we cried for the mercy of God to be gracious and kind. Whether in the midst of thunder, earthquakes or the stillness of the wind, our yielding souls connected to His listening ear and He heard our cry. God will never fail us nor will He forsake us. He knows all about us and is no further a distance from us than the *"reach of prayer"*.

The principle for healing is simple even though it continues to elude us. The challenge is still the same; we should be able to turn water into wine and deliver visible results of our faith. The optimism of faith is centered in our belief which we can *"extract the surety of God's promises with the same delegated power of His Creativity."* God's hand is never shortened He can't reach us nor His power weakened He can't touch us. Despite turbulence, rushing winds and waves of angry seas, His Omnipotence is the invincibility of our faith.

When was the last time you called upon *"The Lord"* and He healed you? Was it instantaneous? Did you see confirming results of your dilemma? Or did the tasking of perseverance purposed to produce character in your waiting cause you to waver? Periodically, the search for healing can lead to fanaticism by seeking remedies not conceived in your faith. Becoming frantic displaces courage for patience needed to *"wait on the Lord"*. An encounter with courage delineates the audacity of faith invariably challenging every part of your constitution.

To become frantic is a discouragement of patience. It will open the door for anxiety that is rooted in fear. Healing begins within the heart of faith and needs time for patience to do its perfect work.

"There is no separation of the Holy Spirit's power within you and power God invested in you. They are one in the same of God's ability to heal you"! It is by the same Spirit of Heaven's power connected within the nucleus of your being you can experience greater achievements of faith. Faith will never separate you from what you believe but will extend its influence as a recognizing agent of God's promises transforming your weakness into strength.

If we would truly apprehend this principle, we could accomplish what Jesus has given us power to do for ourselves. We could feed five thousand from five loaves and two fish; calm travailing seas and quiet the storms of our fanaticisms and fears; or turn water into wine by the maturation of faith using what He has already released into our spirit. In the natural, this may seem impossible, but we need to discover the maturity of faith born of God's Spirit residing within us.

As a rule, it is imperative we see faith through the eye of belief. It requires submission to a cause greater than ourselves; a life inundated with God's Spirit that gives us power to live in His Spirit. It is then we can walk by faith knowing our footsteps have been ordered in God's designated path. The revolutionary energy of the *"Holy Spirit Residing Within Us"* is an allocation to distribute His influence surrounding our lives.

Because of the obedience of Jesus, the power of Heaven came to dwell not just amongst us but also dwell within us as a living dynamo; *"The Anointing"*. When the curtain of Heaven was rent in two invitation of His Spirit was released with unanimity of power to anyone who would accept His Grace. *"Dunamis is the Holy Spirit's power of His Internal Presence"* given to the converted life of every Believer.

> *Whoever believes in me, as Scripture has said out of his belly shall flow rivers of living water.* **John 7:38 KJV**

> *As for Me, says the* LORD, *"This is My covenant with them: My Spirit who is upon you, and My words which I have put in your mouth, shall not depart from your mouth, nor from the mouth of your descendants, nor from the mouth of your descendants' descendants," says the* LORD, *"from this time and forevermore."*
> **Isaiah 59:21 NKJV**

What's in you will flow out of you with power to change everything around you. As a Prophet of Faith, I have *"witnessed"* sovereign acts of God performed out of my stillness as an expression of His ability to do what I could not do for myself. But I have also seen experiential power of His Spirit working through me as an extension of His Creativity connected to my gifting.

Out of the purity of our thoughts we are vested with the ability to speak healing from within and command a performance of faith that can alter the outcome of our circumstances into the richness of a testimony. Yet there are battles in our stillness God chooses to exercise His sovereign ability as the only Omnipotent power ruling the Heavens. He will never allow us to rise above *"His Greatness"*. Neither will He allow the usurping nature of the intentions of pride elevated in man's imagination to distribute power when He has not appropriated it. Without the assignment of God's Anointing, unquestionably you will receive the same treatment as the Pharisees; *"Physician, heal thyself."*

Dualistic Kingdoms

As Believers, our existence is dualistic comprising of two kingdoms; Kingdom of Heaven and the Kingdom of Earth. The Kingdom of Heaven is spiritual; the true life living within us but our outer house is a composite of Earth fueled by breath of God's living soul.

Flesh standing on its own has no conscience of its existence. It is evidenced in every cemetery we see; empty vessels with souls withdrawn left for Earth to reclaim with no life to continue. The dead doesn't exist amongst us though there are dead men walking in our midst without eyes to see and the response of ears to hear. Flesh is the product of dead things dependent on an internal power to sustain its existence from the source of life giving blood flowing through our veins.

There is no difference in Heaven above and God's Heavenly Spirit occupying our hearts. The Holy Spirit is the same Spirit that was with God in His beginning. He is the active power of Trinity bringing the Presence of Heaven into our midst. Must we continue to deny Heaven's Existence when His Spirit came to possess our souls? I am convinced if we dig a little deeper; we will tap into true purity of God's power enabling His gifts to manifest as never before. We have been lacking a closer exposure to the power of His Presence that is radicalized only in prayer. Because of our dogmas, perceptions and suggestions of truth, we are further alienating our submissions from provisions intended to amplify His Presence so central to our faith.

> *In this manner, therefore, pray: Our Father in heaven, Hallowed be Your name. Your kingdom come. Your will be done, On earth as it is in heaven.* **Matthew 6:9-10 NKJV**

God does not rule in our hearts at a distant apart from us. We can apprehend Him at the end of every thought, every action by His Spirit living within. Truly *"God is a Spirit!"* Why continue making concessions fabricating that His Spirit is somehow different than *"His Eternal Presence"* streaming from above bringing Heaven within our reach? Don't get it twisted! I am not advocating doctrines of new age mysticism but more than anything else appealing to your senses. The Spirit of God is the *"Holy Spirit; God's Spirit living within us"*. There is a Heaven above! Convergence of His Presence emanating from above and the Holy Spirit personifying Presence occupying our hearts are equally validating.

The persistent cry of the Holy Spirit is in search for supremacy as the ruling authority connecting God's life with ours to establish the Kingdom of Heaven in every corridor of the heart of man. When our minds are renewed and our thoughts supplanted for His, our conscience will be reshaped reflective of an Image born of His desire. His eternal love shed abroad in our hearts will spark the fire of faith to manifest a power that's been prophesied for two thousand years to do greater works through the *"collectivity of faith"*. As we prep our mantle invigorated by prayer to adorn our garments with power from above, it will instigate an anointing streaming with life flowing from within to complete every assignment God has purposed for us.

Where Healers Fail

Healing is a corrective power; a power delivering peace spoken to raging seas and disruptive winds that has brought so much disorder into our lives. I often pondered in my spirit of my inadequacies when the demand for healing encounters my faith. It remains a puzzling scenario of my understanding of *"why we make exceptions of faith"*. The foundation of my belief is pillared upon the premise; *"Because God says it is so; I can lay hands on the sick and they shall recover!"* But somehow truth of His promise, at times elude me. Jesus didn't heal all. He didn't empty every hospital ward of those suffering in pain.

God's Word is a constant but our faith quite often succumbs to variability, not always connecting to the power center of belief. It lends credence to the question of *"Where healers fail"*. With a deficiency centered in our motivations, we are failing in our commitment and execution delivering results of faith. Have we invested our trust in man more than we ought? God is the giver of all gifts and we should never think more highly than we ought of the personalities of men believing they have power above their measure to deliver what God has not provided. God's energy is radicalizing. If you ever encounter it you will be changed; visibly changed identifiable by every action of your being.

There are times we vacillate in pursuit of healing seeking answers from those who do not have power to give. We run to and fro in our query and can't find lasting solutions to our dilemma. Written in the Book of James; when the burden of our afflictions exceeds the limits of our faith, we are to call on the elders of the Church who are coalesced in belief to deliver God's healing solutions and He will use whoever He chooses.

Without immediate solutions in our pursuit of faith, it can become very discouraging if we fail to acquire answers we relentlessly are seeking. If we waver in weariness of our struggles, we could resolve to accept a counterfeit solution that lacks power to deliver upon God's promises. God has provided us with wisdom of discernment to know the difference by directing our steps into a *"Knowing"* secured from fear and unbelief. We are to be very careful who we allow to speak into our lives. Itching ears can be compromising with a vulnerability to seductive influences *(Familiar Spirits)* that have already mastered your need.

The Solitary Place

Find your closet in the friendliness of darkness and make it your daily retreat. The most precious treasure you will ever possess is awaiting your arrival. It is a place of stillness conferencing with reverberation of God's Spirit as the only voice you will hear. From the chambers of solitude endeavoring connection with seeking souls, from a repository of our own belief we can awaken faith even in the lives of others.

> *Now in the morning, having risen a long while before daylight, He went out and departed to a solitary place; and there He prayed. And Simon and those who were with Him searched for Him. When they found Him, they said to Him, "Everyone is looking for You."* **Mark 1:35-37 NKJV**

In intimacy of the morning hour, the closet of faith invites us into solitude of surrender waiting to explore possibilities of faith looming in our expectations. Many of our solutions can be found searching early in the morning light; pressing Heaven's Gate for grace and mercy to connect with our lives. Every new day has its own challenges; some carried from the day before with perplexities only to be discovered in the light of day that awaits us. Faith is simple but our circumstances can be compounded from one day to the next that can dampen our hope of recovery.

The solitary place is a place of singleness separated from the pressings of those seeking to connect with our faith. With a greater frequency, migration of our faith is targeted for the lives of others as a vehicle of compassion delivering its goods at every flag waved on our road of destiny. Simon told Jesus; *"Everyone is looking for you; everyone wants a piece of you."* If we're not careful we can easily exhaust ourselves of power only to receive a diminished return of our investment. We all have been given a measure of faith but it must be maintained to be an effective source to accomplish the demands put upon the activity of our gifts. If our hands are weakened in the heat of battle the reservoir of strength immersed in our faith can be depleting in our efforts to do the work required of us. As vessels of light abounding in faith, we need a continual supply of oil to fuel our flickering flames. Scripture says; *"if you faint in the day of adversity your strength is small"*.[1] In our engagements fighting the good fight of faith power flowing through our lives must be replenished.

In doing the work of ministry at times can be very exhausting when we have committed ourselves to do as God intended. When we find ourselves depleted in desperate need of rejuvenation, it may require that we seek collaboration with those connected to our faith to carry us until our strength returns. There will always be opportunities where faith seeks to draw from our lives for the sake of others. Collaboratively, it would be much better if we are not dependent on our own strength but work in unison with a woven strength of power that only our togetherness can bring.

> *On the same day, when evening had come, He said to them, "Let us cross over to the other side." Now when they had left the multitude,* ***they took Him along in the boat as He was****. And other little boats were also with Him. And a great wind storm arose, and the waves beat into the boat so that it was already filling.* [2]

Seeing that we are our brother's keeper; we should follow the example of the Disciples; *"They took Him along in the boat as He was."* Our ability to accept the burdens of others is characteristic of our strength. We who are strong ought to bear the infirmities of the weak but our strength must be resolute, emboldened and quickened in our stance against any defiance of the enemy's attempt to prevail over our faith.

It is a given; your battles of yesterday will follow you as an antagonism of your hopes and dreams. Seemingly they resurface at the most inopportune time; from all appearances when peace and tranquility has settled in. There are times, we may have thought we have conquered the demons lurking in our path but they reappear with a vengeance driving our faith to the limits. It follows the principle of a house swept cleaned but when the enemy returns, he has gained mastery over our victories further fortifying himself in a confluence of strength. May I suggest before crossing over to the other side; renew your strength. There are greater contentions ahead that could render your faith in jeopardy with greater consequences.

Every new day is born with its challenges; some carried from yesterday that has not met its resolve; some yet to be discovered with no indication of the solutions they will require. To achieve the merits of faith requires refueling to maintain its effectiveness in a stance of unshakeable belief. After you have done all you can do; *"Stand"*. While you are still standing; *"Don't move."* You cannot do both at the same time.

Standing in faith is the precursor of a life of walking in the Spirit. It is imploring that we do as Jesus did; *"Find a place of rest to renew your strength"*.

The Divine Light of the Holy Spirit is a lamp aglow that can search through any storm brewing in our lives. At night when our physical man is resigned from the contest of a day's venue, opportunities of faith will beckon at our door. God's Spirit will awaken us with a new assignment of faith; illuminating as a mirror of His reflection upon our imagination from visions and dreams discovered in the night. Often it is the perfect idea of God we discover in a night's journey that needs the Light of His Revelation to unveil secrets immersed in our faith. The Holy Spirit will refresh memories of our secret rendezvous of a nights encounter and take you where your spirit has traveled. For some, it is simply called *"Déjà Vu"* without consciousness that it is the Light of God they encountered.

Divine Umbilical

Recently, I visited with a friend whom I hadn't seen in quite some time. She told me she was in the midst of a pregnancy. While visiting with her, I noticed she had a serious craving for ice cream. I mean lots of ice cream! As I sat there, I pondered on the thought of creation occurring in her womb. I know she was eating a lot but I knew she was not just eating for herself. There was another life inside of her who was sharing her consumption; even the consumption of love. Love is consuming always in search of continual fulfillment.

While riding home, the thought came to me of how food was being shared between the two. Imaginatively, I visualized an umbilical extending from Heaven that was attached to my abdominal cavity. The thoughts were quite lucid but true in the sense to consider they portrayed an accurate image defining my spiritual connection to the nursery of Heaven.

The *"umbilical"* is simply a conduit instrumental in transferring nutrients to sustain life developing in the womb of a woman. It is relational meaning that it is an established relationship developed between the mother and embryo. At the instance of birth, the umbilical cord is severed with no more dependent life the womb provided. However, dependency still continues beyond the womb until a level of maturity is reached when the child can sustain on its own.

Connection of the umbilical is a *"onetime"* event we all experienced. It indicated the beginning of a new season in preparation to embrace a world waiting for our arrival. Severing of the umbilical was a catapulting event launching us into a path pre-determined in our secret beginnings. There would be no reconnecting; the time of return had since past. Across the spectrum of life, the only shared life we took from the womb is a distribution emanating from the fountain of love. It is a love that continues well beyond the time when we were offered to the world while in pursuit of our destiny.

Attachment of God's umbilical established a divine relationship developing in the womb of faith. Immersed in privacy of our secret beginnings, there is a level of suspicion in the developmental stages of life. It is the same as a seed planted in the Earth not knowing what it will yield until coming forth to embrace the light. The umbilical of nature and the spiritual lifeline securing our lives are paralleling events. Where they differ; once severed as a onetime event the day of our conversion, we were born into a new world. But through the Holy Spirit's connection from Heaven above, our spiritual lifeline is reattached to the veins of faith as a *"lifetime"* event permanently connecting our lives to the placenta of *"Heaven's Supply"*.

The *"placenta of faith"* connected to the core of our belief provides essentials needed to construct a pliable heart sensitive to the demands of faith. The placenta is a filter eliminating unnecessary distractions forming in our conscience. As blood is exchanged through the lifeline of faith, the stirring of life is invigorated. The purified blood of Jesus sacrificed on *"The Cross"* was a placenta of redeeming life. By divine connection, we are brought into oneness of *"The Cross"* with our Heavenly Father who facilitates the needs of faith. The Cross of Christ is a connection from Heaven above to our yielding hearts below; yearning as a young bird with mouth open wide to receive life from our Father above. With our mouths opened panting for fulfillment, He promised He would fill it!

The Holy Spirit is a living organism of spiritual life that pulsate the life of God throughout our chambers. As an extension of God's life connecting with our lives; His life now becomes our life sharing together as one.

Do you remember Jacob's dream; the laddered stairsteps that extended from Earth to Heaven? It was a lifeline! With angels ascending and descending upon those laddered steps is indicative of our prayer life. When we consistently pray; pray without ceasing for God's entrustment, He will answer with confirmation He has heard our pleadings in the form of answers.

Years ago, I ventured out to work in the fishing grounds of the Bering Sea. It was a memorable time that is very difficult to forget. During that time, I lived in Seattle and accepted a job on a fishing boat that was headed to Alaska. You may have heard of the show; *"The Deadliest Catch"*; they were not the first. I did not realize what everything would entail or what remarkable events awaited me. I was informed when the boat arrives at Dutch Harbor, I was to meet them.

With a ticket in my hand, I flew to Kodiak, Alaska for connection to my final destination. The only access to the fishing grounds was by plane; not just any plane but a *"sea plane"*. Any of you who have a fear of flying; this would be your worst nightmare. I boarded the plane in Kodiak headed for the sea. As if the flight wasn't intimidating enough, as we descended through the clouds, a ship appeared in the middle of the Bering Sea; in the middle of nowhere. As the pilot circled the ship; it then dawned on me; this was my destination. It was a converted freighter ship made into a floating processing plant positioned in the midst of troubling waters. For all the fishermen, this was an easier way to unload their goods without returning to the dock.

The plane landed in a surge of cresting waves and continued to drift toward the side of the ship. A small skiff the size of a rowboat came to welcome me. In my mind I was thinking; *"Lord what have I got myself into! This is unreal"*. The waters were unsteady with waves rocking from side to side as I looked up and discovered a greater challenge. They had lowered a rope ladder from the side of the ship which was the only way to get onboard. Wow; I had to climb the ladder! Every step was a step of fear; fear of the water; fear of what was waiting on the other side. The ladder provided access to everything I needed for the journey ahead. It was a transfer point to acquire provisions to take on the boat waiting my arrival docked to the other side of the ship. After I gathered myself and collected my provisions, it was time to descend to explore the depth of the sea in search of a bounty that would justify all of my fears. Again on a ladder rope but this time a shorter one.

I have to admit coming down was a lot easier than going up. If you did it once; you can do it twice. Going up has its challenges but coming down is a signature of achievement. I realized, the very thing that I feared was what I needed; *"a ladder; an umbilical connecting me to my destiny"!* My confidence grew in my repeated steps encountering the ladder every time the boat came to dock. My experience reminded me of Jacob's dream; as my prayers went up in the midst of my fears; the blessings continued to come down again and again. God will never fail us when He is perfecting us to move beyond our fears for a greater reward of faith!

Sacrifice of Prayer

Achievements of prayer will manifest as evidence of our private encounters with the Holy Spirit well in advance of being publicly displayed. Without a devoted prayer life, we lack the power of bringing results in our search for healing. *"Prayer is the key to unlocking the door of Heaven bringing us closer to our victories."*

The transformational Presence of the Holy Spirit encountered in prayer is life changing converting our ears as receptors of God's Prophetic Words. Seeing through the eye of faith, our eyes will coalesce as an eye within an eye to discern revelation of His Presence. Our tongue will have the creativity as Elijah's faith; our hands transformed as instruments of war bending the strongest of bronze and brazen steel.

Faith in prayer is a trodden path of certainty that always delivers an outcome proven in the intimacy of a hidden life. Why healers fail can be concluded as a *"systemic depravation of prayer"*. The solitary place for communion needs to be cultivated to connect with passion centered in faith. Passion is fire that fuels the burning of love. It exudes as an invisible hand with fingers as tentacles; reaching, stretching for a love that seeks not its own but fills every thirsty soul searching for replenishment. Love is a fanning flame of power that becomes increasingly stronger in the growing of faith attesting to a greater love yet to be encountered.

The premise for maintaining the strength of faith is a *"lifestyle of unceasing prayer"*. Prayer is synonymous with *"Sacrifice"*. The sacrifice of prayer dictates that we should pray when we are commanded to pray just as Job when enlisted to pray for his friends; praying in the midst of threat and danger as Paul and Silas being locked away in prison; praying when it's time to bear our cross with a burden that outweighs our strength. The relational aspect of prayer delivers an Anointing unequal to any subservient natural power.

Quiet Hands

In confidence and quietness is our strength. It comes as an assured action of our belief to move in a subtle determination of faith. The widowed woman with the *"issue of blood"* sought out Jesus as the only solution remaining in her pursuit for healing. As she waited in the wings of an endless search, she stealthily moved in a crowd for a secret encounter with faith. Her determination was seeded in humility; transparently existing above variability of doubt and unbelief.

> *Now a certain woman had a issue of blood for twelve years, and had suffered many things from many physicians and had spent all that she had and was no better, but rather grew worse. When she heard about Jesus, she came* **behind** *Him in the crowd and touched His garment. For she said, "If only I may touch His clothes, I shall be made well."* [1]

After twelve long years of seeking, exhausting all of her resources by the hands of man, she encountered grace at the cost of sacrifice. It was a radical move but when all else had failed she did what we all will do at some point in our journey; cry out as we have never cried out before. At times the presentations of life will invoke inquiries for settlement but with an undeniable determination, we will ultimately connect to that place where our sacrifices will yield the reward of faith.

The sacrifice of believing that produced the miracle of faith is a sacrifice that says; *"If I can."* Have you ever been there? I most certainly have! More often than not, afflictions have a tendency to rob us of our strength depleting our mobility to even access the portal of faith. My mother before she journeyed home made a remarkable statement. She said; *"If you don't have health, you have nothing left to service your gifts."* When our lamps begin to diminish in power and our sight to see the trimming of our wick, faith will yield a greater resolve to embrace peace and rest from the weariness of our battles.

Our failures do not always stem from a lack of faith but customarily, it is the impediment at the root of our inner life; the life of belief. Belief is the eye sight of faith requiring *"uni-focal"* vision with precision just as a periscope in search of its target. Jesus said;

> *"Whosoever shall say to **this** mountain be thou removed and cast in the sea but **believe** in his heart and shall not doubt."* [1]

The possibility of success is born in our belief and speaks with the pleading voice of hope; *"If I can touch the hem of His Anointing"*. Often in pursuit of healing our belief is challenged because of clouds appearing casting shadows over our expectations. Belief precedes faith but hope exists as a conduit to resources needed to fuel our projections. Belief is settling but volatility of restlessness, anxiety and wavering can conquer any attempt of gaining success in our battles.

Hope has a looming presence instigating faith but can easily drift with the winds of uncertainty causing doubt as an obstruction to things we truly believe. Hope is buoyancy of the threshold of faith keeping our expectations from sinking into doubt and unbelief. As the widow woman persisted in her search for healing, despite peculiarity in an uncommon pursuit of faith; she expressed hope exceeding the boundary of denial. She had a determination in her confession of faith as an extension of her belief; *"I will be made whole."*

The quiet hands of faith that touched the hem of Jesus' garment were disguised in hope; hidden in a crowd of seekers pursuing the same thing as her; His attention! In some of our greatest battles, we tend to disguise our faith from crowds seemingly when there is a void in our expectations. Hope then will reappear as a blurred attraction but also provide a protective hedge over our faith. Hope can exist simultaneously while an internal fire of faith may be burning within consuming every ounce of belief we may have.

Life is a journey filled with unexpected detours and turns. It's a one-way street not knowing where or when it will end. Obstructions can alter our path consuming time and energy designated to complete our course.

There are no exits to turn around only a rest stop for an opportunity to refuel. Time for refueling may be far and in between and not so accessible while competing on the freeway of faith. At times we may be running out of fuel burdened with the hope to continue on in our journey. Hope will begin to speak; *"If I can just make it to the refueling station"?* But belief speaks with the voice of affirmation; *"When I get there I will have enough to complete my course".* That's the positivity of faith; just letting me get there fulfills all that I hope for believing that through my faith, God will do the rest. Hope is indicative of the expectations of faith that says; *"If I can"* touch the hem of His garment; but true as well belief is a determined outcome that also speaks with the voice of positivity; *"I will be"* made whole.

> *Immediately the fountain of her blood was dried up, and she felt in her body that she was healed of the affliction. And Jesus, immediately knowing in Himself that power had gone out of Him, turned around in the crowd and said, "Who touched My clothes?" But His disciples said to Him, "You see the multitude thronging You, and You say, 'Who touched Me?'"*
>
> *And He looked around to see her who had done this thing. But the woman, fearing and trembling, knowing what had happened to her, came and fell down before Him and told Him the whole truth. And He said to her, "Daughter,* **your faith has made you well***. Go in peace, and be healed of your affliction."* [1]

In some of our battles that have persisted over time, we tend to hide behind a deceit of smiles struggling to maintain an appearance of strength though our hearts may be heavily weighed down in a cloud of confusion. At times our faith requires a stealthy approach that does not broadcast fear and desperation attaching to our need but advances reverently in confidence in our search of an undeniable promise.

The gathering of crowds has a commonality; they all are seeking the same thing; *"Solutions"* exceeding their abilities. Crowds can be so unforgiving, relentless and will disregard you in a selfish search of their own. The Pool of Bethesda was a venue for healing but if you weren't careful, you could have been trampled in a rush to encounter *"God's Healing Angel"*. Starting out you may have had only one problem in your search to encounter God's Healing Angel but because of your vulnerabilities, you returned with a greater contention; bruises of disappointment further diminishing any hope of healing. In times of desperation, pejorative of crowds can be an impediment and quite disparaging.

When the widowed woman heard about Jesus, she came **behind** Him in the crowd believing and touched His garment not knowing her faith had preceded her. Jesus discerned power released from the virtue of His Mantle by a soft touch of faith concealed from His sight. The touch from behind was an action of humility when connected with faith delivered an anointing with power to reconcile all of the impediments hindering her victory. The touching of His garment put faith on alert for an exhibition. The widowed woman believed if she could but touch the Mantle of Jesus she would encounter an anointing to heal her desperations.

Typically our private battles are reserved for private solutions sequestered in our own belief. Discouraging voices can rob us of our faith. Voices of unbelief will echo as voices of fear like Saul and the people of Israel when David confronted the threats from the giant of the Philistines who looked upon him with disdain. There are times when faith must be defended just as David responded to his brother Eliab with boldness of faith; *"What have I now done? Is there not a cause?"* [1]

Submission is the key to the performance of prayer when we submit our lives as a sacrificial offering cast on the burning Altar of Faith. There is only *"One"* who has power to heal and deliver and His solutions are not ours to determine the when and how of things. God could assign visitation of His angels or as written in the Book of Psalm; *"He sent His Word and healed them and delivered them from their destruction."* [2]

Jesus asked a question that you and I may have encountered in pursuit of faith when we believed to see actualization of a promise; *"Who touched Me?"* Could it have been you? Did you pursue Jesus in silhouette, shadowed in a crowd of circumstances in the disguised possibility of faith? The world does not need to see your tears; nor need to know all of your struggles. They will never know you even had a problem until the release of faith produces evidences of its completion just as Jesus asked; *"Who touched Me?"*

"I can imagine as she was glowing in the excitement of faith testified; It was me Lord, only Me! I am the one who suffered for twelve long years; I've suffered many things by the hands of many physicians; physicians of medicine and physicians of faith who had no connectivity to the wisdom and power flowing from your Mantle. Your Mantle is Your Power; Your Power delivers the promise of faith."

*"Daughter, **your faith has made you well**. Go in peace, and be healed of your affliction."* [1]

In our private encounters faith needs uncovering as an effective testimonial of God's healing power. The words *"who touched me"* is intended to put on display the privacy of faith in our secret movements testifying of God's power for the world to see. Faith harbors our testimonies reverberating with the voice that says; *"I am the one that's been touched"*. The knowing of faith is in the evidence it produces. Even without physical manifestations. *"Faith is a harbinger of the promise of faith forecasting as evidence of the surety of God's Word."*

The true power of God's Anointing is attached to His approval of our submissiveness just as the woman with the issue of blood bowed in surrender at the feet of Jesus. It was an encounter of audacity marveling at such greatness of faith. Our eyes at times are crazy and do not know the true depth of their perception; but love does. Love not only sees; it feels and can touch comforting our lives as well as those who cross our path. In our surrender there is no end to love as it seeks unification in the consciousness of faith.

At times, before healing can be realized, fractures we encounter in pursuit of faith need to be mended. Healing is not always instant. For some of us, we've been crying out for years; *"Lord take this cup from me"*! Have you considered God can give you the length of days to outpace your affliction? The result of bad choices we've made in earlier days of our lives can last a lifetime existing as a torn in our flesh. Though it may appear inconvenient and discomforting at times, we still must maintain gratitude for the breath of life that continues to sustain us despite our battles.

Peace

> *Daughter, as a father says to his child hears the affirming words of love spoken with affection. "Go in peace, and **be** healed of your affliction".* [1]

Jesus said; *"Go in Peace and Be Healed"*. His words were absolute when He uttered them; initiating the *"motion of faith"* towards its progression as a testimony that indeed says; *"it came to pass"*. The evidence of faith can evolve into an asymptomatic performance meaning there are no further symptoms, but the root cause of our problems may still exist. *"Whatever God says is to be will be even though we may not yet see the end of what it is intended to be. His Word will never return unto Him void but will accomplish the intended life incubated by His power!"*

A Word of Peace spoken in the midst of our battles brings comfort and quietness to our spirit. The gentle wings of *"Peace"* usher in a rest from the weariness of our warfare with enough power to sustain us in our beliefs. When our faith comes in contact with the Anointing, God's power is released initiating a process to bring visibility to the Word of Faith to do what it was sent to do.

The underlying principle of our meditations is a declaration of positivity; *"being confident of this very thing, that He who has begun a good work in you will complete it until the day of Jesus Christ"*.[1] When we pray; *"let the words of my mouth and the meditation of my heart be acceptable in Your sight, Oh Lord my strength and my Redeemer"*,[2] we are praying to see as He sees and to know as He knows. By accepting God's Word as the unadulterated truth, any variance of fear and unbelief that may arise in pursuit of faith becomes ineffectual. Even as Jesus was thronged in the midst of a multitude, healing was delivered only to the one who searched in belief extrapolating the possibility of faith. The rewards of faith will manifest infallible proof of God's ability to produce results He has promised. When we enter our secret chambers, we enter resolved of God's ability to complete what our faith had started.

Do You Believe

Have you examined your motivation that compelled you to follow Jesus? What provocation emerged from your battles that had such an encumbering affect on your faith beyond your ability to recover? Have you lost your sight along the way with no one to lead you as a guide in the night? The Lord has a compassionate ear and surely will avail His strength to the beckoning of your cry. Compassion is reinforcement of faith with an ability to see and feel outside of ourselves purposed to touch the lives of those immersed in their battles even in times of desperation.

> *When Jesus departed from there, two blind men followed Him, crying out and saying,* **"Son of David have mercy on us!"** *And when He had come into the house, the blind men came to Him. And Jesus said to them,* **"Do you believe that I am able to do this**?" *They said to Him, Yes Lord. Then He touched their eyes saying* **"According to your faith let it be to you." And their eyes were opened.** *And Jesus sternly warned them saying* **"See that no one knows it." But when they had departed, they spread the news about Him in all that country.** [1]

There were two blind men who followed Jesus. How amazing; blind but still drawn to the Light! Faith is a beacon of hope, illuminating a path even when we may not know the way. Conceivably, there may have been many more searching for their sight but didn't have the audacity of faith to cry out for Jesus' guidance. To a certain degree, we all were blind in need of God's guiding Light to make His footsteps our pathway.

The voice of Jesus is sight to the blind. What we cannot see; hearing of the word of faith transforms our hearing into seeing. The patterns of faith framed in our imagination give us an ability to transpose darkness into light recovering sight to see from the impressions of faith. *"If you can believe it, you can see it; if you can see it, you can reproduce it."* We are only limited by our belief in things we perceive as truth. Our perceptions are artistic framing images into our imagination. They transmit indelible imprints searing into our conscience as a portrait etched in granite. *"Faith transforms static imprints into a 'cinema' of what we believe to see; with movement breathing the breath of faith".*

Faith is the active part of our belief structure that make things happen. I once heard a man of God say; *"God will never part the waters until you get your feet wet".* How remarkable! I can believe it but there comes a time I must do it. Launch out in the deep beyond the shallow contentions of faith. That is the place of faith's greatest rewards. Every vision received from God must be exercised through the channels of faith. Without a commitment to faith, what we perceive as vision has a vaporizing affect and will disappear before your eyes as if you never received anything at all. We need both; the vision of God and the faith of God.

We often find ourselves in the same predicament as the two blind men searching the healing streams of faith for resolution to life's dilemmas. In the passion of night, we cry out for mercy with a reverberation that reaches Heaven above with no greater sight to see than the blind. The blind can't see but can discern the company of the blind. Neither one of them can lead without power to illuminate their path. *"Verbalization without the visualizations of faith is handicapping."* Be very careful who you choose to follow. Everyone does not have your destination in focus. The price for sight is a sacrifice in the orchestrated path of faith and if you are not rightly connected, it may very well cost you valuable time needed for the journey ahead leaving your faith at risk of not completing your destiny.

Faith is a challenge just not limited to the blind but rather; *"do you have the strength of faith **to believe** in the possibilities that God can open blind eyes?"* Belief is an absolute requirement for our spiritual sight which is not dependent on our natural senses for recognition of faith. Whatever we may conceive in our belief can be substantiated. Our conceptions we hold as truth can be animated into a performance for healing from an inner image born from the spoken Word of Faith. If we are able to capture God's impressions as a template for faith; *"Then He touched their eyes saying,* **"According to your faith let it be to you. And their eyes were opened.** *And Jesus sternly warned them saying See that no one knows it."* [3] How astonishing! Eyes opened and still no sight to see! Jesus stood before them but they had no recognition of who He was. They only saw the Son of David.

The instructions of faith are authoritative dictating the boundaries of God's Word. Healing is completed by our obedience to every word of God's instructions. If we are predisposition with a variance of patience, we could lose what we just received. The reason being; *"God is protecting us until faith is fully developed in us".* We should never misconstrue the actions of God with the performance of man. *"To God be glorified!"*

Void of recognition of Jesus greater than an Earthly vessel as the Son of David, revelation of His identity of *"Christ Our Redeemer"* eluded their understanding of accurately authenticating their perception of Him. The prerequisite for accurate spiritual interpretation is very much dependent on our ability to believe in the Holy Spirit's executions as He illustrates the Word of Faith. He is the personification of Christ Our Deliverer who defeated darkness giving *"light for sight to the blind"*.

> *Now as they went out of Jericho, a great multitude followed Him. And behold, **two blind men sitting by the road**, when they heard that Jesus was passing by, cried out, saying, "Have mercy on us, **O Lord**, Son of David!" Then the multitude warned them that they should be quiet; but they cried out all the more, saying, "Have mercy on us, O Lord, Son of David!" So Jesus stood still and called them, and said, "What do you want Me to do for you?" They said to Him, "Lord, that **our eyes may be opened**." So Jesus had compassion and touched their eyes. **And immediately their eyes received sight** and they followed Him.* [1]

Disobedience will disable your ability to advance further in the things of the Kingdom. You may have started out looking for a private encounter with Jesus but now you're sitting by the road amongst a crowd who are seeking to silence your voice considering their needs are greater than your own. Beware of hindering and controlling spirits. They would rather drown you in a sea of fear than allow your faith to flourish.

It is easy to follow Jesus when there is no one else around. But in the midst of a multitude, it becomes more of a challenge when surrounded by distractions. Multitudes have their place authenticating an elevated level of expectation. Their voices echo through the crowd, all seeking relief from the only One who has power to give. In our cry for relief; *"we call on the Lord; the only name we know who can conquer our pain and discouragements."* God hears our cry and all of Heaven stands as a witness to our supplications. Though some of our problems were not fully eradicated when we first encountered Christ; our faith is a progressive element of trust directly interacting with God's ability that can weather any storm surging in our life. What God has for you is for you. It has a life cycle designated for your achievements not to be mimicked in any other way.

There is a proverbial expression we all have heard; *"I will serve no wine before its time"*. Everyone does not need to know where you're going or for that matter, where you've been. Listen people! Some things need to be left at the *"Altar For God's Ears Only"* without any further disclosure. In our first encounter with God, He demonstrated His power as the Great Physician our healer; *"Jehovah Rapha"*. But His desire for our lives is for a fuller revelation of His embodiment. It takes time to develop a relationship for a deeper experience in the life of faith for discovery of *"Christ Living Within"*. How many times have I seen people get healed and settled there; never to be seen again until they have another problem just as the two blind men?

God is not limited to the performance of yesterday. You may have followed Him in the path searching for healing just as the blind men who followed Him but now will you follow Him as the Lord's Witness to testify of His power? As scripture suggest; "*So Jesus had compassion and touched their eyes. And immediately their eyes received sight, and **they followed Him**.*" [1] You can't follow Jesus without eyes to see the sighted path where He is leading you. The first instance of our eyes being opened is one thing but can you see? The return of faith to receive sight is a far greater achievement. Faith flows dimensionally in continuation of our belief for a fuller revelation of the identity of Christ and the power of His testimony.

The healing anointing Jesus demonstrated resides *"Within"* giving us the ability through the conduit of faith to perform even as He did to open blind eyes and give sight to those searching in the dark. Execution of faith is founded upon the premise of the Word of God and His infallible promises which we can duplicate.

Miracles

Miracles are sovereign actions of God beyond our ability to regulate. They are determinative exhibitions intervening in our affairs as a demonstration of God's supremacy above all actions of man. Miracles are breath defying. If you have ever witness one, it will radicalize your perception as an undeniable expression of God's Existence. By divine intervention, miracles exists in defiance of all natural laws and possibilities.

Everything that moves in our universe is defined by a law; *"The Law of Motion."* Motion is an identifiable relationship between the momentums of force acting on the motion of something else. For example; take the motionlessness of a withered hand being touched by the motion of an Anointing that restores normalcy to its movement. *"Movement is observer dependent."* The multitude saw the still motion of Lazarus as being dead except Jesus who saw him as only sleeping. Something that's moving from my point of view may be standing still in yours. Perception of change differs from one to the other. But believe me if it moves, it can be calculated. If it can be calculated, it must be seen even down to the smallest atom. Though motion is an invisible force, I can recognize its power when I see the wind by movement of a breeze passing through the trees. I can calculate motion of the Earth by the rising and setting sun and disappearing moon receding to light. But not surprisingly, I recognize movement of the Anointing by healing of a withered hand as it stretched forth in faith reattaching to the gift of life.

Movement is calculated by the results it produces. Miracles are no different. I can see miracles every time I look in the mirror and recognize a wonder of God's creation; a converted life of darkness turned into light.

> *"But you are a chosen generation, a **royal priesthood**, a holy nation, His own special people, that you may proclaim the praises of Him who called you out of darkness into His marvelous light."* **1 Peter 2:9 NKJV**

Miracles can be found throughout scripture from beginning to end. They speak with a commonality in the performance of God's actions as He implements His authority. It is a common theme of God to precede the exploitations of miracles by an *"Undeniable Word"*. Miracles are in His sovereign jurisdiction as testimony of His Omnipotent power defying every natural law in the realm of Earth. As an exhibition of His supreme authority, His creative energy confronts the powers of darkness with irrevocable evidence of His supremacy. God's originality defies our imagination with creativity performing beyond the exhaustion of our faith.

When Moses came to decisions of the Red Sea with no other possibilities existing in his arsenal of faith he was forced to consider; will the failing of my faith turn me backwards into bondage and I die by the hands of Pharaoh; should I take a plunge in the sea escaping at the risk of drowning; or should I just wait on God for a miracle because He has not failed me yet? The latter decision was much greater than the first; he did wait on God. Betwixt with threatening and fear, the miracle of faith intervened and God parted the waters as a means to escape. The test of faith can be challenging sometimes bringing you to a standstill where you can't go any further. It is a provocation to dig a little deeper exploiting the depth of new found possibilities. Greater will be the expanse of awe-inspiring testimonies of God's intervention even the performance of miracles infused in the affairs of men. When faith comes to its determined end; miracles will begin.

Miracles are significantly centered in the passion of love our Father has for His people. Their birthing is in Heavenly places. Scripture says; *"You are the God who performs **miracles**; you display your power among the people"*.[1] When God gives a directive as He did with Moses in the parting of the Red Sea, it was a miracle according to His instructions. When the bitter waters of Mariah were made sweet; that too was a miracle. What we lack in faith, God will do for Himself to prove His Omnipotence; just as in the day of Elijah when He rained fire from Heaven consuming the satanic waters of idolatry. The provocative actions of God resist the profundities of wisdom accumulated in the depth of man's failing understanding in his attempt to rise above His authority.

> *When the Sabbath came, he began to teach in the synagogue, and many who heard him were amazed. "Where did this man get these things?" they asked. "What's this wisdom that has been given him? What are these remarkable **miracles** he is performing?* [2]

God will do for us when we are not able to do for ourselves. Exhibition of His power is an agent of faith still performing *"signs and wonders"* as the ultimate authority in all of creation. We, the collective body of Believers are in need of restoration to stem the tide of darkness that is seductively dimming our light. But we must first take a self examination of our state of affairs and be true to thine self! Call it what it is! But Believe!

13
Lawfulness Vs. Lawlessness

When the woman saw that the tree was good for food, that it was pleasant to the eyes, and a tree desirable to make one wise, she took of its fruit and ate. She also gave to her husband with her, and he ate. Then the eyes of both of them were opened, and they knew that they were naked.  [1]

The Principle of Lawfulness can be traced back to the Garden in Eden. Obedience legitimizes lawfulness as the *"lawful actions of faith"*. It is a conceptual idea framed in the heart of our Creator. Without guidance of the Holy Spirit's interpretations to the instructions of faith it is impossible for our human nature to adequately apply our obedience to perfection of an image of God's envisioning. As Adam discovered, the makings of flesh and soul does not have the power of sustainability to overcome the burden of obedience. Our free will choices often impede completion of faith.

Obedience is a burden if you truly consider the cost of sacrifice; *"Persecutions"*. It's been said; the shortest distance between two places is a straight line. *"The straight line of faith is with sufferings challenging our willingness to continue."* The inquisitive nature of our free will spirit, more often than not, will continue to lead us down the forbidden path; away from the true intentions of faith. Amidst competition for the interest of our faith; *"Faith has to be centered"* as the nucleus of our expectations without infringement of wavering to achieve any possibility for success.

Fabric of soul and particles of dust held together by water and blood lacks in superiority to the influence of the Holy Spirit's ruling authority. Flesh will always be in opposition to spirit. Within the composition of the anatomy of flesh exists a barrier separating soul and spirit. The consciousness of soul has an identity to speak for itself but not flesh, which will never have a life of its own. It was dead in the day of its formation. Synergistically, flesh and soul share dependency of each other; combining in a singleness of conscience as in the day of Adam's creation. Without the rule of the Spirit as the engine motivating power within their chambers, together their actions are unpredictive.

Tree of Good and Evil

Lawfulness is twin to expediency with authorization to battle in the channels of faith. We are sanctioned to do good but there is a penalty for our unlawful actions. We are compelled as servants to maintain a standard in the Earth operating with a conscience of urgency to reclaim *"God's Order"* He intended for our humanity. By the way, we are only allocated with so much time to do it and the clock continues to tick.

God's creation was implemented to a specific order. Firstly He created an ovum for a firmament to house an Earth for Adam's habitation. He was instructed to maintain God's order in the Earth with given authority of His Word to be fruitful and multiply by expansion through the gift of faith. Everything was in its rightful place void of contamination by the marring of sin. Sin is a disruptive disorder antagonistic to acceptance of God's arrangements. To be void of contaminants is to live a life of purity; the signature of God's approval.

Lucifer was first to challenge the sanctity of God's order in his attempt to usurp his authority over the Throne of God which led to his demise. It was repeated again by Adam's disobedience in the Garden of Eden by suggestion of three seductive words the enemy has and will continue to use; *"But Did God Say!"* [1] If we are not clear of God's instructions, a cloud of uncertainty will surface as an impediment to our understanding with disqualifying results in opposition to our faith.

The *"Tree of Good and Evil"* stood in the midst of the Garden as a judge on the outer limits exceeding Adam's lawful choices. It possessed enough power when awakened to transform obedience into sin as a naked betrayal of faith. Obedience is purity without the need for the coverings of flesh and outer garments of concealment. There are times we veil ourselves as Adam in a disguised apron of leaves only to encounter God's judgment.

Leaves separated from their source will wither to the elements of time as a disappearing veil exposing the naked truth lying beneath. As Adam discovered, leaves temporarily disguised his deception until God removed the mask of his disobedience. Disobedience is void of power to correct itself. There is no other option; it must undergo unveiling by a power greater than itself. If allowed to exist apart from God's correction, we will be exposing ourselves as fools living in a fool's paradise parading in our own deception. We need the grace of God in operation to secure a victorious life by governance of His Spirit. Sufficiency of God's plan of grace and forgiveness without sacrifice of the law is intended to accomplish what the law alone could not do. God further fortified our ability to fulfill His vision by empowering our lives with the gift of the Holy Spirit. We are no longer bound by the law with atoning blood of animals prostrated on an Altar of fire. The fire is now inside of us fuming from kindling of God's love shed abroad in our hearts.

Mirroring of life is fluid always surging, declining with peaks and valleys in a movement of change. We vacillate from emancipated joy as a witness emanating from our victories to a depressive decline born of our defeats. The battleground of our conscience is under constant surveillance by arbitrating powers in a battle thrusting for supremacy as executor of our decisions; *"will of the spirit vs. will of the flesh; Wars of the Mind"*.

Step back for a minute and *"BREATHE"*. Evil as we know it is not a good thing; *"It is what it is"*. But have you ever considered the underlying motivation of evil? It's meant to be a teacher *"A teacher of what not to do"*! At some point we all will testify of its power. Evil has a way of being a featured attraction. When truth exposes our conscience in bare nakedness, any reference of evil will render an indictment against our faith. In many situations we have created by no fault of anyone else, we cried out; *"How long Lord until my cup fills?"* Truth be told, it's only after you have suffered awhile to learn from the practices of evil. Needless to say; evil prevails as a counterfeit of truth.

Principle of Lawfulness

Indifferences comprising our human nature are an inherent contradiction to a spirit led life legislated by the Holy Spirit. A lifestyle of obedience is not bound by signpost at every turn in our lives and is immune from an outer dependency of *"thou shalt nots"*. The sacrifice of obedience is a performance of faith distinguished as an outward display of our inward acceptance of what God has legislated upon our hearts.

In all of society, rule of law and its enforcement mechanism exists as checks and balances to maintain order and civility in our humanity. For without it, we would truly succumb to catastrophes of lawlessness. Lawlessness is a consensus of corporate chaos. It is *"societal anarchy of randomness"* existing in defiance of God's rule of law. Conversely, lawfulness establishes boundaries of trust with a penalty for variances that exceeds its standards. Standards of God's Theocracy are lawful actions instigated as protocols to judge our obedience to instructions He expects us to perform. Adam's unlawful application of this principle ushered in lawlessness of chaotic proportions at its root is the cause of so much violence and chaos seen today.

The origin of the test of lawfulness originated as a contest of words; *"Did God Really Say."*[1] If you are prone to forgetfulness lacking spiritual discernment of who's doing the asking, your natural inclinations will lead you in a downward spiral in violation where you would surely encounter a direct response from God. The power of forgetfulness has a dynamic affect upon your senses. It's laden with suggestive powers with the ability to lead you into confusion of God's intentions.

A Withered Limb

> *And He entered the synagogue again, and a man was there who had a withered hand.* **So they watched Him closely**, *whether He would heal him on the Sabbath, so that they might accuse Him. And He said to the man who had the withered hand, "Step forward." Then He said to them, "Is it lawful on the Sabbath to do good or to do evil, to save life or to kill?" But they kept silent. And when He had looked around at them with anger, being grieved by the hardness of their hearts, He said to the man,* **"Stretch out your hand."** *And he stretched it out and his hand was restored as whole as the other.* **Mark 3:1-5 NKJV**

Mark records the travels of Jesus initial encounter at the synagogue. During His visit, Jesus cast out an unclean spirit who recognized His authority. Beware of *"Familiar Spirits"*. They have the ability to tell you what you want to hear. They have already mastered all that you know! In our churches and synagogues we have allowed the presence of an array of influences to take root in our assemblies. Primarily, the religions of man continue in opposition to deny rule of the Holy Spirit as God's operating authority. Without the gifts of the Spirit in operation, the *"Spirit of Discernment"* needed to unmask deceptions sitting in our midst is nowhere to be found.

Jesus commanded the man with the withered hand to *"Step forward"*. Faith will never lead you backwards; it is always progressive searching for the beacon of light to discover grace needed for our battles. Stepping forward indicates acceptance; an acknowledgement as if saying *"Yes, it is me. I am the one with the problem. My hand is withered and lost its power to respond and despite the naysayers I am not ashamed"*.

The Words of Christ spoken to the man with the withered hand were an invigoration of faith. They were powerful enough to effectuate an internal decision to accept the grace given for his healing. Faith lies within and commands a response of our senses and abilities.

After the initial response of acknowledging our need we are to present our problem; *"Stretch out your hand"*. Faith requires action, stretching! Stretching can be painful with a greater demand of courage for hope in the visible return of faith. The greatest of faith is the surrender of all in belief.

Faith is compelling; stretching, always reaching out at times it appears most challenging. Stretching is the extension of faith moving beyond where we have been; beyond a withered trodden land into new dimensions waiting for our occupation. Stretching comes with a power to move mountains from before us and calm troubling seas of despair surging in our lives. I've stretched before and witnessed its achievements that were proven in faith. I had a withered hand and so did you but as we reached for the promise of faith, we connected with a stream of invisible power that gave infallible evidence of the performance of faith.

Abraham was commanded to leave his kindred land of familiarity and stretch out in faith for a promise awaiting his obedience. Stretching has the ability to enlarge and broaden the scope of our vision. It allows us to penetrate deeper into unknown dimensions to apprehend a greater promise. Just as the man with the withered hand, we will discover by expression of our own actions of faith; *"the power of believing from within will restore one hand as the other"*.

There are some who stand on the sideline judging lawfulness of our actions. Do we measure up to their expectations or fit their protocol of how to and when to? Controlling spirits will inhibit your gift suppressing any increase of your faith. Religious spirits aren't any different. They are very judgmental always critiquing exactness of your movements. They are *"Svengali"* which means a person who manipulates or attempts to exert excessive force over another. How familiar is that? The svengali's of this world have a measure of hardness seeded into their heart not susceptible to change; never allowing the reward of patience and compassion outside of their selfish ambitions.

Actions of the Holy Spirit are spontaneous never calculated to fit into any format or program of design when gathered in our assemblies. The Holy Spirit is boundless and endless reaching to empower the lives of God's people. But we must be sincere and willing to cooperate by intersecting our gifts with His power to deliver on His promises. We have the power to perform but it is no better than our use of it.

Jesus ignited a revolution defying traditions of the Sabbath Day. The religious leaders were incensed and humiliated with contempt and anger, persecuting Him as a derelict because He went against their established doctrines. He asked a question that now I am asking you; *"Is it lawful on the Sabbath to do good or to do evil, to save life or to kill"?* [1] We save on Sunday then why can't we heal on Sunday? A healing is a healing no matter the day. The Sabbath was made for man and man for God and it is His desire that we all be saved and healed of all our afflictions.

God rested after His six days of creation and left the rest for us to do. Unpopular as it may be we do not get to take a day off. *"God does not take a day off";* how inconsiderate that would be if He only serviced the needs of our lives just six days with the seventh day left for us to fend for ourselves. There is a lot of life to live in a given day and it doesn't take the proving of a Sabbath Day to be any different than any other day. *"To do good is to do good no matter the day."* Evil and wickedness doesn't take a day off so why should we? Our faith should be a lifestyle commitment!

Communion with God is intended to be a seven day lifelong experience of fellowship. Sabbath is a time for reflection upon grace bestowed upon our lives. We can learn more of Him but it should be accomplished in our secret encounters where we gain perspective of His Omnipotence. God can do anything He desires to do despite our interferences constantly getting in His way. With a myriad of promises to enrich our lives for a greater production of faith, we then stand a better chance to empower the lives of others. At any cost, we are called to reach the lost and the hurting whenever and wherever they may be found. On the street corner, highways and byways they are waiting for solutions.

Men of pride maintain a watchful eye to control the performance of things they do not understand. Years ago, I belonged to an aspiring congregation growing towards completion of its call. To my surprise a line of demarcation was drawn in the sand separating those who were commissioned on the beaten path from those who were progressively fulfilling the callings of the *"Fivefold Ministry"*. Those with a prophetic mantle and inspired gifting were discouraged the most. Prophets see and can uncover with the gift of discernment the failing practices of pride. In their submission, they can give God's solution with a corrective response. Perhaps that's what man fears the most; the fear of correction.

I remember falling prey to interpretations purposed to keep me glued to my pew every Sunday morning. You probably have heard a considerable amount of query; *"Remember the Sabbath Day, to keep it holy."*[1]

What makes my life holier on one day than any other? There is nothing new about Monday through Saturday and never forgetting Sunday; the day God rested! We are living in *"The Day of God's Sabbath";* a reflection of grace preserved in memory of His accomplishments in our humanity. Holiness is a preservation of purity; keeping things in the finished order of His creation. The Grace of Sabbath is no different than the Grace of Yesterday. It's not a one day event we expense our lives in *"remembrance of Him"* but a lifestyle devoted to worship and thanksgiving set apart in the sanctity of *"communion with Him".*

By submitting to protocols of my leadership; it was impressed upon me; *"not forsaking the assembling of ourselves together".*[1] It was conferred as a mandate to keep me bound within the confines at every instance the doors of the Church were opened. I am always in remembrance of the sacrifices of my brethren in their commitment of faith. However, I do understand there is a different calling upon our lives with bifurcating paths. If your commitment is in the house then serve the house but in the byways where very few travel there should not be any lesser of a commitment.

Some traditions of man are binding to old covenant laws of Moses. For nearly two thousand years, after the sacrifice of the Cross we've existed under a new law; *"The Law of Grace."* In this new covenant God says; *"I will put my law in their inward parts, and write it in their hearts; and will be their God, and they shall be my people".* [2]

> *Jesus said to him, You shall love the LORD your God with all your heart, with all your soul, and with all your mind. This is the first and great commandment. And the second is like it: 'You shall love your neighbor as yourself.*[1]

Grace is liberating in our ability *"to do something"* and freedom *"to be free from something"*. Being freed from the law is fulfillment of *"The Law of Love"*. It is an allegiance of love; the love of God our Father and love of all He created as reflected life created in His Image and instigated by His Creativity.

When Jesus cleansed the Temple, His actions were deemed as being radical disregarding the practices of man. He was committed to a cause that is no different than the obligation of our own destiny of faith; *"To do the will of God descriptive of His instructions to amplify His Existence throughout humanity"*. Jesus removed distractions of marketing that inundated every corridor of His Father's House but somehow we have managed to reinstate them; same practices, prolific systemic methods ever so dangerous unmitigating as a steroidal influence catered to man's convenience.

Our choices are without exceptions to the call of faith. In pursuit of our own interest separated from the life God intended for us; we are without excuse. Why is it we are so resolute venturing backwards away from grace that secured our deliverance? Although Jesus removed the impediments of faith when He cleansed the temple, vision of the modern day Church no way resembles the cost of His sacrifice. What could be our motivations justifying the apathy and complacency?

For years now, moneychangers obsessed with greed have been fleecing the flock for no apparent reason other than filthy lucre; justifying it as blessings of prosperity. They have adorned themselves as angels of light, *"The Anointed"* in a falsity of pride. Their refusal to accept the mantle of simplicity as the true garment of Christ is infectious. The widows, poor and down trodden have experienced the wrath of their greed and manipulation; yet we are still sitting on our hands in the pride of faith allocating space for their devices.

There is so much preaching flooding our airways, but where is the power? The Anointing extrapolates beyond words in a demonstration of the Gifts of Faith. Apostle Paul desired more than wisdom of words but continually sought power emanating from the Spirit of Christ. If the greatness of some of our leaders who continue to preach a different Gospel for gain, we are deceiving ourselves and will surely suffer the wrath of God's correction.

> ***Therefore let no man glory in men.*** *For all things are your's; Whether Paul, or Apollos, or Cephas, or the world, or life, or death, or things present, or things to come; all are your's; And ye are Christ's; and Christ is God's.* **1 Cor. 3:21-23 KJV**

Desperation of Faith

Desperation of faith can lead you into making a frantic error of judgment; *"Seeking men for a share of their gifting."* You will become *"Men-Pleasers"* given to *"Eye-Service"* of deception; courting them who stand in the light of their pride. It is truly a form of idolatry running rampart in our churches. The Holy Spirit is controller of our gifts and He alone will make room for any expression of His Anointing. However, because of our insecurities, we often search for an association outside of what our faith alone is purposed to produce. Without a vision our usefulness will be challenged by unfruitful endeavors filled with restlessness while we are waiting to apprehend the perfect will of God.

God is not a formula; He is a Spirit that can't be bound but yet we continue to limit His expressions to deductions of our perceptions. God is unique in His imagination. He envisioned us as an Image born of His reflection accommodated with a purpose on the day of our creation. Every human being has value connected to the purpose of their existence that empowers them to be who they are. Humanity is consistent as in the day of its creation and has not changed.

Many years ago as my dreams were bubbling to the forefront of my imagination, I traveled to the distant shores of Africa seeking something out of my zeal not realizing what I was seeking God had already provided. How naïve I was in my faith supplanting a hope not inclusive of His vision for my life? While in Benin, West Africa, I realized that in all my searching; *"I discovered faith emerging from a gifting I already had"*. Because of youthfulness and an uncontrollable zeal, I sprung a desire to be something, to do something more than the measure I already had received. Though it may seem rather admirable, it was not what God intended.

> *Be not deceived; God is not mocked: for whatsoever a man soweth, that shall he also reap. For he that soweth to his flesh shall of the flesh reap corruption; but he that soweth to the Spirit shall of the Spirit reap life everlasting.* **Galatians 6:7-8 KJV**

Still seared in my conscience as a testimony I will never forget, I emerged convicted of a principle residing in my faith; *"God will not be mocked."* Unknowingly to me, I was guilty of mocking in pursuit of an alternative direction after God had clearly stated what I was to do and it came with consequences. At issue, it wasn't changing who I was but inventing my own space as an exception to directions already in my possession.

> *When Simon saw through the laying on of the Apostles' hands the Holy Spirit was given he offered them money, saying, "Give me this power also, that anyone on whom I lay hands may receive the Holy Spirit."* **Acts 8:18-19 NKJV**

Simon had the same opportunity we all have asking God for the Gift of His Spirit. Our human nature is visually dependent. What we see creates desires within our conscious that will apprehend our visualizations. We often fail to take into account the cost of sacrifice for acquisition however appropriate it may be. There are no shortcuts for the Anointing. *"To receive power you must accept the gift."* There is no other way; you can't buy your way into it! Just as a dying man who is gasping for his last breath; you can't buy time hoping for an extension beyond its limits. Your choices have already been made. Hopefully the choice for life and its extension have been concluded. When we accept the Holy Spirit as the *"firstfruit"* of God's investment, it will secure eternal continuation to apprehend the ultimate promise of faith; *"Eternal Life"*. It is a price no money can buy.

Simon was a sorcerer who realized there was a power greater than his. His desire for the gift of the Apostles was an attempt to become equal in power, but with a different pretense. His desire is no different than desires of men today; seeking something beyond their measure for inappropriate reasons. What we take out of the lives of others should never be meant for profit. The culture of today conceptually is inundated with *"Monkey See Monkey Do"* mentality mimicking the success we see in others. That is clearly an indication of *"hijacking";* fraudulently perpetrating what's not conceived in your faith. Simon's request for power was seeded in greed desiring to merchandise the Anointing for a greater source of livelihood than his sorcery could ever provide. However, he didn't take into account the consequences of his actions.

I have seen a number of men adorn the office of leading a church for the sake of money with a gift they don't possess. They are called *"Hirelings"*. There is an inherit tragedy to their exploits; by their cunningness they are able to attract gifting from Believers who are not discerning enough to realize their intentions. At any rate being gullible is quite dangerous. In Scripture it teaches; *"The simple believes every word but the prudent considers well his steps"*.[1] The nature of flesh attracts to the exhibition of talents, oratory skills and silvery tongue of men who are disguising enough to disarm you. But the *"Anointing"* is sensitive able to bring recognition of familiar spirits operating in our midst like the sorcery of Simon. The discerning eye of the Holy Spirit features a level of distinction offered to our perceptions to unveil their schemes and disguises.

There are many Simons operating in our midst with a bounty to the highest bidder. I have witnessed men sacrifice their gift in exchange for acceptance and the privilege of notoriety. Truly it's power they are seeking; power that will compromise their faith. I'd rather give my time snatching souls from an eternal doom than to sacrifice God's precious gift accomplished with blood, pain and tears suffered by the obedience of Christ on the Cross of Calvary. Life is a privilege lived within the confines of our choices but they must be founded upon the pillars of truth.

Some Believers seek confirmation of men without consideration of bearing their own cross. Scripture says; *"Many are the afflictions of the righteous but God delivers us out of them all"*.[2] For many, afflictions are not an appealing proposition for the price of sacrifice. It is a risk but faith itself is a risk. From one day to the next, we do not know where the road ahead will lead. The risk of faith is embedded in our mantra; *"We walk by faith and not by sight"*.[3] There are no other options afforded us; *"The Just shall live by faith"*.[4] But who are the willing who will pick up the cross purely for the sake of righteousness? Bearing our cross is identifiable in our motivations revealing the truth of our character and integrity. We all have a cross to bear and it will testify with confirming evidence of our willingness to adopt the pattern of Christ.

Some men will say follow me; my question to them; *"Have you been where you are trying to lead me? If I stumble, do you have power to keep me from falling?"* God will never lead you in a path He has not already accomplished for your future. Even though you may stumble along the way, He will keep you from falling.

Lawlessness

Lawlessness prevails when enactments of our faith are separated from the *"Tree of Life"*. Lawlessness is simply disobedience. We are living in a time of *"revolt"*. Our spiritual foundation is eroding being supplanted by ungratefulness and stagnant memories of the price paid for our deliverance. Murder, hatred, perversion, racism and bigotry have catapulted us into a world of despair. Reliance on the strength of our hands to do it our way is taking us backwards without need of God's provisions. It is possible; we could relinquish all of our successes in pursuit of an independent life of our own accomplishments. There is but one truth; it is the *"Truth of God"* and cannot be colluded with the truth of man as if they are the same. God's principles are His principles and they are indeed absolute! There are no variables or adoption of appendages to His truth but man's principles are selective; conveniently borrowing from the principles of God to validate his intentions which quite frankly are at odds with God.

The influence of greed has replaced compassion; with no further commitment as our brother's keeper. Our culture has become so insensitive and impersonal embarking on a path away from provisions of grace. Materialism has now become our daily bread. When the mantle of God is removed from our public arenas, homes and churches, He will no longer contend with our *"exaggerations"*. Then it will be too late! Wisdom is crying out but we have electively chosen a path away from the concourse of God's civility.

> *How long ye simple ones will ye love simplicity? And the scorners delight in their scorning and fools hate knowledge? Turn you at my reproof: I will pour out my spirit unto you, and I will make known my words unto you.* [1]

Bear With Me a Little

Job was considered righteous in the eyes of God. He was a prosperous family man whom God offered up to Satan for his proving. God allowed Satan to test him with horrendous disasters that took away everything of value to him; his offsprings, his health, his wealth but not his life. Job struggles to understand his situation and begins a search for answers to his dilemma.

In the Book of Job, you recall Elihu's dissertation contradicting Job as he tried in desperation to defend himself having been a faithful servant. Job's righteous assessment of himself drew the critical eye of Elihu as he made an attempt to justify God's actions. In defense of our faith, conceivably we have done the same thing as Job thinking we've done all the right things. At that moment of consideration, we make every attempt to elevate our righteousness above the circumstances that may be descending upon us. And come upon you, it will and maybe not for the reason you may think.

> *The Lord said to Satan, have you considered My servant Job, that there is none like him on the Earth, a blameless and upright man, one who fears God and shuns evil?* **Job 1:8 NKJV**

Substitute your name; have you been there? As in the case of Job, it was a test of integrity to see if his righteousness was indeed true. Severity of the situation can be buffeting to the point you decide to curse God and die as Job's wife suggested. It's my choice if I decide to ask God to get it over with and take me home but still it's my choice and mine alone. The measure of your response to faith to withstand pressures exerted on you should never be determined through the eyes of others. As a watchman standing guard in the night, we are to pray unceasingly and tend to the affairs of faith. Don't waste your time trying to understand everything; just pray and believe in the God of your faith! He will figure the rest out. You may discover from the very beginning, God was in control all along! We are not to underestimate the power of faith. It's required of us to believe and trust in the performance of God's ability.

> ***"Bear with me a little**, and I will show you that there are yet words to speak on God's behalf. I will fetch my knowledge from afar; I will ascribe righteousness to my Maker. For truly my words are not false; One who is perfect in knowledge is with you."* **Job 36:2-4 NKJV**

As Elihu said to Job; *"bear with me a little";* I don't want to make a fool of myself as Apostle Paul said; *"professing to be wise"*. Personally, I desire not to be a professor of the word; had every opportunity and still do. That's dangerous territory; theoretically opening the doors to all kinds of stuff debating *"The Truth"* as a subjective argument. Like Apostle Paul, I want to not just hear the word and speak the word; but bring a performance to match the expectations seeded into my faith. Through exhibition of the power of God it brings into view a reality through the eyes of faith that words alone cannot achieve. *"For Some Seeing is Believing but for the True Soldiers of Faith, Believing is Seeing"*.

As lawyers in a court room, we find ourselves at the sidebar arguing in defense of our opinions and ideas. The chief advocator is there to litigate our arbitrations. Believe me; He is not pleased with either one of us. His truth is absolute despite our seductive arguments and perceptions. His ruling is against both of us.

Job was in an untenable situation; arguing God's intentions after he had lost everything. He was not alone; I did too! I lost 2 million dollars in a transaction gone badly. You think I didn't have an argument? I guess I still do. Argue I did to the point of depression.

I was in a situation just as Job struggling to ascertain truth in a battle that overshadowed my understanding amidst a cloud of uncertainties. Considerably, it was a very painful lesson to learn but further down the road, I mustered enough faith to accept that it was purposed even while in the midst of a whirlwind of persecutions coming in from the outside; *"Believers"* contending with my faith. For every challenge of faith there are naysayers committed to rejoice in your demise.

That's how that stuff usually works; to test your faith, building character. During this ordeal, I had concluded that I didn't want to hear anymore about character; I already had enough. That was my flesh speaking! It spoke, I listened. It had its chance to do all it could do with no lasting consequences. Materially what I lost turned into a greater gain; I learnt how to abase myself in the light of truth for a much greater apprehension of faith.

What are the motivations behind the arguments of faith? We must realize and do it quickly; it is a weapon the enemy uses to divide the full strength of the Body of Christ to deliver on its mandate. Resultantly, the power of deception has inundated our society, notably amongst our younger generation. It is going to take a vigorous effort on our part; vacating our differences to combat the forces of darkness seeking to control the minds of our children. We can ill afford any further dampening of our faith. For so long now, we've been kept away from the power center of prayer. It's time to escalate and do it with a sense of urgency.

In our familiarity, we have attained a certain level of knowledge of God based on our interactions with Him but that is not to say we *"Know Him in Fullness"*. But believe it or not; it is possible to become too familiar with God; not truly knowing Him but familiarity of Him. We should have learnt from Elihu's experience; familiarity does not equate to having perfect knowledge of God. Characteristically, as *"Believers"* being born again in the Image of His Likeness as creatures of faith walking in the sight of belief with His Spirit to lead and direct us; bearing similarity of His attributes should bring us closer to realization of our limitations which are limited to the absolute power of His authority.

God does not need the proliferation of our words; not even in our prayers. He already knows our issues and carryings emerged from our daily battles of faith. It does not matter how long we pray but how sincere are our intentions. *"Pray in the Spirit!"* That's a sure way to get God's attention! Our migrations from time of learning words as babes to maturity of expression as full grown Saints; we have already articulated a profundity of words. We can teach and teach to no end and still teach never moving beyond the portal of faith. Hearing of words creates images that must be brought to life for performance of the works of faith.

At some point in our progression before we attained a fuller expression of praise; we were caught up in what I refer to as *"Think Praise"*. Think Praise is an extrapolation of our inner intentions that does not go further than our thoughts. We've all sung the song;

"When I think about the goodness of Jesus and what He has done for me; my soul cries out hallelujah; praise God for saving me". Thankfulness concluded in our thoughts is not a bad thing; it's edifying and we should all be grateful for our salvation. But it should be a motivation to expand beyond the initial conception of faith and extrapolate on an experiential level to show gratitude as a true witness of faith. Do something more than saying something! Furthermore, for years now we have been taught; *"When praises go up the blessings come down"*. Is that to say we praise God solely for blessings? Why not praise Him firstly for who He Is beyond any material interest or how He performs in our lives! Is that such a phantom thought?

"Phantom Praise" is no different than a phantom thought of randomness seeking for a cause in why we should praise which is no different than the expense of our time trying to fathom the depth of oceans or trying to determine the life span of the sun. Praise at times may not be so convincing of the justifying purpose to praise when surrounded by so many distractions and vexations forming in our spirit. As a liability, vexations will consume all of our energy forgoing an encounter to experience God's Presence so needed in our lives. If you don't know by now the truth of your hearts intent, you might want to consider looking around you and *"Count your blessings and name them one by one"*.

The *"Praise of Faith"* is not a thought; it is an action expressed in gratitude when we encounter power from above purposed to touch the lives of others as well as our own. The Praise of Faith is horizontal movement extending outward after being in contact with the Presence of God; *"Heal the sick, raise the dead, cleanse those with leprosy, drive out demons. freely you have received; freely give"*. [1] If we pray right; we can receive a private touch achieved in our secret dwelling place. But in our public portrayals relatable to our traditions, we do give thanks with yielded hearts fellowshipping with each other for God's performance in our praise.

It's incomprehensible how our aspirations have changed consumed with activity of our day to day lives without the challenge of faith. We are running but from what; I have not yet determined. Maybe it's what we are running to; could it be *"Glitter"?* Glitter always attracts seemingly as an easier appeal because of its superficial nature. But the subtleties of faith require labor necessitating digging deeper beneath the barren surface for discovery of treasures hidden in the path before us. By the way; we should be very concerned of the envisioning of our youth. As a collective conscience they have chosen a different path than the one we have taken as rejection of our hypocrisy. They are emerging with their own standards as an adjustment of their reality which is a considerable distance away from our vacillating persuasions. They want no part of it. Corporately, some of them view our lives as being *"hypocritical"* because we have voided the statement of faith in pursuit of our material agendas. They can't see the difference! What they see on the inside of the Church is the same as their experiences outside the walls of our isolation. If you don't believe me, take a look at the census data and see where it's trending. When we're gone what will they choose?

Have we provided them with enough of a foundation that they won't make the same mistakes as we have? I pray we have done enough to sustain them. They will be empowered with an existence of their own. From all indications, they may have already been radicalized into a new reality with acceptance of materialism and secularism as their guiding light. Technology hasn't helped serving only as greater distractions. What do you think the future is going to look like? Not like you and certainly not like me; but trust me; it will be something entirely different.

When I was a child curiosity of my grandfather led him to ask; *"Do you honestly believe they put a man on the moon?* I said yes Papa; they did. That man laugh so hard he nearly choked on his chewing tobacco. But imagine the future of our grandchildren? That day is rapidly approaching. It won't be too long when we will be out of here. Then what? Let's pray for revival! I mean the real kind; *"God directed"*. Not that kind of stuff we put on the calendar every year; same month; same day and same time but *"The Holy Ghost Kind"* that changes everything it comes into contact with.

Elihu's Rebuke

The width and breath of God and the expanse of His Eternal Presence will never be determined. It is beyond our ability to calculate! He is forever morphing from one dimension to the next. Voyages deep into space, Scientist, Astronomers cannot ascertain the dimensions of God and His boundaries. Can you fix the limits of God? We are restrained in the knowledge dispersed in our understanding of Him. But Job's friend, Elihu, the one who professed to be so wise made an attempt to define the measures of God only to receive His rebuke. What was his motivation speaking into Job's demise? Have you encountered people like that? Elihu's words were quite troubling in his attempt to speak on God's behalf.

To speak out of our humanism without a clear path to discern God's wisdom and instructions concerning the lives of others are recipes for disappointment and failure. The lives of God's people are precious and should not bear the brunt of our intrusions that can lead them down a path God never intended. Every voice speaking into your life is not the Voice of God and we should be aware.

> *"Who is this that obscures my plans with words without knowledge? Brace yourself like a man and you shall answer me!"* [1]

Remember when Elihu told Job he would fetch his knowledge from afar? Get ready you asked for it and you're going to get it. Are you listening Elihu? Job are you hiding yet? The *"Footsteps of God are coming"*! Did you ask Adam? He would have told you not to try it! At times God is really merciful and kind in His correction of us but not always. Selectively His demeanor can be considered condescending; but that's His prerogative.

I've learned to not get ahead of God speaking things void of His acceptance. Speak when God tells you not to speak; go when He tells you not to go; eat when He tells you not to touch; I guarantee you if my name ain't Willie; in truth it's not; it is my grandfather's name; Ham that is, *"Willie Ham";* you will suffer seemingly with vexation coming upon you. To be in defiance of God's correction is indicative of a hardened heart without pliability to accept His mediation.

Message to Job; are you still ready to defend your righteousness? Elihu are you listening? God took His time going through a litany of events in recognition of His authority, wisdom and power. But it is noteworthy of His description of Leviathan; *"The folds of its **flesh** are tightly joined; they are firm and cannot be moved"*. [1] Our flesh is no different! It is tightly resistive to things of the Spirit. *"It's waterproof but not God proof"!* Do you remember when God sealed up the flesh of Adam with no point of reentry after the rib was taken from him? Flesh united unto itself yielding its obedience to its rightful source; *"bone of my bones and flesh of my flesh"*.[2] In contrast the Holy Ghost does not need the cutting of flesh for access into our lives. He is a Spirit who enters however He chooses.

A word of caution; we need to stop the nonsense of conflating God's interest with the agendas of man. Without discernment, we could be like *"Mr. Intelligent"*, Elihu, who considered everyone a mannequin but himself. Have you seen that type before? He found out the hard way in his condescending attitude dealing with Job. There is a penalty to think of ourselves more highly than we ought. It is a very painful lesson to learn not speaking the truth about God or lending your voice in opposition to one of his children who stands righteous before him; *"Touch not mine anointed and do my prophets no harm"*.[3] In the final analysis, Job was commanded to pray for Elihu's deliverance that God would not deal with him according to his reckless endangerment of truth immersed in *"folly"*.

> *So now take seven bulls and seven rams and go to My servant Job and sacrifice a burnt offering for yourselves. My servant Job will pray for you and I will accept his prayer and not deal with you according to your folly. You have not spoken the truth about Me as My servant Job has.* [1]

Does seven bulls and seven rams ring a bell? Job was blameless and stood upright with the fear of God woven into his fabric. I have a deep admiration for his faith. However, in understanding completeness of his journey of faith, it no way resembles the beginnings of my own struggles but remarkable nonetheless.

There was a time during my younger years upon returning from the war stricken battlefields of Vietnam when I so desperately needed God's intervention. The day of reckoning came upon me with the swiftness of my tears. I began to cry out as never before. I needed God's comfort to ease the pain of my troubled soul. *"Where there are great sins there is great grace."* This is not poetry, pulp fiction or an exaggeration but an accurate testimony of an *"Upper Room"* experience that satisfied my hunger. I distinctly recall the channels of life receding from my conscience when a power came upon me so great I humbled myself in a sea of tears. I had no recognition of the Holy Spirit not even to know His name but I felt His Presence as He entered my body sealing me from head to toe. When I looked in the mirror there He was looking through the windows of my eyes contacting the world around me. My house now became His house! A revolution had taken place radicalized by a power that continues to sustain me. Wherever I go; He goes; wherever He goes; I am sure to follow. More precious than gold or money can buy, an experience with the Holy Spirit bears the signature of His uniqueness. Your encounter with Him may differ from mine; no lesser or greater of God's quest to enter into our lives but when He enters His life is consuming reflective of His remarkable Presence.

God can take things away from you to test you at a time He is developing you but will add value back into your life from the same things He took away but with an increase of double for your trouble.

> *"The LORD restored Job's losses when he prayed for his friends. Indeed the LORD gave Job twice as much as he had before.* [1] *the LORD blessed the latter days of Job more than his beginning."* [2]

*Now the whole earth had **one language and one speech**. And it came to pass, as they journeyed from the east, that they found a plain in the land of Shinar, and they dwelt there. Then they said to one another, "Come, let us make bricks and bake them thoroughly." They had brick for stone, and they had asphalt for mortar. And they said, "Come, let us build ourselves a city, and a tower whose top is in the heavens; let us make a name for ourselves, lest we be scattered abroad over the face of the whole earth."*

But the LORD came down to see the city and the tower which the sons of men had built. And the LORD said, "Indeed the people are one and they all have one language, and this is what they begin to do; now nothing that they propose to do will be withheld from them. Come, let Us go down and there confuse their language, that they may not understand one another's speech."

Genesis 11:1-7 NKJV

14
Return of Babel

Come, let Us go down and there confuse their language, that they may not understand one another's speech." [1]

Revelation of Christ is surely missing in our day. We have been feeding on stale manna for years and it has begun to make us sick. We have vacated the intimacy of gaining perspective of God's Heart accomplished in the solitude of prayer but would rather satisfy our itching ears for a copious supply of knowledge. After Jesus cleansed the Temple; swept clean with a braid of cords to constrain ungodly pollution that occupied space in His Father's House; we still continue to offer intercessions amidst fumes of strange fire operating in our churches.

We are living in perilous times like in the days of Babel when the whole Earth conspired to violate the sovereign omnipotence of *"The Great God Jehovah"*. The nature of man is predictive; wait a season in time as in the Book of Judges he will resolve to repeat the same patterns of his demise bearing even a greater consequence for his action. How quickly did we forget our allegiance to faith after such great promises?

From the time of Adam's eviction from the Garden to the Great Flood in the days of Noah, the nature of flesh and soul have proven to have a mind of their own. Even after the covenant promise of God with the seal of the rainbow, man continues down his own path that will eventually encounter the judgment of fire and brimstone awaiting his betrayal.

Since the beginning of time, the wisdom of creation has not changed. The consequence of betrayal of its order and purpose will continue to encounter God's judgment. We can never exist apart from our Creator with our lives separated from the only source of power that can sustain our survival. We will surely fail at any attempt to exalt our wisdom above *"His Originality"*.

God's universe bears uniqueness of resiliency with ability to purge itself of man's compromising solutions. We are living in times of great upheaval and disrespect of God's order; totally disregarding the principle of love and purity. The principle of love is pure and without compromise. Scripture indicates that God loved us so to the extent He deemed it important enough not to leave us to ourselves. He provided us with a precious gift to share His life with ours. It is by the Holy Spirit's availability our lives are connected to His. Our shared life is a communion of faith with renewable bonds in a relationship accomplished in prayer. The Holy Spirit defines the parameters of God's expectations of love. Without an unmitigated love of God of our Father and love of our brethren what miserable anarchic creatures we would become.

Love is missing in the lives of so many people; for some they continue to search in the night to connect with a love of their own only to be found wandering as a vagabond sifting through recycles of yesterday. Hate, frustrations, racism and bigotry we see demonstrated in our daily encounters exemplify how far we have moved away from respect of God's humanity. God loves us but what is the problem we cannot exercise love of ourselves? He delegated His trust in us to maintain His standards in the Earth legislated by the greatest commandment of all; *"Love"* and we are failing miserably. As simple as it is, we need to pursue love as never before for civility and respect of humanity; love ourselves and through love, love our neighbor.

In all of the woes of mankind, we have devalued the purpose of our existence. Whether it's our neighbor who does not bear similarity of color; the division of politics causing one to hate another or divisiveness of our beliefs setting religion apart from each other; we have become fractured components of our choices. Whether we are cognitive of its significance or not, our future generation is dependent on our leadership. If we were to squander away such a great opportunity, they will fill the void with choices not conducive to our own.

We live in a *"thin skinned"* society without tolerance to accommodate differences. But why the pursuit for supremacy? That's a real problem! Society of yesterday had a belief in each other anchored in the Church. But today; Walls! *"Walls of isms"; materialism, separatism, racism but greatest of all; "isms rooted hypocrisy"!*

The Day of Babel

Now the whole earth had **one language** *and one speech.* [1]

Humanity is on the cusp of becoming *"One Speech";* blurring the lines of demarcation that differentiate our language. Language is an expression that identifies patterns of commonality vital for speech recognition. Verbalization of speech captures our thoughts and ideas reflected as activity of the language we speak. The motivating power of speech can be interpolating as a means to radicalize the perceptions of others by transforming the spoken word into a reflection of our ideologies bridging the gap of commonality. Speech without understanding babbles in confusion.

Being a Computer Science major, I understand the accomplishment of technology has mastered language into one binary protocol. It is a binary notation of *"zeros and ones, yes and no's, on or off, for or against".* This is the language of computers that have emerged as the universal language encapsulating every culture and every idea on our planet. From the far reaches of space, the emergences of satellites have a controlling influence over our firmament with intrusive authority connecting our lives in a dominion of one language. A new consensus of creativity has emerged threatening life as we now know it. With an increasing dependency on the reliability of technology, despite its volatility, it influences every aspect of our day to day lives. Without guarantee of dependability, it can be compromising.

Our technology is not infallible. It is subject to the violent emissions from the sun when the sun burst with a radical emission of energy. One event can knock out all of our satellite transmissions less than the time it takes the sun's energy to travel to Earth. It is not within our capacity to control the heavens. We are at the mercy of universal powers far exceeding our ability to understand. But, there is a power that's delegated to our trust; *"authority over all physical matter of the Earth guarding against our own destruction."*

In the day of Babel, the Lord separated conspiring powers united in their effort to gain dominion over the heavens. He caused mass confusion of their language. Incoherency to understand one another's speech is indicative of what we are currently experiencing in our society. Resolutions of conflict have proven fatal while attempting to resolve our differences. No longer do we exercise a capacity for longsuffering and patience in our dealings with people but we have succumbed to a lesser order of our communications. Increasingly, we have become very combative without the tolerance for listening as our condescending attitudes of judgment quiets the voices appealing to our reasoning. Judge me wrong; look at me wrong; talk to me wrong is a sad narrative of the systemic failure of our civility.

It seems as though everyone is talking passed each other never connecting to the things that bind our hearts together. Without dependency on the counsel of our Heavenly Father, we are inclining to become gods amongst ourselves and it's not impossible to get there.

We are flirting with delineation of *"Atheism; which is the Supreme Achievement of Flesh"*. By all accounts it is an acrimonious conclusion at the core of racism.

We are no longer divided separated by oceans and continents apart; but technology has bridged the gap. It seems we are back together again raising our banner into the heavens. The only accomplishments man has managed to inscribe his signature are his acclaim to wars, poverty and strife; men who have become lovers of themselves living in perversion to an image of flesh seared into their conscience. There is no need for God to confuse us again; *"We already are"*!

The Internet

Man is yet again attempting to frame the world with his signature reflective of his natural instincts. The spawning of technology has evolved by our innovations into conspiracy of one language; *"The Internet"*. Words and systems defining the boundaries of language that are common to a nation, geographical area or people of the same cultural traditions are being circumvented by a new standard radicalized into corporate connectivity via the binary conception of the Internet. What was once divided by our individualism and sectarianism has now been co-opted. Prophetically speaking, it is called *"Globalism"*; the advent of a one world system.

The Internet is a system that combines our planet under one domain. It is global, an interconnectivity of networks that consists of millions of private and public networks on a global scope that are linked by a broad array of technologies. The Internet carries an extensive range of information resources and services on the World Wide Web (WWW). With improvisation; it has transformed our imaginations displaying visualizations even of our thoughts.

In this information driven age we live in, the access to knowledge is immediate at the pressing of a button. A spoken word can become *"universally viral"* within a matter of seconds articulating an imagination at times with dire consequences. Artificial intelligence (AI) can recognize the spoken word and has led to dependency limiting the use of our senses. Human attributes of our voice and ear are being substituted with a variety of *"Technologies"*. Robotic technology has displaced millions from being gainfully employed by replacing their talents, education and gift of creativity. Droning of our culture is evident in every facet of our reality from our homes, businesses and even our churches.

The proliferation of discovering technology can be frightening. Despite the advantages achieved through research in science and medicine, we are headed on an accelerated path void of privacy and uniqueness of our individuality. We are being drawn into a collective web of common sociable influences and secularize beliefs. The uniqueness of faith from one culture to the other is being lost in a battle of extremes only to compromise in the middle without offending another. Despite being an instrument for convenience, enforcement of the Web's protocols lack the mechanisms that can ensure safety and usability without the danger.

Celestial Time

From the beginning of God's creation, He created a binary system of stars, planets, galaxies and even our sun centered in the heavens. Our planets within our solar system evolve around the sun receiving equity of power from its source. What separates one from the other is the distance from the sun's center; some too close while others are orbiting on the peripheral of the sun's attracting beams. They continue to exist as a witness in the day of their creation. Despite being fixed to the gazing eye, they have a trajectory influenced by movement of our universe. Our universe is constantly expanding; it has no center. It is alive; breathing by its own breath. Due to the expanding speed of its breath, there is no conclusion to the endings of its expansion.

> *When we look up into the sky at any distant star, we are in effect looking backwards into historical time. What you see when you look at a star one million light years away is what that star looked like 1 million years ago in time. In reality, that star may no longer be there. It could have exploded 500,000 years ago and you would not see from Earth for another 500,000 years from today. Light travels at 299,792,458 m/s the distance between the Earth and the stars is measured in light-years.* **kjvbible.org**

It's been said; *"We can't see the forest for the trees"*. Our lives are laterally consumed moving from one fixed object or position in time to the other. Predisposition as victims of observational encounters rendezvousing with time and circumstances of a day's progression; we wake up in the morning with the appearance that our lives are no better than the day before; carrying forward incumbencies laden with the burdens of our decisions. A day's encounter and the choices we make become relevant in our decisions of tomorrow.

Days of Vengeance

In the pause of evening; how many times have you focused your attention on the vertical display in the heavens above? Did you notice the moon and stars? Did your spirit migrate upwards to ascertain meaning of their existence? They are there as a witness of times past at the entrance of faith when God spoke light into existence. As remnants of creation their contribution glimmers with hope as a collective power only seen at night. To understand wisdom born of their existence we need look no further than the suns beaming light. Jesus teaches we should look upward into the heavens for revelation of times to come; *"And when these things* **begin** *to come to pass, then look up, and lift up your heads; for your redemption draweth nigh"*.[1]

The cosmic display in the heavens are bound to an empirical testimony of prophetic events recorded by all the Major Prophets of old; Isaiah, Jeremiah, Ezekiel, Lamentations and Daniel. From the beginning of the New Testament to the Book of Revelation; from the star in the east at the birth of Christ to the ending of time seen by the apostolic revelations of John, they all give testimony of visions of signs in the sun and in the moon and stars. That's the time clock of our universe waiting in readiness for the day of their departure. For some; they will be around to witness those grave and dreadful days. But not us; by then we will have made our journey home.

> *And there shall be signs in the sun, and in the moon, and in the stars; and upon the earth distress of nations, with perplexity; the sea and the waves roaring; Men's hearts failing them for fear, and for looking after those things which are coming on the earth: for the powers of heaven shall be shaken. And then shall they see the Son of man coming in a cloud with power and great glory. And when these things begin to come to pass, then look up, and lift up your heads; for your redemption draweth nigh.*
> **Luke 21:25-28 KJV**

Truth stands upon a pillar of its own. It needs no other appendages. More often than not, our human nature subtracts more from truth rather than accept its true value designated for our empowerment. It boils down to a matter of belief and our trust of faith. Our senses are visually dependent relative to our physical existence interacting with the natural laws of nature. The motto of our senses is experiential; *"I can believe it if I can see it"*. However, the spiritual manifestation of faith sees through the eyes of belief.

We can accept the testimony of the Prophets and the cosmic testimony of the heavens as truth and glean from all they have to teach us; or we can simply consider it all to be a fable and bear the consequence as in the day of Noah. Ignorance occurs when we trust more to our visualizations than to accept wisdom gained from our interactions with faith.

> *For this they **willingly are ignorant** of, that by the word of God the heavens were of old, and **the Earth standing out of the water and in the water**: Whereby the world that then was, being overflowed with water, perished: But the heavens and the Earth, which are now, by the same word are kept in store, reserved unto fire against the day of judgment and perdition of ungodly men.* **2 Peter 3:5-7 KJV**

There is a river of life above our firmament called the *"Sea"*. Some refer to it as the *"Sea of Time"*. We will never be able to travel to the end of it to see what lies beyond. Only until our souls are reclaimed and we are released from time will we see time in its beginnings. *"He who comes from above is above all; he who is of the Earth is Earthly and speaks of the Earth. He who comes from Heaven is above all."*[1] Time is a place of division separating God's Heaven from all visible forms of life. The heavens are three dimensional; the 3rd and highest Heaven is timeless, place of God's occupation, the 2nd is of our planetary system and lastly, the 1st heaven is the atmospheric dominion of man.

In the day the Earth was created, it was immersed in water until God divided the waters and created a firmament in the heavens that is called our universe. Our universe is surrounded by a sea of water. Not the oceans of Earth but the Seas God separated for our habitation on Earth. When the Light of God penetrated darkness; it exposed water lying beneath in frozen tundra. The Spirit of God hovered over the waters of the deep and God divided the waters. Our firmament was made from the same water which was vaporized by the Light of Creation. God's Light is never-ending!

> *Then God said, "Let there be a firmament in the midst of the waters, and let it divide the waters from the waters. And God made the firmament, and divided the waters which were under the firmament from the waters which were above the firmament;" and it was so. And God called the firmament Heaven. And the evening and the morning were the second day. Then God said, Let the waters under the heaven be gathered together into one place, and let the dry land appear; and it was so.* [4]

The Great Fall

> *By the abundance of your trading You became filled with violence within, And you sinned; Therefore I cast you as a profane thing Out of the mountain of God; And I destroyed you, O covering cherub, From the midst of the fiery stones. "Your heart was lifted up because of your beauty; You **corrupted your wisdom** for the sake of your splendor.* [5]

In Pre-Adamic days, Lucifer possessed power as the ruling authority of God's materiality along with a host of angels. He ruled the firmament of the heavens and all things on the surface of the Earth. Scripture clearly indicates that he was in Eden in the Garden of God.

Lucifer and his host of angels were the first immortal beings to sin; it was the original sin of corruption born from the splendor of Lucifer's pride. He made a fatal conclusion to believe he could usurp God's authority by rising above God's seat of power.

Before Lucifer fell, he entered into a conspiracy with a congregation of angels who sought establishment of their own kingdom; a kingdom above God's Throne. What we should realize, though he is a fallen vessel of light who was defeated at the Cross, he has mastered the visible principles surrounding our existence here on Earth. Lucifer had a catastrophic ending that has impacted our lives by his influence which was induced in the life of the serpent. The Book of Revelation says; *"So the great dragon was cast out that serpent of old called the devil and Satan who deceives the whole world; he was cast to the Earth, and his angels were cast out with him".* [6]

> *You were the anointed cherub who covers; I established you; You were on the holy mountain of God; You walked back and forth in the midst of fiery stones.* **Ezekiel 28:14 NKJV**

When Lucifer had authority to rule the heavens, remarkably he had the power and access to go back and forth by extraterrestrial travel from Heaven's Mountain to the dominion of Earth. The passageway was amidst fiery stones of the constellations occupied by the celestial existence of stars and planets; lords of the universe populating the expanse of God's creation. Lucifer's motives were the same as I see seeded in the heart of man; *"Lust for supremacy of power".*

The same temptations Christ was subjected to; the *"lust of the flesh, lust of the eye and the pride of life"* [7] engineered by seduction of Lucifer and his fallen host of angels continues to maintain their presence in the affairs of man.

"Pride of Power" by the enemy's deception has led some to believe they have legitimacy to a Kingdom that never was intended. Ask the rich man and see how he fared. We are warned not to think of ourselves more highly than we ought. You may think for the sake of your splendor, just as Lucifer did; you have power that can ascend through the heavens raising your throne above the Stars of God, but you will fail miserably.

The Devil is still in search for occupancy in any vacant chamber in need of his power. Accumulating of his attributes is corrupting. We all have heard the expression; *"the Devil made me do it"*. I don't believe that and neither do you. The blame is on you. You did it to yourself by allowing his influences to take root in your life. You gave him the right to destroy God's good intentions purposed for your success and now you are searching in the dark for a way out. The Devil is a usurper who encroached beyond his measure but is contained with restricted access into the operation of our lives. His kingdom will never reach the heavens again for he is the fallen star which has lost its power.

We are instructed to give *"no place to the devil"*. In the vanity of our imaginations he will play games with our mind. Once his corruption enters in his usurping tendencies undoubtedly will compromise our faith.

Bricks and Mortar

> Come, let us make bricks and bake them thoroughly." They had brick for stone, and they had asphalt for mortar. And they said, "Come, let us build ourselves a city, and a tower whose top is in the heavens." [8]

Bricks baked in the fiery furnace of conspiracy, indicates the rebellious nature of man's heart that has hardened and turned away from God's providence of grace. The mixture of brick and asphalt is a sealant of rejection anchored in idolatry. The imaginations of man gives cause for believing he is a god unto himself. God's Spirit will never allow the fusion of His Spirit with the mitigated imaginations of man's idolatrous attempt to exist independent of Him.

It is a haunting thought to see how our churches have changed from a beacon of hope to reach the lost, hurting and needy at the expense of embellishing their own success. Some of them have been too successful in their endeavor by propagating personalities to fuel expansion of their empire. What happened to the Anointing? Did we get left behind at the dissecting point of our indecisions? Did we go one way when God chose to go another? Can it be the result of our refusal to hear? *"God is a Spirit and He changes not."* Healing of yesterday is the same as His healing of today with the same availability continuing in the days to come.

The Holy Spirit is more than a teacher. Is this where we have settled? Why aren't the Evangelist and Prophets beating the streets with warnings of the days that are soon to come? God's methods haven't changed but we have. We are not as spiritual as we once were. We would rather spend our time listening to a message than taking the time to sacrifice on bended knee. On any given Sunday, the church parking lots are full of prosperity seekers who have itching ears satisfied only by the smooth sayings of man that does not challenge their faith. They barricade themselves behind walls of separation; expanding their presence brick by brick to build their towers into the heavens. They are seeking a name to validate their accomplishments to brandish their pride amongst men.

Where is the Anointing to do the work the Church is was entrusted to do? God's divine energy embodied in The Holy Spirit is intended to empower our gifting for the performance of faith. Why are we continuing to harness His power in pursuit of fruitless things? Every saved vessel of God can teach or preach the Gospel by testimony of their faith and not just the ones elevated in our midst. It suggests to me we have a serious need for deliverance to free up our gifts and allow the Holy Spirit to use us as He so chooses. The Spirit of Christ is the engineer of our faith but we have managed to supplant His usefulness for our own endeavors.

There is a difference between talent and gifting. You can learn talent if you are endowed with the natural ability to adapt. Even though it is learned behavior it has a self-gratifying capacity of doing something and can exist independent of anything else. But our gifting gratifies through obedience of what we are sent to do.

Our gifts are dependent on our cooperation with the *"Gift of Faith"*. It is a spiritual commission activated by the power of an anointing with a targeted destination. *"A gift is not a gift just to be a gift!"* It differs in having a talent to sing than having the gift of singing; praying minus power to pray; healing without the anointing to heal. Spiritual exploits rendered from our faith are not dependent on the talent of our hands but by a power greater in creativity. Without movement of God's power our gifts are limited as vain expressions of any attempt to bring satisfaction to faith.

If you haven't realized this by now; I may be a little different than some of you. I have been called peculiar at times to say the least. Destination of faith requires me to speak *"Truth to Power"*. It is a gift serviced by the *"One and Only"* who has given me the boldness to speak and power to participate in the performance of faith. Individually, we all have to discover that place which has our unique signature of what God requires of us. Discovery of His will for our lives to answer the call of faith is paramount for fulfillment of our destiny.

Artifacts

> "But He turned and said to Peter, Get behind Me, Satan! You are an offense to Me, for you are not mindful of the things of God, **but the things of men**." [9]

Some churches exist in name only. They disguise themselves behind artifacts of the Cross of Christ; aligning themselves in a conspiracy of building cities for a habitation of an idolatrous tower penetrating into the heavens. There is a name for them: *"501(c)(3)"*. For you who may not know the term, 501(c)(3) refers to non-profit organizations such as our churches that qualifies for special tax status under section 501(c)(3) of the U.S. tax code. You may say who cares? I most certainly do! Our churches have become no different than organizations that pursue profit mirroring each other's accomplishments. Rolls Royces, Learjets and Yachts are the calling card of attraction. They have a religious footprint but their actions parallels with the agendas of this world. Where does it end? When is enough, enough? We are using the power of the Cross to profit. There is a word for that; *"USURY"*! Usury is extortion, stealing; taking something that does not rightfully belong to you and acting as if it is your own. Seemingly we have normalized vanity and corruption and accepted it as our *"norm"!*

It is rather disturbing how vain we have become. We continue propping up personalities as angels of light, merchandising their accomplishments for our gain. There is no substitute for the guiding Light of the Holy Spirit, *"The True Spirit of God"*. The power of the Cross of Christ still avails us but we must turn again to seek His face. But be warned; *"for if we sin willingly after we have received the knowledge of the truth there no longer remains a sacrifice for sins."* [10]

The Church is headed for a collision. Even though we are in this world, we are commanded to restrain ourselves from consumption beyond our measure. To participate in the offerings of this world is one thing but blurring the lines of demarcation from being *"In It"* to becoming *"Of It"* are entirely two different principles! And that's where we find ourselves today; *"fudging the lines of lawfulness towards compromise"*. For some who are living in pride of the Gospel are bending the rules of acceptability. Where is the separation? I see none! Some have thrown caution to the wind through radicalization by accepting the falsity of materialism to be become *"Of It"*. We've been naming it and claiming it far too long. Do we have enough yet?

In an accelerated path to build his own kingdom, seemingly man has rejected the sacrifice of the Cross when Jesus relinquished His Spirit that Heaven would be open to all to receive His power. What possibly can be greater than an anointing to heal, deliver and set the captive free? Is it our obsession with materiality that continues to get in our way; resolving to believe that flesh is more advantageous than spirit? We have used the prosperity of the Gospel without doing the works of faith we are required to do only resulting in complacency with lethargic attempts to justify our righteousness. Where is the hunger? What happened to our thirsty souls unraveling at the seams of our spiritual fabric? Where is the fire that singes the roots of darkness shadowing our faith? We need rekindling to renew the fire of our intercessions accomplished in our commitment to prayer. Surrendered vapors of our submissions are a sweet aroma in the nostril of God's detection. With a liberated spirit; freed from the access of man, God will release fresh vigor of His Anointing.

> *Let us make a name for ourselves, lest we be scattered abroad over the face of the whole earth.* **Genesis 11:14 NKJV**

We are good at making names for ourselves; always re-inventing from one day to the next. Often names we assign to ourselves and even to others depend on our moods and attitudes. Out of our benevolence, we can be quite accommodating with our words but it is not always; particularly for those who cross our path who exhibit contrarian behavior. You probably will have to close your ears to some of the names we can invent. The things people say are no different than the things people do. An unruly tongue dictates unruly behavior. We are advised to be very discreet in our approach in dealing with people. We don't always discern who it is crossing our path. There could be a stranger in your midst asking for water and food for a long journey awaiting them who very well could be a messenger of God sent for your deliverance.

For the most part, we are very judgmental always comparing one to another. At the root of it, there is a deficiency embedded in our character which indicates the presence of pride which is the *"root of conspiracy"*. Pride is an interruption of faith causing you to believe you are more than what God intended you to be. It challenges the net worth of His grace assigned to your destiny by injecting a superior image of yourself when comparing to someone else. It stands to be repeated counteracting the flaw in our human DNA, we are not to think more highly of ourselves than we ought in *"looking at ourselves elevated above others"*. Humility demands we remain humbled in the sight of all God's people. Every life God created must be given respect and equality rendered on an even platform; with none exceeding value greater than another.

Sometimes God's grace seems insufficient and we wander to and fro seeking connectivity to a cause. We often tend to accept the like *"mindedness"* with others believing they can bring a greater distinction of our purpose. We assign ourselves to clusters, groups and assemblies in an effort of maintaining connectivity to a collaborate cause. But be reminded of this one truth; *"Every cause is not your cause"*. You could render yourself in jeopardy by participating in the cause of others when it was never meant to be a cause of your own. You may make a name for yourselves but at the same time alienated from the truth of God's intentions for your life. We are encouraged to not forsake coming together in our assemblies but it doesn't say where. You can't just go anywhere neither do anything. You will discover judgment upon one is judgment upon all and you need to be rightfully connected.

Pride is born of the flesh that the enemy uses as a contradiction of faith. Humility is the cornerstone of faith; a lifestyle anchored in our submissiveness and the only known antidote for pride. Humility focus is never inward but extends outwards as an expression of love and compassion. Pride will always precede a fall but for some, pride of this life will render immutable consequences beyond their strength to get back up.

Show me a man full of pride and I will show you a man with an obsession of greed instigating corruption as an agent for his fulfillment. His cup will never get full. Greed has no limits; curtailed only by apathy for pride.

We are living in perilous times. As Believers it is imperative we humble ourselves and pray. God has made an appeal to the Saints occupying His tabernacle as we are attempting to make a name for ourselves at the expense of sufferings on *"The Old Rugged Cross"*. Redemption came with a price; a horrible price but a necessary one with forsaken tears descending upon the mantle of Christ. He separated from the heart of *"His Father's Love"* with a cry still echoing as a beacon of hope for weary souls tossed in the raging seas of life. It was God's gift of love pinned upon a towering Cross lifted into the Heavens for man's redemption for the entire world to see. The tearing display of the Cross has a subliminal presence seeded in the consciousness of man. It is an invocation for the choice of life only sponsored by the redeeming nature of Christ. He is the way; the only exclusive path into the Kingdom of God. There is no other access except through Him.

> *But the* LORD *came down to see the city and the tower which the sons of men had built. And the* LORD *said, "Indeed the people are one and they all have one language, and this is what they begin to do; now nothing that they propose to do will be withheld from them. Come, let Us go down and there confuse their language, that they may not understand one another's speech.* [12]

It is rather striking how God first came down alone to see the city and tower the sons of man built before returning with an emissary to deliver judgment upon the *"Kingdom of Babylon"*. Has He come down to look at your city and idolatrous tower? Have you seen His emissary yet? *"He's coming!"* Even though, the Tower of Babel was an essential part of the city of Babylon's interior commerce which featured man's idolatrous achievements actualized as an exhibition of his pride; he can never escape the searching eyes of God and his throne will never succeed above the Throne of God.

> *Twelve months later as the king was walking on the roof of the royal palace of Babylon he said; Is not this the great Babylon I have built as the royal residence, by my mighty power and for the glory of my majesty?* [13]

In a blink of an eye God's supreme power can tear down all the years of your labor and bring destruction upon you. If your motivations are self-rewarding of your accomplishments caught up in *"pride of power and glory in the majesty of pride"*, certainly you can expect a direct response from God. With your heads held high basking in the affluence of glamour of your achievements, the blinders of pride will distort your perceptions elevating your accomplishments without any regard of grace that came from above. It is quite troubling when we take for granted God's grace which enables us to have what we have and do what we do. The inverted nature of pride knows no gratitude.

God has angels at His disposal He can dispatch to do His bidding. They may appear as Messengers or an Angel of Mercy or an Archangel of War. Regardless, God can bring confusion upon a city of congregated minds incensed against Him. Even an idolatrous tower propagated in the heart of pride is discoverable to His query and cannot escape His judgment. Whether He chooses His judgment at the pinnacle of pride's achievements or bring correction into our lives before it even begins as a warning of pride; however His appearing may be; His eyes are never removed from our presence.

Apart from God's delegation of angels, He retains the sovereign right of an independent visitation of His own. At His appearance, mercy and grace will not be in His quiver; only judgment meant for our correction. He may cause a cloud of confusion to overshadow our understanding with intentions to reconstruct our Altar in neglect; He could rain hails of fire and brimstone from above scorching any path leading to pride or cause torrid winds of tornadoes and hurricane forces destroying everything in its path. In any event out of His provocation, God can usher in terrifying events as an instrument of His wrath to destroy the pillars of idolatry we have propagated as a god unto ourselves.

We are living in very tenuous times. For Christians we have reached a heightened level of persecution. We are witnessing the rise of totalitarianism and isolation. I've often pondered on how restricted movement of the Church has become to fulfill its call abroad which I have been very much involved. As a nation, we have inbreeded enough while expansion is evolving outside our borders. It's not a call to all; everyone does not have the Anointing to go. Still the doors of Samaria must be opened for the willing to spread the Gospel. That's the mantra of faith; *"Go"!* Freedom must be secured without inhibition of our gifting to go where God sends us. More likely than not; He will send you off the beaten path for an encounter not necessarily conceived in your faith. Faith is willingness to go as you are being sent with instructions delineating a path pre-inscribed for you to follow.

> *Now behold, an angel of the Lord stood by him, and a light shone in the prison; and he struck Peter on the side and raised him up, saying,* **"Arise quickly!"** *And his chains fell off his hands. Then the angel said to him, "Gird yourself and tie on your sandals"; and so he did. And he said to him, "Put on your garment and follow me." So he went out and followed him, and did not know what was done by the angel was real, but thought he was seeing a vision.*
> **Acts 12:7-11 NKJV**

Apostle Peter encountered an angel on assignment for his deliverance while imprisoned. Visitation of an angel will forever leave you stricken only if you are able to discern his presence. As the angel of the Lord stood by Peter with supernatural lighting all around him, he still had no recognition he was even there. After being struck to the ground; raised up by a power not of his own strength; hearing a voice speaking into his ear; chains falling from his hands; iron gates opening by an invisible power; Peter still concluded he was in the midst of a vision. We are no different; still immersed in delusions of a dream; hearing voices while sedated in defeat with our hands still bound as the bondage of Lazarus; we are entombed in our own imprisonment. If the Angel of God can't wake us up; then who can?

> *And when Peter had come to himself, he said, "Now I know for certain that the Lord has sent His angel, and has delivered me from the hand of Herod and* ***from all the expectation of the Jewish people****."* [1]

Being lackadaisical in faith is not a good place to be. There are times our spiritual senses need to be awakened. Just like Peter, we need to snap out of it; come to ourselves; in stillness and quietness to know God as He truly is. An intimate experience with Him is life changing. When we are traveling in the night with our conscious laid bare we could have encountered Him but in our waking moments we say it was just a dream; *"déjà vu"* all over again. The Presence of God is a remarkable experience; one you will likely not forget.

15

The Constitution
"A Variable Conception"

Every living organism breathes sustained by the breath of life. It is said of our Constitution here in America; *"It is a Living Document"*. If it lives, it must breathe in the breath of its people exhaling the interpretation of its principles. It is of no greater value than the people who accept the morality and ethics of its doctrines. The Constitution exists as a foundation, a system for governance of its citizens but transient in the sense that it allocates provisions for amendments. Counter intuitively the first ten amendments, the Bill of Rights, protect us from the Constitution itself.

The founders of our Constitution are dead. Their voices can still be heard echoing across the tops of every mountain across this land. They are not here to offer corrections to their original intentions, but made it possible to amend their steps. I amuse myself at times when I consider what would be their response to today's reality? I am not sure; they were different men of a different time. So who's to say? I do know some of what we see today they never could have envisioned.

Throughout our history, there have been variances in opinions and interpretations of the meaning of their words. In the writings of Thomas Jefferson, principal author of the Declaration of Independence wrote;

> *"We hold these truths to be self evident that All men are created equal and are endowed by their Creator with certain unalienable Rights among those are life, liberty and the pursuit of happiness".*

Wait a minute; not so fast! We had a civil war fighting amongst ourselves losing 620,000 of our own people in a battle challenging the meanings and purpose of an array of foundational principles he articulated.

If Jefferson were still here today; would he have said something differently? Should he have explained exactly what he meant by the words *"All men"?* Did he mean black, white, red or brown? Was the invitation to all to feast at the table of democracy with equal shares of participation? In his draft submitted to Congress, part of it was stripped out. I doubt very seriously the majority of you did not realize that Jefferson advocated against slavery at the same time understanding the contradictions of his argument in framing a defense for independence before King George III who was spearheading continuation of slavery amongst the colonies.

When men use men at the expense of inflicting pain and sufferings upon another without respect for the principles consistent with life, liberty and pursuit of happiness of every human being, it's considered a crime against nature. Sadly, there are always those waiting in the wings of suffering to capitalize for their gain with no regard for the endowment of life God has given to all of us. If not reckoned with, it will produce a cancer eating away the fabric of one's conscience.

Jefferson himself over the course of his lifetime was owner of 600 slaves on a 5000 acre plantation. For his own justification, He later contributed removal of the passage to delegates from South Carolina, Georgia and Northern states that represented merchants actively involved in the Trans-Atlantic slave trade. Jefferson was not an activist by any stretch of our imagination but was fully aware of the injustice perpetrated against foreign nationals enslaved in this country.

Inclusive in the presentation of his argument, did Jefferson *"use"* the suffering of slaves to advocate his argument unjustly? Or was it passion seated at the core of his principles of what was right or wrong. In his writings, he emphasized certain truths that are self evident; understood as being an obvious interpretation in the mind of every human being that ever existed; *"the trusted endowment by our Creator assuring a right to live life and liberty of one's personal expression to pursue happiness"*. We know in truth that has not always been the case beginning with the denial of the life of Abel murdered by the hands of his brother Cain.

In the good conscience of faith determination of the right to happiness is an individual response exercised in the choices we make and not by the denial of our choices by those infringing upon our rights. God given rights instigates freedom to move beyond the restricted boundaries of man's limitations. The passage removed from Jefferson's declaration indicted the King of Great Britain of his infidel powers that violated the sacred rights of life that exploited the sufferings of slaves.

He has waged cruel war against human nature itself, violating its most sacred rights of life and liberty in the persons of a distant people who never offended him, captivating & carrying them into slavery in another hemisphere or to incur miserable death in their transportation thither. This piratical warfare, the opprobrium of infidel powers is the warfare of the **Christian King** *of Great Britain. Determined to keep open a market where Men should be bought & sold, he has prostituted his negative for suppressing every legislative attempt to prohibit or restrain this execrable commerce. And that this assemblage of horrors might want no fact of distinguished die, he is now exciting those very people to rise in arms among us, and to purchase liberty of which he has deprived them, by murdering people whom he has obtruded them: thus paying off former crimes committed again the Liberties of one people, with crimes which he urges them to commit against the lives of another.*

Did you read that? Were you moved? Well Change! I have never heard so passionate a response in defense of human rights as I have read in this document. That is why it is so important to know for yourself beyond perceived conceptions and propagated ideas of men which tend to radicalize your thinking. Jefferson did what I see in people of today who tend to scrutinize the actions of others when they themselves are doing the very same thing. And even after coming into the truth, they still will use the sufferings of others in violation of their own hypocrisy. The principle of faith teaches;

"Judge not lest you be judged." Sometimes it is not the most appealing sight to see when the table is turned and mirror of your reflection renders an indictment against you; *"Be True to Thine Self"*.

By the standards written in the preamble of our Constitution it references *"Natural Laws"* meaning the intuitive laws of nature that should be visible to us all. It also references the *"Laws of Nature's God"*. The only measurable commentary of *"Nature's God"* in existence is the Word of God itself. *"It is the truth and nothing but the truth."* From beginning to end, the Bible vindicates arguments of God's Creation and rule of governance for humanity; *"today, tomorrow and forever"*!

In high school, we were required to memorize part of the Preamble where it states; *"Secure the Blessings of Liberty to ourselves and our Posterity"*. Is the word posterity relevant to you? The context of its meaning is quite simple; *"A future generation of people"*.

The Preamble for the life of all Believers is etched in the heart of faith; *"John 3:16"*. It is not meant just to be recited from memory but intertwined in our fabric as our mantra advocating the true intent of faith: *"For God so loved the world that He gave His only begotten Son that whosoever believeth in Him, shall not perish but have eternal Life"*. [1]

Love is centered as the feature of faith for all intent and purpose to bring identification of the Existence of God's life in all of humanity. Despite the uniqueness of our individuality and biases developed through our perceptions interpreting the motivations and life of others, the influence of which should never diminish our understanding that *"We all are God's Creation; Human Beings identifiable as His Humanity"*. All Life Belongs to God! Our conscience must evolve into a fuller recognition that there is no life created outside of His exception. The pathway back into the center of His vision is a challenge laid before all of us; *"To Believe in His Redemptive Plan by Acceptance of His Grace"*. It is a matter of belief from one to the other to render an accountability of life given to each one of us.

Central to the creation of man, God gave us all a measure of faith instigating reflection of His Existence through the expression of love. Love is a vehicle of conveyance bringing to the surface recognition of His identity and defining purpose justifying the reason for our creation. The laws of man are not absolute in their reflection of God's intent. Even more so, they can be outright contrarian opposing Kingdom principles in his rendering of opinions and exposition of his intentions.

Man's laws are transitional and arbitrary without absolute meaning of their expressions. For example; when Jefferson drew up his draft, did he mean to say *"Our Creator"* rather than *"Their Creator"*? For me, it implies a pluralistic meaning. Was Jefferson saying whatever god you serve; you have the same liberties and freedoms of the God of his conviction? Was he articulating the freedom of religion? If so, then why do we continue to victimize those who view their faith just as significant as our own? We should make every effort to bring others into a deeper revelation of truth but because of our differences, we continue to ostracize those who may not think like us; look like us; talk like us or for that matter believe as we believe. We usually find it much easier to diminish the value of their God given existence rather than respecting their humanity when we ourselves don't have a heaven or an island of the Hades to put them in. So, why the hate?

What rights did the Indians have? In essence they were denied the very freedoms in their own land that Jefferson propagated. They already had life and liberty and without a doubt were pursuing happiness by their own standards but were annihilated, ostracized with the remainder bound on reservations of treaties.

The American Indians lost everything by invention of the repeating rifle comparatively to proliferation of today's automatic weapons bundled in the hands of a stealthy militia. They lost their land; the plains where the buffalo roamed; graves of their ancestors covered with the sacrifice of blood and shame from wailings of surrender. But more significant than anything else; they lost their national identity to be an American even though they are native to the land of their ancestors.

With stealthy tactics of deception and the maligning of enforceable treaties or overt measures of threat with weapons of destruction; the sacred treasures of the American Indians were stolen by *"European Settlers"* regardless of their origin, authenticating themselves as *"The True Americans"*. What they stole even the bounty of human life of Africans grafted into the American ideology oblivious of indifferences was extended a share of the ill-gotten gains in lieu of searching for their own identity. *"Descendants from Africa now the African American is still in search of their grandeur."* What's next? Are you settled yet? Everyone else is! It may come as a surprise for some of you to discover all the different shades of Africa. They resemble any other Black American with the same diversity of colors and you know exactly the reason why! We wear the shame in the consequence of someone else's action. Legacy of nearly **"12.5 million"** enslaved Africans harvested from the soul of Africa only began their journey on board the *"White Lion"* in 1619 just *"1600"* years after Christ left this Earth! Are you quick to forget?

From the days of my youth; my mother instilled in me a valuable principle; *"If you take something that does not rightly belong to you; you are a thief"*. Whether it was Easter eggs I stole from the church Easter Egg Hunt while hiding in the bushes or candy from the neighborhood corner store; I still was a thief and paid a dear price at the expense of her wrath. Listen people of this nation; ask yourself; *"do you want to get this thing right and move on from our improprieties or keep it as status quo"?* If it's the latter; we will not be able to withstand conjugation of internal pressures that are seeking our demise. Even as of today, the tentacles of racism are brewing in our midst like a bubbling teapot whistling with pressure.

Across the landscape of America we have nearly forgotten the Indians and their resiliency to survive. I often wonder how our Creator views the sacrifices of a nation of people at their core who were denied their right to be. It is estimated that as high as 18 million Native Americans were here before their continent was nearly purged of their existence. As of today it is only 4.5 million. If the world then was sophisticated as it is now; would other nations have sat on their hands and allowed genocide of a nation of people to continue? Would they have defended the sovereign right of the Indians to remain autonomous? I believe those kinds of questions will never be answered for we exist in a different world than that of yesterday. But even in our ultramodern day culture atrocities of Sudan, Rwanda, Bosnia and the apartheid of South Africa indicates the needle has not moved very far. The European and American model of *"Eugenics"* Hitler used for ethnic cleansing to eliminate the Jews is indicative of human nature's inability to learn from its failures. Truly, it is a generational cycle that continues to evolve.

The words we speak convey meanings. They frame images of our perception and if allowed to linger can be infectious enough to sway our beliefs. As a result, what we perceive as truth justifies the condition of our heart. When our biases are brought to the forefront, we tend to render conclusions based solely on our observations which can be quite dangerous. It creates opportunity to erroneously provide validation of our preconceptions. Even the writing of history is reflective of biases which some use as a means to substitute truth repaginating sequencing of events to alter our perception for their own justification.

Pretentiously, American history is reflective of its own biases failing to come to grips with truth of its emergence. By concession, there are consensuses that say rather than correct the wrongs of yesterday; accept an oblivious choice of not recognizing that they ever existed. That's how the spirit of pride speaks veiled in a superior perception concluded in the consciousness of denial. So why am I saying these things; *"To speak truth to power of the elusive attempts of denial rooted in the chronology of the American Manifesto."* Truth being; Indians aren't savages never were; they're Americans; true Americans, human beings just like you and me.

Bible vs. Constitution

Unlike our Bible that exists as a document of truth; line upon line, precept upon precept; the Constitution mimics some of its principles but does not holistically reflect the fullness of its tenets. Remarkably, there is a fundamental difference in their underlying principles. *"God is a theocracy; the Constitution is a government of men immersed in a collaboration of ideas and principles not absolute in all of its appendages."*

Articulation of truth in scripture has no variances; *"it is what it is and will always be what it is"*! Strange as it may seem, the Constitution itself has rendered a verdict against all of us by giving power and access on an equal platform through naturalization to those in opposition to our beliefs. How subjective is that? But yet we still complain as we continue to victimize those who are seeking the same freedoms and opportunities we have acquired. Are we to close our borders? Have we crossed the threshold saying enough is enough? We are all immigrants regardless of the way we got here; some by choice, others by indentured labor while yet there are others who arrived through no choice of their own still being penalized simply for the fact that they are just here! However it may be; we all are fighting for a piece of the pie; some want to share it while others desire to keep it all to themselves. *"Some say it is my way or no way while others contend it is our way; We the People"*. Which way are we going to have it?

In truth, the reason for so much unrest experienced in our nation is that we have lost our way by living in compromise of principles engineered for our faith. What happened to the *"Beacon of Light"* shining on the hill showing others a more excellent way? Erosion in our culture has jeopardized our traditions and now we have become frantic. I can tell you hot off the press; *"It's too late! Our house is already divided"*. It is rather sad that the division between us has lasted so long. We are succumbing to internal pressures charitable by outward influences allocated with equal sponsorship helping to facilitate our demise. Will somebody please take the lid off! How much more of this suppressive heat can we withstand without erupting into perpetual chaos? Let me know. I might be inclined to help you.

There is no nicety in war; the winner takes all. Our vision is blurred and we cannot see the forest for the trees. We are being buffeted by an array of influences seeking to compromise us more than we already are.

Seductive persuasions have us fighting against each other in our homes, on the street and even in our churches. Take the blinders off can't you see what's going on? It is the enemies plan to sow seeds of doubt and discord impeding our destiny. But be reminded; the day will come when the rooster returns to roost and finds us shackled in our own deception.

From a colony to a colonized power of imperialistic dominance, we've exported *"democratized capitalism"* as a vehicle for world commonality. It is now a flailing commodity dependent solely on the success of the rich and powerful. Our allies share our corresponding ideas and conceptions in an intricate stream of cooperation. But yet as of today, we are confronted with challenges of an unsettled future. Distribution of financial wealth of the most privileged in our society is shared only in the hands of a few who have controlling interest in our everyday decisions.

Our spiritual conscience here in America has been vastly eroding. What was once considered as truth is perverted to be lies. Integrity, honesty and civility are but bywords in our daily interactions. The greed of a few has violated every principle of compassion laying bare a wasteland full of deception. Strikingly, hatred has punctured the bowels of love and compassion causing so much unwarranted suffering and pain. Is that the reason why we have so much poverty amidst our greed? What's up with that? I don't always have to agree with you but I can be sensitive to your sufferings and certainly always a friend to your need.

Instigations of fear permeate within our culture in violation of security and trust needed for our survival. Murder and indiscriminate killings of our citizens have but all demonstrated our lack of civility in our love for God's humanity. It seems as if we are reluctant to call anyone our brother for that matter not even a neighbor because our ideologies won't allow it. The color of our skin; where we worship, how we worship gives greater credence to some of us than the investment of life God deposited in all of His humanity. After all, we all are human beings! Tell me; whatever happened to the concept of forgiveness; what's that about? Believe me; it is a whole lot easier to forgive than to carry the weight of vindictiveness. That's the kind of stuff that will definitely destroy you. It will consume you as a cancer; eating you up from the inside out. It is the same as revenge which is indicative of our attitudes we have for one another that stirs up so much strife. Be advised; *"Don't let the sun go down on your wrath"*.[1]

One could say in observation of the state we are in; *"It's Mental Illness, something that has affected us all"*. I refuse to accept that! It's too convenient of an excuse to justify our actions. If that's the case why don't we all take *"Prozac"* and call it a day. But America we are suffering from an illness deep down in the soul of this country that all the Prozac in the world can't help. It's spiritual! When a nation forgoes the power of believing, praying and loving; in its betrayal, it will suffer the consequences indicative of a nation blindly headed on a journey towards its own demise.

Listen to me citizens; *"When did we forget how to live"?* Simple answer; *'It was the day when we stopped praying together".* Consequently, we are witnessing a spiraling diminishing of faith, compromising to accept the fruits of money, power, greed in a society resistant to inclusion and change. It has become much easier to exist in the shadows of the pride of men than muster enough courage to fight against their rebelliousness. *"The choice is yours; you choose. Might I suggest to you, do it soon before it's too late."*

But now we have taken a step further but this one has greater consequences. Men of pride have emerged dominating our cerebral space without influence of the Holy Spirit's guidance putting us all at risk. I believe we as a people have the same aspirations; security in the environment we live, love of our family and friends, a consistent livelihood without threat of termination, freedom to go where we want to go, do what we want to do and a place where our choices are uncontested.

Riding on the Wings of the Devil

The devil has wings and he can fly. He flies at the speed of spirit and you do not have the ability to keep up with him unless you have the Holy Ghost. The Holy Ghost flies fast, I mean real fast; faster than you can think. He does not rely on familiarity of your thoughts; He is before them and knows them from beginning to end; they are not original. The impressions of your mind have been seen before; *"Revelation Knowledge"* will surely attest to relevancy of all that preceded you.

What would inspire me to take a free ride on wings that does not have enough power to take me where I need to go? I am on one wing but who is riding on the other? The answer is simple; somebody just like me and anyone else who is willing to take the chance. What am I willing to sacrifice knowing where this road is going to take me? Know this, the Lord didn't buy you that ticket; it was you, the devil and everybody who has bought into his persuasion. God tried to warn you but you didn't listen. You did not want any part of His counsel because your zealous aspirations exceeded the boundaries faith allowed. Meaning you just didn't have the capacity to wait! Did we forget what it means to be a witness? *"A true witness delivereth souls but a deceitful witness speaketh lies"*. [1]

In one of my moments of meditation a Word was dropped into my spirit that I was quite reluctant to share. I am of the understanding that everything that you hear and see isn't always for public consumption. But this was one of those rare moments up until now. The voice speaking into my inner ear demanded my attention; *"Riding on the wings of the devil"*! I have heard things before but this was quite unusual. In consideration of my immediate response; I had none! I know the devil can fly but I was not on his manifest. I did not give it any thought that I could possibly be one of his passengers; surrendered, trusting in where he would take me. That was not my thought. However, my spirit was impacted as I waited for the Image of the Word to reveal itself.

When Samuel grew old he appointed his sons as Israel leaders. The name of his firstborn was Joel and the name of his second was Abijah, and they served at Beersheba. But his sons did not follow his ways. **They turned aside after dishonest gain and accepted bribes and perverted justice.** *All the elders of Israel gathered together and came to Samuel at Ramah. They said to him, "You are old, and your sons do not follow your ways; now* **appoint a king to lead us, such as all the other nations have.**" *But when they said, "Give us a king to lead us," this displeased Samuel; so he prayed to the* L<small>ORD</small>. *And the* L<small>ORD</small> *told him:* **"Listen to all that the people are saying to you; it is not you they have rejected, but they have rejected me as their king**. *As they have done from the day I brought them up out of Egypt until this day, forsaking me and serving other gods, so they are doing to you. Now listen to them; but warn them solemnly and let them know what* **the king who will reign over them will claim as his rights.**" *Samuel told all the words of the* L<small>ORD</small> *to the people who were asking him for a king. He said, "This is what the king who will reign over you will* **claim as his rights**: *He will take your sons and make them serve with his chariots and horses, and they will run in front of his chariots. Some he will assign to be commanders of thousands and commanders of fifties, others to plow his ground, reap his harvest, and others to make weapons of war and equipment for his chariots. He will take your daughters to be perfumers, cooks and bakers. He will take the best of your fields, vineyards, olive groves and give them to his attendants. He will take a tenth of your grain, your vintage and give it to his officials. Male, female servants and the best of your cattle he will take for his own use. He will take a tenth of your flocks, and you will become his slaves. When that day comes, you will cry out for relief from the king you have chosen,* **but the** L<small>ORD</small> **will not answer you in that day.**" [1]

It took a little time digesting the above passage of 1 Samuel 8:1-18. Parallels during the waning days of Samuel's tenure are reflective with an insightful query translatable to things we see today. The words spoken into my spirit; *"Riding on the wings of the devil"* had never left me after nearly three months of ponderings, but it became increasingly quite clear what was being revealed. As the images continued to translate in my deliberations as to their relevance, my curiosity still remained heightened as I got closer to realization of God's indictment against the elders of Israel. Samuel's words seared deep into my conscience. Contextually, I trust I can make sense of what I perceive of their meaning. Truth is a witness unto itself. It speaks truth to power without any arguments of our perceptions.

Let me just get to the point without further pause; *"The coronation of 2016; our presidential election"*. Wow! What a ride! Configuration of lies, corruption, deception and everything the enemy could have used seemingly was set into motion to invalidate the eternal good of this nation. Somebody please tell me and tell me now; *"What's going on"?* I have reached the point of resignation! I don't necessarily cast all the blame at the feet of Trump he had help and not the kind you think I am talking about. Just don't blame Trump; Trump is Trump. Trump does what Trump does. It is not a secret. As a citizen of this country, I clearly heard him tell us before we elected him; this is who I am and this is what you're getting. But No! What did some of you do? A delegation of Christian leaders across this land the *"Big Fish Type";* who I rather not name but you know exactly who they are; collectively ventured to Manhattan to the king's tower and laid hands on him; anointed him and prophesied into his future broadcasting as a witness for the world to see. Regrettably, now he has convinced himself he is the chosen one! Did they ask God? Or were they not in need of His counsel? Whether they knew or didn't; I believe without God's directive they initiated a self-fulfilling prophesy for their own correction.

Scripture says; *"Lay hands suddenly on no man, neither be partaker of other men's sins; keep thyself pure"*.[1] I know what it means but do you? I doubt very seriously even as of today, Trump still doesn't know what was going on. He was a deer stuck in the head-lights. Seemingly, they all wanted a king who would champion their desires and every cause under the sun. With an aggressive agenda, they promoted him as their last opportunity. Opportunity for what might I ask? I have my suspicion but I elect to keep it close to my vest. Resoundingly, he rendered himself a servant to their cause and all of his methods dictate that to be true. Christians, Russians and Trump's own pride triangulated their efforts to secure his appointment. With their minds made up; it really didn't matter much concerning what were his beliefs, character, morality or truthfulness indicative of a walk of integrity.

From all appearances, you would expect a higher disposition from a leader of a Christian Nation. Does it matter anymore? There was never a disguise of his faith and subsequently it's been proven he was not sufficiently rooted. He was blinded by the success of his riches, fame and glamour of pride. Anyone who tells you they live above repentance as to never see fault in themselves is saying they are *"God Proof"*. That's some scary stuff! *"To become mesmerized over other people's achievements is a sin against your own."* Don't get blinded! Do you hear me leaders?

"Fear is very ambitious thing" and will override your senses and reasoning ability to accurately calculate your steps towards the completion of faith. Fear exist as an impediment and will dislodge you from any hope in God's ability to deliver answers to your prayers. God has answers and most certainly the devil does too if you listen to his persuasions! The devil has mastered *"the art of familiarity"*. In our desperation, he knows how to supplement our wanting out of the knowledge gained in the midst of our fanaticism. Fear mixed with adventurism in our response to faith is quite negating. It assaults surety of our beliefs by randomly pursuing causes of indifference not connected to our faith.

As I see Trump wailing, twisting in knots like a pretzel truly I have sympathy for the agonizing position he has gotten himself into. Nothing but persecution on every front! The Bible says; *"A wise man will hear and increase learning and a man of good understanding will attain wise counsel"*. [1] Leaders veiled in their own deceit had their worldly agendas and they used him but little did he know they didn't have the power to keep him from falling. They can't pick him up; that's something he has to figure out on his own. They didn't care about his lost soul searching in the dark that needed deliverance they had attained. However, I am no judge of man's soul but I do recognize he is in need of deliverance; the same deliverance that inspired me to change from a life succumbed to belligerency. He couldn't see their light; his light was brighter; blinding them by the superficial light of his attracting glitter more than their pretentiousness.

It seems rather remarkable how silent their voices have become and their actions truncated to no more than a puppet suspended in the wind; dancing to a choreographed diatribe of rhythms secluded in his mind. And now there they sit; *"Complicit in Silence"* with muted voices surrendered to arguments no more valuable than expended air. So tell me; through the exercising of your faith can you truly say you heard from God? Are you now able to honestly answer the question; *"Did God Really Say"?* [1] Are you still holding on to your inflexibility that you indeed heard from God and continue to passionately use scripture in defense of your suppositions? Since God is a Spirit; why is it that I didn't hear the same thing you heard? What's up with that? Tell Me! I am on a need to know bases.

Consequently, the actions of these leaders inspired a community of Believers to error in their judgment at the expense of their leadership. Next time somebody tells you who they are; *"BELIEVE IT"!* And stop trying to make people into the product of who you want them to be. *"That's a poster for witchcraft"!* Are we to blame

Trump's woes solely on the devil or the Russians; *"No! The culprit is quite obvious; "Blame the Church"*. Where was the gift of discernment to accurately give God's counsel of wisdom? It really didn't matter; they didn't care. They were just ecstatic to have a seat at the king's table to accomplish their agendas. Have you seen that type before who are fully obsessed with greed and power and will use anyone and anything to achieve success? Pray for our leaders even Trump; it's only God who delegates power for reasons of His own.

Where is the Faith

The challenges facing our nation are enormous but we must not conclude that God is not big enough to solve them if we would only come together in prayer. A praying nation is a winning nation. It is secured above policies of governments which can change from one legislative cycle to the next. Scripture teaches that; *"Render to Caesar the things that are Caesar's and to God the things that are God's"*.[1] Loyalty to Caesar has not been our problem but what about our loyalty to God? What is it that belongs to Him that is not a part of our considerations? The answer can be seen across the changing landscape of these United States. Our states are fractured from one to the other in different shades of the *"Covenant Rainbow"*; some red states, blue states and the confused states of purple. They all are failing faith with variances in their commitment and confessions that indeed it is *"In God We Trust"*!

The sacrifice of faith is a burden to bear that is being voided in the disruptive channels of division of black vs. white; poor vs. the rich; separating those who have from the have-nots. The cares of this world will always be the cares of this world. My father told me to always *"lift up my eyes unto the hills from whence cometh my help. My help cometh from the Lord, which made Heaven and Earth"*.[1] I continue to look, watching and waiting with the gift of faith in readiness for God's response in our time of need.

There is a general consensus of the public's attitude towards the Church which by all accounts is quite condescending because of misappropriations of the enormous wealth the Church has accumulated. It is very concerning to the degree that the appropriations which come into the Church's treasury; they never reach the lives of those whom we come to serve. Man continues to stand in his stature and pride and has insulated himself from fault. If he considers he is being victimized by his own success, seemingly he could be justified. In his defiance, the intended recipients of our contributions are falling through the cracks of his lofty intentions and they are suffering. My beloved mother taught me a very important principle; *"If it is within your power to do good and you withhold your hand; woe unto you"*. I'm afraid the Church will suffer from its own woes because of insensitivities in regards to their ministry to the less fortunate. If you don't know this by now; the poor will always be amongst us.

What God supplies or for that matter does not supply is still His sufficiency. Desire for God's grace at times does not always appear to be so immediate and easily attained. Every so often, for our learning, it will take patience with a willingness to wait on the Lord to see results of faith. There are times we pray for God's grace and mercy to shine upon us and do not readily see his solutions and suffer seemingly just for the sake of suffering and even get discouraged in our movement of faith. There is no other alternative to consider in our despondency but to exercise patience in waiting for God's provisions. Remember; *"The devil can't take you where God has destined you to be nor is he able to complete the finishing of your faith"*.

In my observations, I have encountered the actions of some who have withdrawn from the press of faith reneging from any further expectation of God fulfilling His Word. For them; they settled abandoning hope just waiting for the *"Chariots of Glory"* to carry them home. I refuse to get caught up in the clouds when they have not yet fully developed into a formation indicative of the times of my surrender. Until then there is work to do without invoking a mechanism of escape into a reality that has not yet arrived. But I continue to look up for my help comes from the Lord! What is on the other side is on the other side. It will be there when I get there. But until then, I will wait on the Lord and try my best to be of good courage.

"To be empathetic is Earthly; limited to the natural movement of your senses. But to be compassionate is spiritual; an unlimited distribution of Heaven's love moving in your heart." LLW

Trust in the Lord with all your heart and lean not on your own understanding in all your ways acknowledge Him and He shall direct your paths. [13]

Message to the Church

In some of our churches, there is a question to be asked; where is the Altar? I can easily recognize the pulpit but why is the Altar buried beneath the modern day pleasures of the Church? If I may implore you; be committed to the life of prayer restoring the fallen Altar as the center of God's appeal. Greater than the value of the promotion of our gifts, the Altar of God is the most valuable asset available to the life of every true Believer in maintaining connectivity to the Throne of God. The active stream of God's productive life can heal our nation but we must be committed yielding our sacrifices for the service of humanity.

The pulpit is symbolic of an office; it is but one gift. But where are the remaining gifts? We all have a part in ministry to do the designated works of God. There should be enough room at the table for expression of every gift God has assigned to the Body of Christ.

Seductive Influences

Seductive influences rooted in materialism have corrupted many of our leaders. Some boldly embraced worldly principles as a substitute for provisions of faith. We have to be very careful. The responsibility is laid at our feet. The spirit of covetousness is running rampant in our assemblies making merchandise of the Saints. If you are not vigilant, you will become captive in your own faith to their deceptions. We have made idols of some of our leaders and our contentions have made a mockery of faith by pitting one against another as to who is the greatest amongst us. Why should it matter who has the greater anointing or achievements or who has the most money. Church, we are dealing with some goofy stuff! From Church to Church; why does everything look like it just came from the factory; the same format; same visuals; same performances? Whatever happened to uniqueness giving distinction of our gifts from one to the other? Is it possible that we've become too successful in our materialistic pursuits?

Because of pride and self-righteousness, we have misappropriated intent of our gifting of seeking the lost and those destitute of faith. Being prideful offers no resilience to change. It indicates our expectations are suffocating in fear. Fear has power to move our hearts away from *"God's Trust"*. The voice of God's stillness needs reclaiming in the strength of our meditations to rediscover Him as He Truly Is!

We are living in very perilous times with our days rescinding under shadowy clouds filled with so much uncertainty. Wars and rumors of wars, poverty, strife and the *"Spirit of Greed"* have catapulted us further into despair. The looming decline of our faith demands intervention. Must we continue to wander aimlessly as a ship without a rudder in unpredictable waters that will only yield God's judgment upon us? As a guiding light in a sea of darkness the compass of God's Spirit is a beacon of hope for all who are seeking in faith.

REFERENCES

Subject matter of the following subjects all researched on the World Wide Web; Pottery, Hematology, Water Properties, Sankofa, Law of Motion, Internet, Stars, 501c(3), Eugenics, Side-Meat, Single Parents, Constitution, Deleted Page from Declaration of Independence, Bill of Rights, Music Lyrics, Indians, Slavery, Tobacco. *Word search*: Dictionary.com

Cover source image
    Image: Cool Amazing Space
    Artist: Bruna Source
    Improv: Lester Wingate
http://www.bruna.cat/bkey/amazing-space-wallpapers

Vector graphics courtesy of: www.publicdomainvectors.org
    Image: *Black Swan*
    Image: *Decorative Text Dividers*

https://www.literarydevices.net/euphemism (Pg. 71)

http://www.madehow.com/Volume-4/Pottery.html (Pg. 84-85)

https://www.mayoclinic.org/departments-centers/hematology/sections/overview/ovc-20201283 (Pg. 87)

https://pmm.nasa.gov/education/water-cycle (Pg. 118-119)

https://en.wikipedia.org/wiki/Sankofa (Pg. 196)

https://jamesclear.com/physics-productivity (Pg. 286)

https://en.wikipedia.org/wiki/Internet (Pg. 326)

https://kjvbible.org/katabole.html (Pg. 328)

https://en.wikipedia.org/wiki/501(c)(3)_organization (Pg. 338)

https://www.history.com/topics/native-american-history/native-american-cultures. *Indians*: (Pg. 353)

https://en.wikipedia.org/wiki/Eugenics (Pg. 355)

Side Meat: (Pg.198)
 https://www.urbandictionary.com/define.php?term=side%20meat

Tobacco: (Pg. 221)
 https://www.ncpedia.org/anchor/tobacco-farming-old-way

Single Parents: (Pg. 242)
http://www.pewsocialtrends.org/2018/04/25/the-changing-profile-of-unmarried-parents/

Amazing Grace John Newton 1779 (Pg. 221)

When I think of goodness James M. Capers 1948 hymnary.org (Pg. 312)

When praises go up 1995 Chicago Mass Choir newreleasetoday.com (Pg. 312)

Count your blessing hymnal.net 1897 Johnson Oatman Jr. staugustine.com (Pg. 312)

Declaration of Independence: (Pg. 348)
https://www.constitution.org/us_doi.pdf

Deleted Passage from Declaration of Independence: (Pg. 350)

https://www.blackpast.org/african-american-history/declaration-independence-and-debate-over-slavery/

Constitution: (Pg. 347)
https://billofrightsinstitute.org/founding-documents/constitution/

All scripture references attributed to Biblegateway.com
King James Version: KJV, AKJV; New King James Version: NKJV
New Living Translation: NLTV; New International Version: NIV
Amplified Bible Classic Edition: AMPC
English Standard Version: ESV

Page	Version	Scripture
IV	NKJV	2 Peter 1:19-21[1]
VII	NKJV	Matthew 16:17[1]
	KJV	1 Corinthians 3:2[2]
IX	NIV	Mark 10:30[1]
IX	KJV	Luke 6:38[2]
XX	NKJV	Genesis 1:1-9[1]
XXII	NIV	Genesis 1:1[3]
XXII	NIV	Genesis 1:28[4]
XXII	KJV	James 1:17[5]
XXIII	NKJV	John 3:16[1]
XXIV	NKJV	Revelations 2:7[1]
XXV	KJV	John 1:1[1]
XXV	NKJV	Hebrews 11:1[2]
XXV	NKJV	Mark 11:23[3]

Chapter 1

1	NKJV	Job 28:12[1]
2	NKJV	Isaiah 55:11[1]
5	NKJV	Acts 9:3[1]
5	NKJV	Acts 9:5[2]
5	NKJV	Acts 9:6[3]
6	KJV	Acts 22:11[1]
7	KJV	Acts 9:7[1]
7	NKJV	Acts 9:6[2]

Chapter 2

12	ESV	Revelations 21:1-3[1]
13	NIV	2 Peter 3:5[1]
14	KJV	1 Kings 3:12[1]
14	KJV	Genesis 1:3[2]
19	NKJV	Philippians 4:6-7[1]
	NKJV	2 Corinthians 10:4-6[2]
20	NKJV	Genesis 2:9[1]
22	KJV	Genesis 3:24[1]
23	KJV	John 1:6-9[1]
24	NKJV	Exodus 3:2-5[1]
26	KJV	John 1:12[1]
27	NKJV	1 Corinthians 15:45-49[1]
30	KJV	Colossians 3:2-3[1]
31	NKJV	I John 4:16[1]
33	KJV	Romans 3:23[1]
34	NKJV	Mark 4:21[1]

Chapter 3

37	NKJV	James 1:17-18[1];
	NKJV	1:18[2]
40	AKJV	Ecclesiastes 3:15[1]
42	NKJV	Ecclesiastes 3:2[1]
42	KJV	Philippians 2:12[2]
46	KJV	Joel 2:31[1]

Chapter 4

51	NIV	Job 42:3[1]
57	KJV	Genesis 1:29-30[1]
58	NKJV	Genesis 2:8[1]
65	NKJV	Exodus 32:16
66	KJV	2 Chronicles 7:14[1]
69	NKJV	2 Timothy 4:7[1]
72	NIV	Genesis 2:18[1]
72	NIV	Genesis 2:21[2]
72	NIV	Genesis 2:22-24[3]
73	NKJV	Genesis 2:24[1]
74	NKJV	Genesis 3:6[1]
76	KJV	Genesis 3:6[1]
76	KJV	Romans 15:4[2]
76	KJV	Romans 15:1-2[3]
77	KJV	Romans 15:3[1]
77	NKJV	Genesis 3:12-13[2]
78	KJV	Genesis 5:2[1]
81	KJV	Psalm 51:11[1]
82	KJV	Amos 3:3
82	KJV	1 Samuels 18:1[1]
83	NKJV	Leviticus 17:11[1]

Chapter 5

89	NKJV	Genesis 3:9-11[1]
89	NKJV	Genesis 3:11[2]
90	NKJV	Genesis 3:22[1]
93	NIV	Revelations 1:18[1]
98	KJV	Genesis 3:20[1]
105	NIV	Genesis 3:1[1]
108	KJV	Genesis 6:5-6[1]
109	KJV	Genesis 6:3[1]
113	NIV	Matthew 24:32-33[1]
114	NIV	Genesis 3:3[1]

Chapter 6

117	NIV	Genesis 2:6-7[1]
120	NIV	Genesis 2:10[1]
125	KJV	Romans 8:37-39[1]

Chapter 7

135	NKJV	Revelations 1:9[1]
138	KJV	1 Peter 2:5[1]
139	KJV	1 Peter 1:7[1]
139	KJV	1 Peter 2:21[2]
139	NKJV	1 Peter 5:10[3]
143	NKJV	1 Corinthians 10:16[1]
144	NKJV	Ephesians 4:4-6[1]
145	KJV	Psalm 46:10[1]
146	KJV	Romans 15:1[1]
148	KJV	1 John 2:16
150	NIV	Genesis 3:1[1]

150	NIV	Genesis 12:1-3[2]
152	NIV	John 11:11[1]
152	KJV	John 11:16[2]
152	KJV	John 11:44[3]
152	KJV	John 11:25[4]
153	KJV	John 11:15[1]
153	KJV	2 Corinthians 10:5[2]
159	KJV	Acts 20:24[1]
159	KJV	Matthew 3:11[2]
160	KJV	Matthew 16:16[1]
160	KJV	Matthew 16:19[2]

Chapter 8

163	KJV	Luke 11:13[1]
164	NKJV	Luke 22:42[1]
165	KJV	Psalm 91:1[1]
171	NKJV	Mark 10:29-30[1]
172	NKJV	Jeremiah 33:3[1]
173	NKJV	Matthew 5:8[1]
	NKJV	Job 37:12-13[2]

Chapter 9

177	KJV	Colossians 3:4[1]
180	KJV	Genesis 1:6[1]
181	KJV	John 19:30
184	NKJV	Luke 3:21-22[1]
185	KJV	Proverbs 29:18[1]
190	KJV	Proverbs 4:7[1]
192	NKJV	Romans 1:18-23[1]

Chapter 10

197	NKJV	Matthew 6:25[1]
204	KJV	2 Corinthians 5:8[1]
207	NKJV	Proverbs 22:6[1]
211	NKJV	Mark 8:24[1]
211	KJV	Mark 8:25[2]
214	NKJV	Matthew 6:25[1]
215	KJV	Philippians 4:19[1]
216	KJV	Romans 4:21[1]

Chapter 11

223	NIV	2 Corinthians 12:20[1]
227	KJV	1 John 2:16[1]
233	NKJV	2 Corinthians 4:18[1]
234	NKJV	Hebrews 13:5-6[1]
	NKJV	Philippians 4:11-13[2]
239	KJV	Mark 10:25[1]
242	NIV	1 Timothy 5:8[2]
245	NLTV	John 8:10-11[1]
247	KJV	Proverbs 23:7[1]
249	KJV	John 8:11[1]

Chapter 12

253	NKJV	Hebrews 4:12[1]
263	NKJV	Proverbs 24:10[1]
263	NKJV	Mark 4:35-37[2]
271	NKJV	Mark 5:25-28[1]
272	KJV	Mark 11:23[1]
274	NKJV	Mark 5:29-34[1]
276	KJV	1 Samuel 17:29[1]
276	KJV	Psalm 107:20[2]
277	NKJV	Mark 5:34[1]
278	NKJV	Mark 5:34[1]
279	NKJV	Philippians 1:6[1]
279	NKJV	Psalm 19:14[2]
280	NKJV	Matthew 9:27-31[1]
282	NKJV	Matthew 9:29-30[3]
283	NKJV	Matthew 20:29-34[1]
285	NKJV	Matthew 20:34[1]
288	NIV	Psalm 77:14[1]
	NIV	Mark 6:2[2]

Chapter 13

289	NKJV	Genesis 3:6-7[1]
291	NIV	Genesis 3:3[1]
294	NIV	Genesis 3:1[1]
297	NKJV	Mark 3:4[1]
298	KJV	Exodus 20:8[1]
299	KJV	Hebrews 10:25[1]
299	KJV	Jeremiah 31:33[2]
300	KJV	Matthew 22:37-39[1]
305	NKJV	Proverbs 14:15[1]
	NKJV	Psalm 34:19[2]
	NKJV	2 Corinthians 5:7[3]
	NKJV	Galatians 3:11[4]
307	KJV	Proverbs 1:22-23[1]
313	NIV	Matthew 10:8[1]
315	NIV	Job 38:2-3[1]
316	NIV	Job 41:23[1]
316	NIV	Genesis 2:23[2]
316	KJV	1 Chronicles 16:22
317	NIV	Job 42:8[1]
318	NKJV	Job 42:10[1]
318	NKJV	Job 42;12[2]

Chapter 14

321	NKJV	Genesis 11:7[1]
324	NKJV	Genesis 11:1[1]
329	NKJV	Luke 21:28[1]
331	NKJV	John 3:311[1]
332	NKJV	Genesis 1:6-9[4]
332	NKJV	Ezekiel 28:16-17[5]
333	NKJV	Revelation 12:9[6]
334	NKJV	1 John 2:16[7]

335	NKJV	Genesis 11:3-4[8]
337	NKJV	Matthew 16:23[9]
338	NKJV	Hebrews 10:21[10]
342	NKJV	Genesis 11:5-7[12]
343	NIV	Daniel 4:29-30[13]
346	NKJV	Acts 12:11[1]

364	KJV	1 Timothy 5:22[1]
365	NKJV	Proverb 1:5
366	NIV	Genesis 3:1[1]
367	NKJV	Mark 12:17
368	KJV	Psalm 121:1-2[1]
370	NKJV	Proverbs 3:5-6

Chapter 15

351	KJV	John 3:16[1]
359	KJV	Ephesians 4:26[1]
361	KJV	Proverbs 14:25[1]
362	NIV	1 Samuel 8:1-18

MasterWorks BookMakers

Email:clariongate@msn.com

www.sardiusstone.com

Other Books by the Author:
- Book of Discipline
- Prophetic Eyes
- Foundational Principles
- Apostolic Restoration
- Life by the Brook-Reflections in Silence
- In the Middle of the Passage
- Mountains to Climb

To request a copy per availability:
Contact: Elijahblue_15@outlook.com

> *"And so we know and rely on the love God has for us. God is Love. Whoever lives in love lives in God, and God in them."*
>
> **1 John 4:16 NIV**

Notes

www.ingramcontent.com/pod-product-compliance
Lightning Source LLC
Chambersburg PA
CBHW050610300426
44112CB00012B/1447